Readings in
Educational Psychology
Today

Contributing Editor, John P. DeCecco
PROFESSOR OF EDUCATION AND PSYCHOLOGY, SAN FRANCISCO STATE COLLEGE

Readings in
Educational Psychology
Today

CRM BOOKS
Del Mar, California

Contents

Introduction

Education and schooling are too often equated in thought and literature. Psychologists concerned with education know that this equation is only one in the whole mathematics of learning. Infants learn vast numbers of things before they are old enough to know what a school is. Many psychologists want to know how human cognitive and intellectual abilities develop—what abilities are inherent in being human and what are learned. Some of the authors in this collection who report on their studies of cognition are: Jerome Bruner, who finds in the very earliest development of infants' coordination, attention, and language an analogy with the unique development of human culture; Joachim Wohlwill, who, although he accepts Piaget's hypothesis of an orderly progression of human logical thought, believes that education can hasten a child through these stages of development; and Rhoda Kellogg, who sees in young children's scribbling a basic human—unlearned—esthetic, which soon becomes *adult*erated by grownups whose rigid conception of literal representation prevents them from perceiving the child's artistic objectives.

Many studies have shown that emotional deprivation as well as socioeconomic deficiencies can block learning. The studies included here by the Harlows and by Gordon Jensen and Ruth Bobbitt of the effects of affectional deprivation—whether maternal love or playmates' attentions—on monkeys' emotional growth have obvious implications for humans.

Infants as young as four months who come from deprived socioeconomic backgrounds show differences in attentional reactions from children whose environments are more affluent; Jerome Kagan reports his studies in this area. How, then, can an educational system be adapted so that schools can help supply these deprived children with what they need in order to come up to the level of their luckier counterparts? Surely, the American society cannot be satisfied with having a continuing class of inferior citizens. How can we supply this opportunity in what is, after all, "the land of opportunity"?

First, we must not prejudge: Raymond Cattell shows that traditional IQ tests, often used to set children in tracks from which there is no egress, have a middle-class, "school-intelligence" bias; he suggests a culture fair test, which is capable of demonstrating more than one type of human intelligence. Next, Theodore Sizer and Phillip Whitten offer a plan for a massive attack on ghetto school problems; Harvey Pressman, also concerned with the atmosphere of slum schools—part of which is an expectation of failure—offers his solutions to some of these problems, including a plan for breakdown of the bureaucratic shackles that hold dedicated and innovative educators in traditional bounds. A. S. Neill, who succeeded in breaking most traditional canons of education, talks about his philosophy of education and the forms it takes at Summerhill school, which he founded and presently directs.

Special children need special teaching. Sidney Bijou discusses some causes of retarded development in children, and James Lent and Todd Risley relate the effects of special programs in teaching such children—Lent's children are retarded from physiological causes; Risley's are developmentally retarded for socioeconomic reasons.

The future of education undoubtedly holds an increased use of machines for teaching. Current classroom methods employ machines (slide projectors, movie projectors, tape recorders, record players, TV sets) to a degree not imagined twenty years ago. William Uttal discusses with great clarity the experiments now being conducted with computerlike machines and what their future use in classrooms might be. Richard C. Atkinson did use a one-year computer-based program to teach reading to first-grade children; he reports the results of the program.

All branches of psychological study contribute to educational psychology. This collection brings the fruits of investigations by developmental, physiological, behavioral, experimental, and social psychologists—as well as those studying learning—to bear on the problem of educating *all* children up to their capacities—and of enlarging these capacities—so that they can lead fulfilled lives of individual human dignity and satisfaction. A society made up of such individuals would be at peace, with itself and other societies.

I
School and Society

Can I Come to Summerhill?

A. S. Neill

A. S. Neill here raises perhaps the two most important questions in education and psychology today: Is American society sick? Do the schools reflect this social illness? Neill describes the American school as a product of a society that represses emotion and sexual desire, that is led by a crowd psychology of dead uniformity, and that is dominated by insane dollar values. His own school, Summerhill, stands for freedom of belief, freedom of dissent, and freedom of children to govern themselves.

In reading this article ask yourself about the relationship of schools to society and what social values make it difficult for schools to become Summerhills. You might also determine what the relative advantages and disadvantages would be of working in a school like Summerhill. Why would you accept or refuse a teaching position in such a school?

Just over twenty years ago I had two books published in New York, *The Problem Teacher* and *The Problem Family*. So far as I could make out, each issue sold a few hundred copies and the rest were sold as remainders at a few dimes each. The press notices I got were either lukewarm or hostile. One called the books old hat. "We have lived through this in the States and there is nothing new for us." Twenty years later the book *Summerhill* became a best seller in the States. Why? I have no idea. I like to think that the United States has come up to date rather than that I have gone out of date. I do not know why I get so large a mail from the United States. It is mostly from young people, and in the seven years since the book was published I can recall only two hostile letters. Many are from schoolchildren. "Can I come to Summerhill? I hate my school. It is all pressurization. The teachers make every lesson dull and dead and originality is frowned upon." Oddly enough, although our British education is all wrong, I never get letters from home children.

The mystery to me is this: Why has America become conscious that its education is not good enough? Why now and not twenty years ago? Surely the schools have not changed all that much. But is it a case of a change of society? Is society sicker than it was a couple of decades ago? I fancy that that is the deep reason. In all countries youth is rebelling. Alas, too often rebelling against all that does not matter. The hippies, the flower merchants show their protests not against war, not against race discrimination, not against the stupid learning we call education; no, all the challenge is the right to wear long hair and leather jackets and blue jeans. That is the impression I get in this country, but from what I hear and read about America, the young, especially in the universities, are challenging real evils—the insane dollar values, the dead uniformity of the people who have been molded and indoctrinated so much that they are automatic slaves to any ideas thrown out by the press and the TV screens. In Britain I think that the average TV program is geared to a nation of ten-year-olds. Our B.B.C. refused to put on *The War Game* because it told of the horrors of an atomic war and it might upset the nice folks who want to think that God is in his Heaven and all is right with the world. The young feel that they have been cheated by the old, lied to, castrated by their parents and teachers. They no longer accept glib answers—in Vietnam we are saving the world from Communism; in South Africa we are preserving the God-given rights of the superior whites; in America we are battling to preserve the white civilization. It is significant that all these reasons involve hate and war and possibly ultimate death to humanity. Youth sees a world full of savagery. Hitler's six million Jews paved the way for a world that accepted torture and death as almost commonplace factors in our modern life. In short, the world is very, very sick, and youth feels it but, alas, cannot do much about it. Summerhill's good friend Joan Baez, recently in prison, has no power over the hate merchants; all she can do is to march in protest and then be carted to prison. It is the helplessness of youth that so often brings despair.

In this American *Stimmung* the book *Summerhill* was launched in 1960. It caught on because it was voicing what so many of the young had felt but had not intellectualized, had not made conscious. For its theme was freedom—real freedom, not the sham thing so often called democracy. Freedom for all to grow at their own pace; freedom from all indoctrination, religious, political, moral; freedom for children to live in their own community, making their own social laws. To many a youth Summerhill became synonymous with Paradise. I hasten to say that it isn't—*Gott sei Dank!* Most of the rebellion stems from home, from what Wilhelm Reich called the compulsive family, the family that strangles youth, fears youth, often hates youth. From my mail I am led to believe that the American family is more dangerous than the British one. I never get the sort of letter I had two days ago from New York. "I am seventeen and I am allowed no freedom at all. I have to be in at certain hours and if I am late my father hits me. I hate my parents." A girl of a middle-class family. I have had scores of similar letters. A boy of fifteen writes, "I hate school and cannot concentrate on my work and my parents bully me all the time because they say that I must go to college and get a good job." I have no idea how much truth is in Vance Packard's *The Status Seekers*, but even if a tenth of it is true it gives a terrible picture of American civilization. A Cadillac-civilization with its sequel, dope and drugs and misery for those who cannot accept the god of cars and furs and wealth.

This looks like an attack on a country by an outsider and it may well be resented by some readers, but I do not mean it as an attack; it is a case of trying to think aloud the answer to the question: Why did the Summerhill book catch on in the United States? At home we have our own miseries and troubles. The growing race hate due to the immigration from Jamaica. The futility of a culture that dwells on bingo and football crowds, on infantile TV programs; a culture that gives the cheap sensational press millions of readers while the more cultured papers—*The New Statesman*, the *Observer*, the *Sunday Times*—too often struggle to keep themselves alive. World sickness is not confined to North America. Russia has its teen-age gangsters also.

One reason why Summerhill appealed to Americans may be that it is, so to say, antieducation. The great American educationists, Dewey, Kilpatrick, and their kind were mostly pre-Freudian in their outlook. They kept linking education to learning, and today in all countries educational journals concentrate on the learning process. I escaped that trap. I was and I am ill-versed on what the educationists did. I never read Rousseau or Pestalozzi or Froebel; what I read in Montessori I did not like, partly because it made play the mate of learning. Learning what? Summerhill is not a seat of learning; it is a seat of living. We are not so proud of David who became a professor of mathematics as we are of Jimmy who was hateful and antisocial and is now a warm-hearted engineer with much charity and love to give out. Summerhill puts learning in its own place. I have more than once written that if the emotions are free, the intellect will look after itself. What a waste it all is! Sixty years ago I could read some Latin and Greek. Today I can't decipher the Latin words on a tombstone. Our schools teach children to read Shakespeare and Hardy and Tennyson, and when they leave school the vast majority never read anything better than a crime story. For my part I'd abolish nearly every school subject, making geography and history matters for the school library, and quadratic equations a luxury for the few boys and girls who loved math. Abolish exams—and my school will have only creative teachers —art, music, drama, handwork, and so on.

Every man has a bee in his bonnet. It was comforting to read in Erich Fromm that Freud had to be in the station an hour before his train was due. My original bee was psychology. In the 1920s my home was Vienna and my associates the psychoanalysts. Like all young fools I thought that Utopia was just 'round the corner. Make the unconscious conscious and you have a world full of love and fellowship with no hate. I grew out of that phase but did retain the belief that education must primarily deal with the emotions. Working for many years with problem children made my belief stronger. I saw that the aim of all education must be to produce happy, balanced, pro-life children, and I knew that all the exams and books in a million classrooms could not do a thing to make children balanced. A B.A. could be a hopeless neurotic—I am an M.A. myself. A professor could remain at the age of ten emotionally. The emotional level of the British Cabinet or the American Pentagon is anyone's guess; my own guess is a low one. Today in any school anywhere it is the head that is educated; every exam paper proves the point.

Now, one cannot flee from reality. I cannot say to prospective parents, "Exams and school subjects are not education and I refuse to teach the ordinary school subjects." That is what the Americans would call flunking out, and, by the way, I get too many letters from students in the United States saying, "I can't go on with my college career. The teaching is too dull; I am flunking out. I want to be a child psychologist." I answer that they won't let one be a child psychologist unless one accepts their qualification demands. I wrote to the last man who had flunked out, "If you haven't the guts to walk through the muck heaps, how can you ever expect to smell the roses you value so much?"

I do not find this flunking-out element in old Summerhill pupils. One of my first pupils spent two years standing at a mechanical belt in a car factory. He is now a successful engineer with his own business. His brother, who wanted to be a doctor, had to pass an exam in Latin. In just over a year he passed the matriculation exam in Latin. "I hated the stuff but it was in my way and I had to master it." That was over forty years ago, when students did not as a rule flunk out. I do not think that youth has become defeatist; rather, it is that society has reached a point of futility and cheapness and danger where youth, frustrated by the mundane standard of success, simply gives up in despair. "Make Love not War" is a most appropriate motto for youth even if youth feels it is a hopeless cry, and it is a hopeless cry; the hate men who make wars force youth to die for country, but when the young demand freedom to have a sex life, holy hypocritical hands are held up in horror. Youth is free to die but not to live and love.

I fear I am rambling, not sticking to the point. My consolation—too many who stick to the point make it a blunt one. I ramble because I am trying to evaluate Summerhill as a factor in the sick world, really asking what value freedom has for youth. One is naturally apt to think that one's geese are swans; one tends to forget or ignore the outside world, so that when a lecturer in education in an American college wrote and told me that over 70 percent of his students thought that Summerhill was all wrong, it came as a shock. I had repressed the idea that when the young are conditioned and indoctrinated from cradle days, it is almost impossible for them to break away, to challenge. Few can stand alone without a supporting crowd behind them. "The strongest man is he who stands most alone." Ibsen.

I like to think that freedom helps one to stand outside the madding crowd. Symbolically one sees differences. The conventional suburban office-goer with his striped trousers and his neat tie and his neater mind on one side. On the other, the creator, the artist to whom exterior things mean but little. Compare the tailoring of L. B. J. with that of a film director or a Picasso. Symbols, but characteristic. Put it this way: Summerhill gets hundreds of visitors, but I do not think that any visitor ever notices that my staff never wear ties. Summerhill hasn't got to the Old-School-Tie stage. But one cannot carry such phantasying too far; my old friend Bertrand

Russell wears a tie, and no one would claim that he is a crowd man.

I think that one aspect of Summerhill is that, rightly or wrongly, it gives pupils an anticrowd psychology. I could not imagine any old pupil following a Hitler or for that matter a Kennedy or a Reagan. This sounds incongruous because the chief feature of Summerhill is the self-government, the making of laws by one and all from the age of five to eighty-four. Pupils become ego-conscious and at the same time community-conscious. Bill can do what he likes all day long as long as he does not interfere with the freedom of anyone else; he can sleep all day if he wants to, but he is not allowed to play a trumpet when others want to talk or sleep. It is as near democracy as one can get; every child is a member of parliament able to speak "in the house." No doubt because this democracy is real and honest, our old pupils cannot tolerate the sham we name politics. Because politicians have to rely on votes, nearly every urgent reform is delayed for two generations. In England a Member of Parliament has—say—a predominantly Catholic constituency or a Baptist one. How can he act honestly when faced with some reform—a bill to abolish punishment for homosexuality, a much-needed reform of the divorce and abortion laws? Was any great man a politician? Any Darwin, any Freud, any Einstein, any Beethoven? Was any big man ever a crowd-compeller, a demagogue?

When children are free they become wonderfully sincere. They cannot act a part; they cannot stand up in the presence of a school inspector because they will not countenance insincerity and make-believe. Tact forces them to make minor adaptations, as it does with you and me. I dutifully doff my hat to a lady although I realize that it is a meaningless, even dishonest, gesture, hiding the fact that in a patriarchal society a woman is inferior in status, in pay, in power. To tell a social white lie is often a necessity but to live a lie is something that free people cannot do. And my pupils feel that to be a member of a crowd must involve living a lie.

This crowd psychology angle is important. It is at the root of the sickness of the world. A neighboring country insults your flag, and many thousands of young men die for the honor and glory of their fatherland. National hatreds everywhere, Greek versus Turkey; Israel versus Arabs; Rhodesian white versus black. And it is not only the nationalism crowd. Our football grounds are full of irrational, partisan hate and violence. Gang warfare is not confined to Chicago. Yet in a way violence is minor. It is the violence that a crowd inflicts on its members that frightens, the violence of intimidating, of molding. A school uniform means: We are members of a crowd, a crowd that will not tolerate opposition. We must all dress alike, think alike, act alike. For the great law of any crowd is: Thou shalt conform. The world is sick because its crowds are sick.

Education therefore should aim at abolishing crowd

psychology. It can do this only by allowing the individual to face life and its choices freely. Such an education cannot lead to egocentricity and utter selfishness, not if the individual is free within the confines of the social order, an order made by himself. The slogan "All the way with L. B. J." shows the iniquity of the crowd, a system that makes crowd members sheep who can feel the most elementary emotions without having the intellectual capacity to connect such emotions with reason. Today our schools educate the head and leave the emotions to the crowd-compellers—the press, the radio, the TV, the churches, the commercial exploiters with their lying advertisements. Our pop heroes and film stars have become our leading schoolmasters, dealing with real emotions. What teacher in what school could have a few hundred hysterical females screaming their heads off when he appeared?

The danger today is undeveloped emotion, perverted emotion, infantile emotion. Millions scream in Britain every Saturday afternoon when their favorite football teams take the field. If the evening paper had a front page in big lettering "Atom War Very Near," most of the spectators would turn to the back page to see the latest scores. Crowd emotions are not touched by news of starvation in India or China. It is this same unattached, unrealized emotion that makes the crowd numb to any realization of a likely atomic war. Crowd emotion is not shocked by our inhuman and un-Christlike treatment of criminals in prison; it does not even realize that the inhumanity is there. And none of us is guiltless. I do not cut down my tobacco and give the savings to the starving nations. We are all in the trap, and only the more aware of us try to find a way out. My own way is Summerhill, or rather the idea behind Summerhill: the belief that man is originally good, that, for reasons no one so far knows, man kills his own life and the lives of his children by harsh and antilife laws and morals and taboos. It is so easy to cry, "Man is a sinner and he must be redeemed by religion" or whatnot. God and the Devil were comfortable explanations of good and evil.

One thing I think Summerhill has proved is that man does not need to become a "sinner," that man does not naturally hate and kill. The crowd in Summerhill is a humane one. In forty-seven years I have never seen a jury punish a child for stealing; all it demanded was that the value of the theft be paid back. When children are free they are not cruel. Freedom and aggression do not go together. I have known a few children who were reared with self-regulation, that is, without fear and outside discipline and imposed morality. They seem to have much less aggression than most children have, suggesting to me that the Freudians with their emphasis on aggression must have studied the wrong children.

Even in Summerhill, where very few pupils were self-regulated, there is a peacefulness, a minimum of criticism, a tolerance that is quite uncommon. When a Negro pupil came from the States, not even the youngest child seemed to notice her color. Our TV showed white faces full of hatred when black pupils were being stoned in the deep South. This is alarming. We can condition children to hate and kill by giving them a hate environment. But we can also give them another sort of environment—were I a Christian I'd call it a love-your-neighbor environment. But then, what is a Christian? Catholics and Protestants beat children in home and school—didn't Jesus say suffer the little children? The Christians see that they suffer, all right. But to narrow the life negation to religion is wrong. A humanist can hate life and children; he can be as anti-sex as any Calvinist.

Summerhill has not answered many questions, the biggest one being: Why does humanity kill the life of children, why does it take more easily to hate than to love? Why did jackboot Fascism conquer a nation of 60 million?

One answer to the question of world sickness is sex repression. Make sex a sin and you get perversions, crime, hates, wars. Approve of children's sex as the Trobriand Islanders did under a matriarchal system and a Malinowski will fail to find any trace of sex crime or homosexuality before the missionaries came and segregated the sexes. Wilhelm Reich, to me the greatest psychologist since Freud, dwelt on the necessity for a full, natural orgastic life as a cure for the sickness of an antilife society. Then came the new American Interpersonal Relationship school of Sullivan and Horney, with long case histories of patients who seemed to have no sex at all. I have a book on problem children written by an Adlerian; I failed to find the word sex in it. And in all this divergence of views on sex, what can one believe? One can make the guess that the torturers of German Jews were sex perverts, but can one safely conclude that the men in the Pentagon are Hawks because of their sex repressions?

I have gone through many phases in the last fifty years, the most exciting my long friendship with Homer Lane and then with Reich. Now, at eighty-four, I simply do not know the truth about sex. Is a teacher who canes a boy's bottom a repressed homosexual or a sadist or simply a man who has never been conscious of what he is doing? I ask because my father in his village school tawsed children with a leather strap, and when I became a teacher I automatically did likewise without ever once wondering if it were good or bad. Looking back now, I see that one motive was fear, fear of losing one's dignity, one's power; fear that any slackness would lead to anarchy. I cannot see anything sexual in my tawsing.

Summerhill society is a sex-approving society. Every child soon learns that there is no moral feeling about masturbation or nudism or sex play. But every adolescent is conscious of the fact that if approval meant the sharing of bedrooms by adolescents, the school would be closed by the Establishment. One old boy once said to me: "The fear of closing the school if pregnancies occurred gave us a new form of sex repression." The difficulty was and is this: How far can a school go in being prosex in an antisex society? Not very far, I fear. Yet one factor is of moment; the pupils are conscious of our attitude of approval. They have had no indoctrination about sin or shame, no moralizing from Mrs. Grundy. Their free attitude shows itself in minor ways. In our local cinema a film showed a chamber pot. The audience went into fits of obscene laughter but our pupils did not even smile; one or two asked me later why the people laughed. Free children cannot be shocked—by cruelty, yes, but by sex, never.

Summerhill products are often said to be quiet, unaggressive, tolerant citizens, and I wonder how much their rational attitude on sex has to do with their calmness of life. They prove that censorship is the product of a life-hating civilization. I never see our adolescents taking from the school library *Lady Chatterley* or *Fanny Hill*. A girl of sixteen said they were boring.

Most of our old pupils are pacific. They do not march with banners against the H-bomb or against racial discrimination. I cannot imagine any of them ever supporting warmongers or religious revivalists or censors. But how much this has to do with a free attitude to sex I cannot know. Certainly sex is the most repressed of all emotions. Most of us were made antisex when in our cradles our hands were taken from our genitals, and it is an arresting thought that the men who have the power to begin a nuclear war are men who were made sex-negative long ago. Anglo-Saxon four-letter words are still taboo in most circles, maybe partly for class reasons; a navvy says fuck while a gentleman says sexual intercourse.

I confess to being muddled about the whole affair of sex. I do not know whether if we all experienced Reich's perfect orgasm, there would be an end to war and crime and hate. *I hae ma doots.* Yet it is true that people who have a prosex attitude to life are the ones most likely to be charitable, to be tolerant, to be creative. Those who do not consider themselves sinners do not cast the first stone. For charity I would go to Bertrand Russell rather than to Billy Graham.

Billy naturally leads to religion. Summerhill has no religion. I fancy that very few religionists approve of it. A leading Church of England priest once called it the most religious school in the world, but few parsons would agree with him. It is interesting to note that I have had many letters of approval from Unitarians in the United States. I asked one Unitarian minister what his religion was. Did he believe in God? No, he said. In eternal life? "Good heavens, no. Our religion is giving out love in this life," and I guess that is exactly what the Church of England priest meant. It is our being on the side of the child (Homer Lane's phrase) that has

aroused so much antagonism among religionists. The other day a Catholic school inspector told a meeting of Catholics that corporal punishment was practiced much more in their schools than in Protestant ones. "We beat the body to save the soul." In the days of that life-hater John Knox I would have been burned at the stake. The widening interest in the freedom that Summerhill stands for fits in with the lessening belief in religion. Most young people, outside the Roman Catholic faith, have no interest in religion. To them God is dead. God to them was father, molder, punisher, a fearful figure. The gods and fathers were always on the side of the suppressors. In Britain the enemies of youth, those who

Schools to Beat the System

Harvey Pressman

When Harvey Pressman argues for the creation of small experimental inner-city schools under private community management, he gives substance to the hopes of millions of ghetto parents and children throughout the nation of achieving the educational equality so long denied them. The public school in the ghetto is presently crippled by metropolitan school bureaucracy and the cynical professional staff that does not expect the ghetto children to learn. Increasingly, no doubt unwittingly, the school has become the symbol of an alien middle-class culture that fewer and fewer children, particularly poor children, can believe in and assimilate.

Pressman suggests some innovations in the choice and use of staff and teachers, subject matter and skills, school governance, and school-community relations. What advantages and disadvantages would these small community schools have compared to present public schools?

After a while the children had come out of their tough shells. Most of them were 11 or 12 years old, and now for the first time in their lives allowed themselves to express sustained curiosity in a classroom. The boys had made a volcano with vinegar and baking soda; they wanted to try more experiments. So their teacher went to the school's assistant principal and asked for science supplies. The assistant principal said there were none, and this is what the teacher reported to his class. The boys in the class snickered. There were plenty of science supplies, they insisted, but they'd never get to use any of that stuff because the school was just a "bean school" in Harlem.

The teacher was flabbergasted; he challenged the kids to show him. He was led to a locked closet, he managed to get a key for it, and he found the closet crammed with scientific equipment. Some was years old; none of it had ever been used; it had come straight from the manufacturer or supplier to that closet. The principal allowed the teacher to use the stuff, but wondered seriously if the kids would really get anything out of it.

This episode is almost wearily reported in Herbert Kohl's *36 Children*, an account of a year's teaching in a Harlem elementary school. It is in many ways typical of the inside stories reported recently in books by sensitive urban teachers. And the motifs and problems in these anecdotes are almost daily being exposed, on a citywide and nationwide basis, by educators, independent investigators, and official commissions. The McCone Commission investigating the Watts riot found that the average fifth-grader in the Negro areas of Los Angeles could not read and understand a daily newspaper; similar stories can and have been told for Detroit, Boston, Pittsburgh, New York, and almost every urban center with large numbers of students from low-income minority groups. Although their reading achievement may well be at or even above grade level in the early grades, minority group students fall increasingly behind national reading norms thereafter. They are the result of the schools' failure to cope with students' learning needs. Arithmetic achievement stays closer to national norms, but here, too, the poor student falls farther and farther behind as he progresses through the school system. Individual IQ scores, questionable as measures of basic intelligence—and especially of intelligence in minority groups—go down in proportion to the time spent in school.

The Problems

In disguised but telling fashion, urban school systems throughout the land have in this decade increasingly admitted their failure by offering compensatory programs, ostensibly to compensate for some hypothetical learning inadequacies in the children of the poor, but in reality to compensate for the failure of their own regular programs to recognize, to nurture, and to develop the very real talents in these children. City schools have been spending more money, providing more special programs and special personnel, and devoting more attention to the problems of educating the disadvantaged in their midst. In California, the McAteer Act has since 1963 provided special additional funds for new programs. In 1965 the Ford Foundation granted more than one million dollars to the Pittsburgh public schools for compensatory programs. Also in 1965, Congress initiated an effort that has since provided almost a billion dollars per year for locally administered programs for the children of the poor. The Office of Equal Opportunity has funded a variety of programs such as Head Start, Follow Through, and Upward Bound.

All of this high-minded and breathlessly reported activity has created the feeling that now, finally, things are beginning to move, that real success is just around the corner—along with the next appropriation or two. The real prospects are not nearly that promising. These current compensatory efforts have a tendency to succeed more on paper, in reports and press releases, than in reality. Often they are merely an attempt to placate an unhappy population and to wallpaper over some of the more obvious inadequacies of inner-city schools.

In 1966 the National Advisory Council on the Education of Disadvantaged Children reported to the President on the effects of $250 million spent on special summer projects for inner-city children, and found these projects ill-planned, fragmentary, and shackled by low, vague goals. The council's January 1968 and 1969 reports were almost as dismal. After a half-dozen years of fanfare and several billions of dollars poured down the public and private spouts, the 1968 Kerner Report on civil disorders stated flatly that "the bleak record of public education for ghetto children is growing worse."

Why? Among the many reasons why our public schools seem to fail the poor, the most important and most difficult to change probably is the expectation of substandard performance, which seems to pervade the atmosphere of most slum schools. Kenneth Clark described it as a "clash of cultures in the classroom," in which teachers and administrative and supervisory personnel assume that both the student and his parents are in some irremediable way inferior. Once the educator assumes the inferiority of his students, once he fails to understand, for whatever reasons, that their innate capacities are as good or bad as anybody else's, his low expectations probably will be internalized by the students' poor results, which reinforce or confirm his low expectations.

Many of these same people who bear negative attitudes about the abilities of poor students work in implementing the new enrichment programs. In addition, there is too little freedom within the public-school system for the necessary across-the-board qualitative improvements to be accomplished. Principals are bound by often irrelevant and obstructive regulations imposed by administrators who are ever conscious of costs and of their public relations. Teachers feel bound to unimaginative and poorly designed curricula, and they are constantly watched by regulation-haunted administrators. Innovators at any level find it difficult to pursue their experiments through to their logical conclusions.

All of this is exceedingly difficult to change. There are too many bureaucratic and administrative roadblocks, too much parochialism, too many vested interests in appointments and promotion procedures. Too much fear, negativism, and, to be frank, incompetence among the men and women who are, after all, responsible for the past failures of urban education—incompetence in $40,000-a-year big-city superintendents and in callous, disillusioned teachers riding herd in countless darkened, filthy classrooms from Harlem to Watts. The many dedicated and talented teachers who still labor in the slum schools of the nation are too often the most frustrated and disaffected people in these schools, their efforts neutralized by the inadequacies of the system.

Solution Through New Schools

While the present situation is in many ways discouraging, it is at the same time revolutionary. Much has been done to raise hopes, but almost nothing has been done to fulfill them. The only acceptable solutions now are immediate, highly visible, and large-scale.

Public schools simply cannot manage such solutions alone. What is therefore required is the creation of a new, national complex of privately managed inner-city schools, completely divorced from the public educational establishment and even independent of one another. These schools must not be designed as small, nonreplicable experiments but as large-scale demonstrations of what good schools can do for large numbers of inner-city students, from preprimary to junior-college grades. Such schools can begin immediately to provide ghetto children with a quality of education that even the best public school systems will require much more time to achieve.

These new schools could not operate according to a single formula or unique solution because there isn't any. But there are already a number of exciting, innovative, and quite different designs for new inner-city schools, all of which should be given a chance to prove themselves in a truly experimental way. Behind all the variations in structure and detail among these models, however, lie three broad assumptions that seem to be borne out positively by currently successful private experiments—and negatively by much of the current effort in the public schools.

These assumptions are: the children of the poor will learn better when they are genuinely expected to learn; they will learn better when their learning materials bear some relevance to their lives; and they will learn better when a bond of humor, mutual concern, and mutual respect is established between them and their teachers.

The new schools should be innovative "leapfrog schools" for the whole nation. And they can be proving grounds for the development, trial, and demonstration of new learning or teaching patterns. There should be short-term fallout in terms of adaptable features or components that can be immediately grafted onto existing urban and suburban public educational systems. More importantly, these schools can drive home on a significant scale the central point for success—the children of the poor, when properly taught in a proper environment, can learn as well as or better than their overprotected suburban counterparts.

If the new schools demonstrate dramatically that the poor results of urban slum schools stem from inadequacies of the schools and not of the students, they may go a long way toward building up the pressure for real change in the urban educational establishment. And they may show that significant improvements are possible in all the schools of the nation.

New instructional materials, new organizational patterns, new staffing arrangements are necessary to the improvement of all facets of the tradition-bound American educational system. But when all that is said, the major difference between the school that will succeed with ghetto kids and the school that won't is not likely to be the matter of which school has gimmicks. The important difference will be that one school has a preponderance of people who care deeply about, believe in, and demand much of their charges.

Thus the first contribution of the new, exciting, and self-reinforcing atmosphere should be vigorous and demanding leaders. Even this relatively simple initial change would be exceedingly difficult to arrange within an existing school system. The first steps would quickly produce other changes—in curriculum, scheduling, and classroom organization—that existing school systems now find difficult, even impossible, to tolerate.

Changes might well include a vastly increased number of student-selected books, magazines, and discussion topics; radically reduced limitations on the kinds of experience and the kinds of language considered appropriate to the classroom; the intensive study of "hot" topics like riots, rent strikes, civil-rights murders, race relations, Vietnam, and so on. Student-created curricula

and highly individualized learning patterns certainly might develop.

The new schools should be able to compete directly with public schools for federal, state, municipal, and private funds. Federal legislative action will be necessary if the billions of dollars now pouring more or less uselessly through Titles I and III of the Elementary and Secondary Education Act are to be tapped by private, nonprofit educational institutions, although some federal funds are already being utilized by new schools.

One State Moves

Enabling legislation recently has—for the first time—been passed at the state level. Massachusetts passed a bill that will give three nonprofit corporations both authority and funds to operate state experimental schools, with the first branch opening in September 1969. The project is headed up by a 21-member commission that includes representatives of various educational and community organizations concerned with inner-city education. More such legislative action is sorely needed. At present, most of the funds for new privately managed schools are coming from foundations and other private sources, and in part from the urban poor themselves, as in the case of the Roxbury (Massachusetts) Community School, and various storefront or freedom schools. Another obvious souce for funds would be private industry, especially the giant industrial, communications, and financial complexes.

One of the major characteristics of any new school, of course, should be concentration on selecting and developing the right kind of personnel. Quality of personnel—not only in terms of teaching skills, but also in terms of human attitudes—probably will be the most important single variable in the success or failure of these schools. A curriculum-development center staffed by specialists and actively involving the teaching personnel probably should be a permanent part of most new schools. Teachers can make continuous and substantive contributions in the creation, selection, adaptation, and revision of curricula that are geared to the special learning styles and needs of their students. The addition of new faculty categories (master teachers, curriculum specialists, supervising teachers) can provide extra rewards of money and responsibility. Master teachers can be utilized to do in-service training, conduct demonstration classes, and head up teaching teams within the school. The improvement of the capacities of the staff should be viewed primarily as a task of the leaders within the school, rather than something the teacher goes outside the school to get. Given the great improvement of staff morale through heightened responsibility, meaningful interstaff communication and in-service training, more varied and intensified creative roles, and reduced bureaucratic and clerical chores, these new schools could prove to be spawning grounds for a whole new group of talented teachers.

Community School Concepts

Most of these schools should also be community schools. The idea of the community school has come to cover a number of very different concepts, from the idea of a school with a community-centered curriculum to the notion of a school with a community service program. A number of these concepts seem particularly relevant. The schools I propose should hire members of the community to fill staff positions. Parents and other people within the community should, of course, have a voice in the decision-making process of the schools. The schools should offer educational opportunities to parents as well as to students and keep facilities open for use by the community.

Every new school should also concern itself with the special problems of the community, both as classroom subject matter and as social and economic problems that the school is prepared to help solve. Vocational programs may be offered, to prepare students for jobs available within the community and to give them a greater sense of control over the machinery of everyday life. The Newark, New Jersey, Community School proposes to offer several vocational programs or projects—such as masonry, home building and repair, auto repair, and home-appliance repair—all taught by community residents and all structured informally so that they are interesting in themselves, economically useful, and emotionally rewarding.

New schools can involve the student more positively and more honestly in what school is all about. The student should not be required to tolerate a school culture alien to himself and his environment. Nor should it be suggested to him that real success consists of embracing that alien, often boring, and false culture, with the accompanying—and threatening—corollary that he reject himself and his environment. Instead, the schools must allow the experiences, needs, and facts of life within the community to generate much of the curriculum, and they must permit meaningful participation by high-school students in governing these schools.

The new schools can and should avoid those common public-school procedures that have the effect of acculturating students to the values and mores of the dominant group in the society. Such procedures ultimately rob children—and society as a whole—of richness and diversity. Children from low-income backgrounds *can* be well educated without being alienated from their subculture in the process. Indeed the curriculum of the poor black children ought to be planned so that it confronts and counteracts the messages of inferiority coming from the larger society, even at the risk of creating anti-white feelings.

The new schools can and should provide to the best of their ability the basic satisfactions that are a prerequisite to learning and that are not provided by other agents in the society. Thus breakfast and midday meals, physical examinations, assistance to parents in the development of a better physical home environment that supports learning in school, and a vastly expanded counseling and guidance program are all necessary in order for the schools to do their job.

One of the most delicate problems of the new schools will be the phasing of growth. Care must be taken so that the school in its initial stage is not so large that the administrative problems of setting up and operating a large enterprise consume a disproportionate share of leadership time. Equal care must be taken, however, to make the growth rate sufficiently rapid so that meaningful numbers of children are rapidly served and so that the overall scope of the effort is not frozen at a size too small for the desired impact. The answer here may be a plan that provides for both a relatively small initial stage and for increasingly rapid advances thereafter. For example (and it is only one example), in its first year the school might serve 10 percent of its ultimate total population, in its second year it might serve 30 percent, in its third year 60 percent, and 100 percent thereafter.

Quality of Schools

Finally, these schools should be *expensive* schools. The inner-city poor have been notoriously short-changed educationally, not only in terms of emotional and cultural rejection, but also in simple economic terms, as can be seen all too easily in the conditions of the school buildings, the size of classes, the investment in equipment. (Many cities that now provide special programs for the poor do so by exploiting the availability of outside funds rather than by a more equitable redistribution of municipal educational resources.)

Anyone who has thought hard about the meaning of equality of educational opportunity will understand that it cannot be achieved by spending the same amount on everybody. The children of the poor haven't had an equal start, in school or in life; almost month by month the catching up becomes more difficult and more expensive until finally the price becomes so high and the burden of repairing past failures becomes so great that nothing seems to work.

I am convinced that the creation of a national network of experimental, independent urban schools must be an important goal of those who desire to respond to the realities of the present urban educational crisis. Given the current funding possibilities and the criminality of what is happening to so many urban children at the moment, even such a large-scale effort at creating a parallel system is not a sufficient response. Our responsibility, it seems to me, must be to make a number of simultaneous efforts in the hope that the totality of these efforts can produce quick results for children whose futures we have too long neglected.

There are several areas in which energies can be applied. We must support present efforts to create full-time new schools as energetically as possible. Boston's

Roxbury is a good example of public mood and present effort. Three new, parent-operated schools already are in operation. Sites have been selected and plans set for the opening of one more school in this same area within the next year. The energy of dissatisfied parents clearly is the key to community self-help.

Part-Time Schools

We must also work now to create a system of part-time independent schools for children who cannot yet be served by a full-time parallel school system, in the hope that we can help them survive educationally with even this limited input. An example might be the liberation school, a school to which black children can go after school hours, or on Saturday mornings, or during the summer months. Imparting a sense of ethnic pride should be an important element of the curriculum of such schools, as well as providing students with techniques for dealing with the public system they must attend. Such schools could be in cheap storefronts, rented lofts, living rooms, or in the churches that abound in our urban slums. We certainly should sup-

port the efforts of local community people to increase their power over the public schools. In response to direct political pressure—perhaps from fear of things getting worse or to head off further trouble—boards of education are beginning to understand the necessity of sharing their powers over ghetto schools with people of the community served. We should support the minority of good public-school teachers in their lonely, mostly abandoned struggle against school boards, big-city administrators, and often hostile colleagues.

The solutions or tactics I have suggested, and others like them, seem worth trying as experiments that may help people who will otherwise continue to be oppressed and victimized. But we must face the cruel but equally likely possibility that none of the programs can do much to contend with the powerful virus that infects all our efforts to cope with the problems of the children of the black ghettos, racism reinforced by the isolation and unreality of our middle class. We must come to the bone-deep knowledge that the freedom and dignity of a people within a nation cannot ultimately survive unless they are shared with all the people of that nation.

A Proposal for a Poor Children's Bill of Rights

Theodore Sizer and Phillip Whitten

In a democracy education is a right rather than a privilege, and therefore equality of educational opportunity is something that the citizens of all ethnic and economic backgrounds can claim as a birthright. But because the schooling of middle-class and poor children has been traditionally unequal, Sizer and Whitten argue that we must discriminate in education in favor of the poor by committing a major share of money, effort, and imagination to ghetto schools. We must shift, they say, from color-blind to color-conscious school policies and expenditures that favor the minorities.

The Poor Children's Bill of Rights would provide a money grant to each poor child and thereby provide him with a choice of which public or private school he will attend. The authors assume, in the sense that good business drives out bad business, that parents will choose the better, integrated schools over the poorer, segregated schools. What are the implications of such a program for the concept of American education? Compare this plan to Pressman's solution for the same problem.

Reliance on formal education as a significant vehicle for social mobility is an unpopular article of faith these days. There is not now, nor has there ever been, an American "equality of educational opportunity." That is historically evident. It is equally clear that there might be. Few other social institutions potentially offer so much as schools, and ingenious men must make them work.

Very simply, we are involved in a struggle by the poor to catch up. But thus far the rich, at a time when the gross national product rises to over $800 billion, become further enriched and the poor get poorer. It is obvious that the poor, particularly the minorities, no longer are willing to accept this state of affairs. That they have abandoned placid tolerance gives us some hope, but only if we correct this disparity. To do otherwise, general society assumes a perilous risk.

Given the general conviction about the urgent need to solve the problem, what does society do?

Ours is a simple proposal: to use education—vastly improved and powerful education—as the principal vehicle for upward mobility. While a complex of strategies must be designed to accomplish this, we wish here to stress one: a program to give money *directly* to poor children (through their parents) to assist in paying for their education. By doing so we might both create significant competition among schools serving the poor (and thus improve the schools) and meet in an equitable way the extra costs of teaching the children of the poor.

The idea of such tuition grants is not new. For almost two centuries variant proposals for the idea have come from such figures as Adam Smith, Thomas Paine, John Stuart Mill, and more recently from Milton Friedman, the conservative University of Chicago economist. Its appeal bridges ideological differences. Yet it has never been tried, quite possibly because the need for it has never been so demonstrably critical as now.

Before we discuss the economics and details of our proposal, it should be emphasized at once that an open society cannot be constructed by good schools alone. As Paul Goodman has warned:

> . . . There is plenty of social mobility, opportunity to rise—*except precisely for the ethnic minorities* [our emphasis] who are our main concern . . . but the statuses and channels are increasingly stratified, rigidified, cut and dried. . . . By plain social justice, the Negroes and other minorities have the right to, and must get, equal opportunity for schooling with the rest, but the exaggerated expectation from schooling is chimera—and, I fear, will be shockingly disappointing.

Even as we educate our poor and equip them with the skills necessary to hold responsible and meaningful jobs, we must ensure absolutely that, once the requisite skills have been acquired, jobs will be available. To fail here will assure a social explosion unlike any we have experienced thus far.

Inequality of Education

There are two reasons why equality of educational opportunity does not, in fact, exist in the United States. First, there is the simple fact that the schools and the children who attend them differ in many respects. Second is the fact that since the time of Thomas Jefferson we have misconstrued the phrase—equality of educational opportunity—as meaning equality of *opportunity*. Thus *Plessy vs. Ferguson* (1896) established the concept of separate but equal facilities. It was not until 1954, in *Brown vs. Board of Education*, that the Supreme Court reversed this principle.

What, then, is meant by equality of educational opportunity? We feel that the stringent demands of our modern industrial society call for an *equality of attainment*. This does not mean that the schools should be attempting to make everybody the same; that is prima facie absurd. What it does imply, however, is that we should make the schools appropriate for people with respect to their environment. That we are not doing that at the present time is quite evident.

James Coleman has reminded us that the home also educates. Homes also differ. Schools, rather than being alike (equal), must differ just as homes do. In short, education must be planned for the child in his complete milieu, not just within school.

The concept of equality of educational opportunity, then, concerns the relative intensity of two sets of influences—school, and home and neighborhood.

Coleman, writing recently in the *Harvard Educational Review*, elaborated on the nature of the problem:

> If the school's influences are not only alike for the two groups, but very strong relative to the divergent influences, then the two groups will move apart. Or more generally, the relative intensity of the convergent school influences and the divergent out-of-school influences determines the effectiveness of the educational system in providing equality of educational opportunity. In this perspective, complete equality of opportunity can be reached only if all the divergent out-of-school influences vanish. . . . Given the existing divergent influences, equality of opportunity can only be approached and never fully reached. The concept becomes one of proximity to equality of opportunity. This proximity is determined, then, not merely by the *equality* of educational inputs, but by the *intensity* of the school's influence. . . .

What all this boils down to is that *we must discriminate in education in favor of the poor*. We must weight the education scales in favor of the poor for the next generation and commit a major share of our resources to providing superior educational programs for them. The U.S. Commissioner of Education, Harold Howe, supports this view: "My plea in this regard is not for *equal* education but for *better* than equal." Howe, quoting former President Johnson, writes, "You do not take a person who for years has been hobbled by chains and liberate him, bring him up to the starting line of a race and say 'you're free to compete with the others' and justly believe that you have been completely fair."

A Poor Children's Bill of Rights

We propose a Poor Children's Bill of Rights that will frankly discriminate in favor of poor children. It would be based on a free enterprise approach to education and would be patterned after the GI Bill of Rights following World War II and the Korean War.

It would, quite simply, give money in the form of a coupon to a poor child who would carry the coupon to the school of his choice, where he would be enrolled. The school chosen could use the sum as it saw fit. And the supplementary grant that the child would give to his school must be large enough to motivate the school to compete for it. Our judgment is that a grant of $1,500 per child per year (about three times the current per-pupil national expenditure) is a necessary figure.

Our research suggests several alternative patterns that provide sliding scales—allowing for the allocation of different amounts of money proportional to family income and number of school-age children. For practical political purposes, as well as equity, it might be better to employ a scheme based on a sliding scale rather than one that would simply provide $1,500 for each child defined as poor. The charts in Figure 1 show how two different sliding-scale formulae would work for a family of four. For families of five, six, seven, or more, appropriate adjustments in the formulae in income relative to a given subsidy would, of course, be made. Regional equalization formulae necessarily would be employed to deal with such problems as the one inherent in the fact that New York, for example, spends $912 per child per year while Mississippi spends only $315.

The charts show what the educational grant—under each of the formulae—would be to each school-age child in a family of four, depending on the level of income. The chart shows quickly the maximum family income level that would be subsidized.

The estimated total cost of the various plans we have

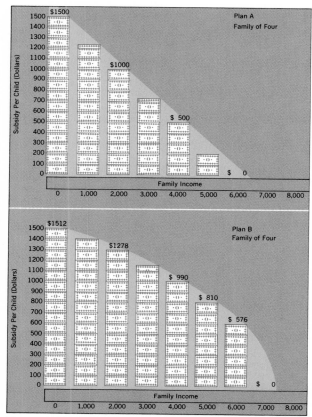

Figure 1. Two sample education subsidy Plans: Plan A is a linear function and cheaper than the exponential function, Plan B.

considered ranges from approximately $11 to $17 billion per year, depending on the formula and on the number of families served. If families with incomes up to $10,000 per year are included, up to half of the population with school-age children would receive an education subsidy. Generally speaking, for the Poor Children's Bill of Rights, formulae that are linear functions (such as A) are cheaper than exponential functions (such as B). However, exponential functions have the advantage of decreasing more slowly than linear functions (as income increases) until the maximum subsidized income is approached. At this point exponential functions rapidly—and, from an administrative point of view, neatly—approach zero.

An Investment That Would Repay Itself

For political reasons it might be necessary to include a large proportion (up to 50 percent) of the nation's children: one guesses that much of the political opposition to the Poor Children's Bill of Rights would come from upper-lower- and lower-middle-class groups. However, if the children of these people were also included under the program, it is reasonable to expect opposition to diminish in some degree.

There are some 10 million children now growing up

in what the Johnson Administration defined as poverty (approximately $4,300 per year for a family of four). Our simplest plan, that of providing a $1,500 subsidy to each poor child, would cost about $15 billion per year, less than the current expenditure for highways and about half the annual cost of the Vietnam war. In straight fiscal terms this would not place much of a strain on a well-managed economy. However, even the $15 billion figure is deceptively inflated. As Christopher Jencks points out, "In the long run there is abundant evidence that this investment would repay itself by raising taxable income and by cutting expenditures for welfare, unemployment, police and other slum symptoms." Michael Harrington elaborates on the expense of maintaining poverty:

The tensions, the chaos, the dislocations . . . are a major item in the budget of every municipality. In some cities a quarter of the annual funds are devoted to taking care of the special fire, police, and health problems created by the slums. The cost of keeping these people at the bottom year in and year out (rather than making an investment in real change once for all) is considerable.

And British educational economist Mark Blaug writes:

A number of studies, in such diverse countries as the United States . . . Israel, Mexico . . . India . . . and Uganda, have all shown that both social and private rates of return on investment in all levels of formal education are typically positive, meaning that *the lifetime earnings of educated people more* than recoup the cost of their education.

One of the principal advantages of the proposed system is that it would give to the parents of poor children the power to choose the kind and quality of education their child will receive (a not inconsiderable benefit as we shall later see), and it would foster competition between schools, public and private, with the inferior institutions eventually being eliminated.

Milton Friedman, who proposed a system similar to the Poor Children's Bill of Rights in 1955, recognized these advantages. "Parents," he wrote, "could express their views about schools directly, by withdrawing their children from one school and sending them to another to a much greater extent than is now possible." Further, he notes, "Here as in other fields, competitive private enterprise is likely to be far more efficient in meeting consumer demands than either nationalized (publicly run) enterprises or enterprises run to serve other purposes."

One can only disagree with Friedman in his emphasis on private enterprise. Competition between public school systems, or even between public schools within a system, easily can reach the same desired ends.

Allowances Are Not New

The allowance scheme here presented is seen erroneously by all too many as new and a most radical form of conservatism. It was in 1776 that Adam Smith wrote:

The public can facilitate this acquisition (of reading, writing and arithmetic among children of the poor) by establishing in every parish or district a little school, where children may be taught for a reward so moderate, that even a common labourer may afford it; the master being partly, but not wholly paid by the public; because, if he was wholly, or even principally paid by it, he would soon learn to neglect his business.

Tom Paine, writing in the 1790s, protested, with relevance for today, that "it is monarchical and aristocratical Government only that requires ignorance for its support," and proposed the distribution of four million pounds to working-class families according to the size and the age of the family. The government was to pay:

. . . to every poor family, out of the surplus taxes, and in room of poor rates four pounds a year for every child under fourteen years of age; enjoining the parents of such children to send them to school, to learn reading, writing and common arithmetic.

In the nineteenth century John Stuart Mill endorsed a similar idea, and in 1926 Francis Cardinal Bourne, Archbishop of Westminster, proposed that each poor parent ". . . would receive an annual . . . coupon for the cost-per-child amount, entitling the child to a place in any recognized school. . . ." He stated that ". . . the adoption of this novel project would . . . relieve poor parents of a social disability and would vivify Education by a spirit of wholesome rivalry. . . ."

In spite of its ideological antiquity, there are a number of advantages inherent in our proposed scheme: it would concentrate dollars on the children who need it most. By taking her child to school X, the mother gives to that particular school as a supplementary grant three times the amount of money spent, on the average, per student for education.

Accordingly, this provides an incentive to middle-class schools to take in poor children.

It would give to the poor some power to choose and control their own destinies. Many believe that the sense of powerlessness and inability to choose and control one's destiny is a major factor in perpetuating poverty. Writing in *The New York Times*, Floyd McKissick bluntly puts the problem:

Public education is a monopoly. Black people have no alternative to public education. They are trapped in public schools until they are old enough to drop out. . . . Boards of Education . . . are not responsible to the community in black areas.

Analyzing the Coleman Report, Michigan psychologist Irwin Katz writes in the *Harvard Educational Review*:

For Negro students, sense of control was clearly the most important attitude. . . . Moreover, the relation of Negroes' sense of control to achievement was considered stronger than that of any family background factor . . . or objective school characteristics. . . .

Mario Fantini of the Ford Foundation adds:

. . . a "parents' lobby" with unprecedented motivation and commitment might arise. Nor should the possible effects on parents in their own right be overlooked. Few people can engage in a social cause and not themselves be transformed.

Fantini predicts that parents may even be stimulated to enlarge their own education, but, most important, it would mean for the parents ". . . a tangible grasp on the destiny of their children and (the) opening to richer meaning for their own lives." The ability to control their own destinies definitely will instill in poor people a necessary pride and dignity of which they have been cheated.

Competition will be developed between schools, public and private. Not only between existing schools, but between present institutions and new schools; there is ample evidence to believe the Poor Children's Bill of Rights will promote this. Responsive to the communities they serve, particularly in black urban areas, they also will compete.

Those who would argue that our proposal would destroy the public schools raise a false issue. A system of public schools that destroys rather than develops positive human potential now exists. It is not in the public interest. And a system that blames its society while it quietly acquiesces in, and inadvertently perpetuates, the very injustices it blames for its inefficiency is not in the public interest. If a system cannot fulfill its responsibilities, it does not deserve to survive. But if the public schools serve, they will prosper.

The plan could cause a kind of decentralization that would promote diversity, pluralism, responsiveness to the needs of the community being served and, indeed, even greater efficiency. Henry Levin, in "The Failure of the Public Schools and the Free Market Remedy," points out that under a market system the motive for success among schools would require that the school meet the needs of its students better than its competitors for any given cost. "Under such a system," says Levin, "the massive inefficiencies and rigidities which currently exist in the public schools would have to yield to more rational use of resources, flexibility, and innovation. In particular, the schools would have to be more responsive to the needs of their particular students in order to retain them and to attract new pupils."

Some Anticipated Problems

There are, of course, problems. By giving power to parents, with all its attendant virtues, one loses some power to enforce integration by race and class. We hypothesize that parents will send their children to the better schools and that better schools are by definition integrated by class and race. We concede that this is a hypothesis of high faith.

Congress must build in a requirement of equal access to any school receiving children's allowances (parallel in kind to the affidavits required of universities receiving government contracts under Title VI of the Civil Rights Act of 1964). This requirement would prevent the use of allowances to support de jure apartheid schools, white and black. But the requirement would have to be policed assiduously—no easy task. Allowances still could create more "separate" schools than we want or need. Further, by giving power to parents, one asserts trust in them for the welfare of their children. Anyone who has taught in any school knows of the scandal of parental indifference or worse. Then, why build on this pile of sand?

We feel, unhappily, that giving parents more power can only be seen as the least of evils. We trust them little, but still more than we trust the present monopoly of lay boards and professional schoolmen.

The latter two entities have power and resources now and will retain most of these. Parents will get significant new power under our scheme and will thus have more leverage than before. Power will be better balanced—and it is a balance that is required. We favor no one's monopoly: parents', teachers', or the state's. All have rights and obligations, but all have weaknesses. Wholly parent-run schools would be too parochial and their power base would shift as children come and go. Domination by teachers has its obvious flaws, as does state control, the present system. Parents, teachers, and the state all have stakes in the schools, but the stakes are different. The child will be best protected if these stakes are balanced off, one against the other.

The Plan in Context

Under our plan, new schools would spring up to receive the new bounty, much as they did in higher education after World War II. There would have to be some form of quick but fair accreditation by regional professional groups and the states to prevent fly-by-night enterprises from fleecing unwitting parents. The last thing that American slums need is Dickensian proprietary schools.

Such accreditation is as tricky to plan and administer as it is necessary. It will require courage and imagination on the part of regional accrediting authorities, and new mechanisms to judge the quality of the output of the schools (rather than merely to judge the visible attributes of institutions doing the educating). We operate now on a system that decides which educational

car to buy by examining the factory that makes it. Yes, this assessment will be difficult—but it must be done. Perhaps the National Assessment Project, launched several years ago under the leadership of Ralph Tyler, can give direction—eventually—to those who will accredit.

And, finally, the plan, even cloaked with a politically classy title such as "Poor Children's Bill of Rights," must be part of a package, one that surely must include some form of guaranteed annual income and the provision for health and welfare services at a level of accommodation far higher than at present. And, as we have said, relevant education will demand relevant careers for its graduates. Brutally put, educated unemployed are considerably more dangerous than uneducated unemployed. This nation can afford neither.

Freer enterprise in education will provoke high quality only if there is a new breed of professionals to make it happen in the various competing schools. Drastically more powerful and flexible curricula will be needed—and these will be costly to develop. The costs of improving education in the purely technical-pedagogical sense to a point where it does become an effective means of social mobility will be immense.

Racial and class mixing promoted by the scheme will result only if there are school buildings available to hold more and varied children: a federal school-building program established to house imaginative and integrated educational programs is essential. And the public, the parents, will have to be informed about education as never before. Our limited trust of parents might be increased if public information about schooling were better and fad separated from fancy more often. (This will be difficult as the education profession itself is notoriously prone to fads.)

If we do all this we will, perhaps, double the costs of elementary and secondary education. Such would be a social reform of considerable consequence and would vault the federal government centrally into support of the schools. We propose that half this increase be in the form of allowances for a Poor Children's Bill of Rights. The use of these allowances would be free, virtually, from federal (or state or local) control. And the total increase would be less than a year's cost of the war in Vietnam.

It can be done. It must be done.

Russian Nursery Schools
Michael and Sheila Cole

The Russian school, like the American, is a reflection of the surrounding society. Because Russian society has only recently achieved economic stability, we can perhaps find in it examples of what we can do to bring the economically undeveloped urban ghetto and ghetto schools into the mainstream of twentieth-century history. The Coles discovered that the Russian nursery school they visited had broken out of the monolithic bureaucracy that once stifled Russian education and that still characterizes urban education in the United States. Despite emphases on good table manners, clean table-cloths, and practicality, there seems to be a humane emphasis on accepting the child at his own level, especially the concrete level of his own sensation and perception in the school's sensory training.

Compare Pressman's inner-city experimental schools with this Russian nursery school. What political and social values do they share? What consequences for children do they symbolize?

It was free-play period at Preschool 67 in the northwest suburbs of Moscow, and it was early summer. Two three-year-old boys were building a castle in the sandbox, occasionally getting in the way of a little girl who was tunneling. A red-faced youngster was hard at work hauling pails of water for the boys from a nearby pond. In a far corner of the yard, two little girls were playing with dolls. Sitting under an arbor in another corner, alone, was a three-year-old girl with short dark hair, singing softly to herself.

We had seen the girl spend the play period that way for several days, and we mentioned her to the teacher, a young woman who had been trained at one of the Soviet Union's pedagogical institutes. "Oh, that's Irichka," she replied. "Irichka is happy to be alone. She's that kind of child—quiet and able to amuse herself."

To us, it seemed odd that a woman who was supposed to be raising children in a collective should show such an easy acceptance of individualism. But the more we learned about Soviet nursery schools, the more

apparent it became that we had brought with us from the United States a full bag of misconceptions.

We spent the summer of 1966 in the Soviet Union, chiefly to help with preparations for the Eighteenth International Congress of Psychologists. In the United States at the time, Head Start programs were springing up all over, and the newspapers were full of heartwarming accounts of children listening to stories and receiving medical checkups for the first time in their lives. A heated debate was also underway among teachers and psychologists about what kinds of programs would best prepare these children for the public schools, whose task in turn would be to make them productive and socially useful members of our society.

Especially because of this situation at home, we were eager to find out all we could about Soviet nursery schools. We spent almost a week at Preschool 67, talking to the children, teachers, and principal. Later, we visited the Institute of Preschool Education in Moscow and interviewed its director, A. V. Zaporozhets. The Institute is responsible for recommending a nursery-school program to the Soviet Union's Ministry of Education, and its psychologists perform the research on which the recommendations are based. Once the program has been adopted by the Ministry, it is used throughout the country.

Nursery schools have been part of the system of universal education in the Soviet Union since the time of the Bolshevik Revolution. Although they are not compulsory, preschools are the first link in the Soviet educational system. The Communist Party assigns to nursery schools the task of ensuring the normal development of all children—preparing them for school and teaching them proper work habits, so that they, like their American counterparts, will grow into productive and socially useful members of their society.

Preschool 67 is just like thousands of nursery schools in the Soviet Union. Its drab two-story building comes from a blueprint used throughout the country for almost ten years, and its educational program and goals are also identical to those in effect elsewhere.

The pupils range in age from two to seven; there are 150 of them, all from homes in the neighborhood of the school. One group of 25 lives in the school's small dormitory, going home only on weekends and holidays. The others arrive between eight and nine in the morning and leave between four and six in the afternoon.

There is a long waiting list at Preschool 67, as there is at most nursery schools, and admission is based on need. Priority is given to children who have two working parents and no grandmother or other baby-sitter, to orphans, and to children from very large families or from homes where there is sickness or some other problem. Payment, which is determined by the parents' income, ranges from $2.20 to $13.00 a month.

"Work" Training

When we arrived at Preschool 67, the children were eating breakfast on one side of a large, airy, toy-cluttered room. The older children used cloth napkins and sat at tables covered with white cloths. These amenities, we were told by Sofia Shvedova, the warm, grandmotherly director of the preschool, were both a reward for good table manners and an incentive to improve. "We ask the children to see how clean they can keep the tablecloth," she said. "But we never shame them when they have an accident."

"We know that some children eat less than others, but we give them all the same amount anyway," Mrs. Shvedova went on. "We let them eat as much as they can. We occasionally feed the little ones. But we don't force a child to love all food. We try to teach him little by little."

At nursery school, the children receive three substantial meals a day—they are not supposed to eat at home on school days except for an occasional snack—and they take their naps there as well.

In other words, the nursery school is responsible for the health and physical development of the child. This lessens the burden on the working mother, and it also reflects the Soviets' very different view from ours of the relation between children and society. The Soviets believe that children are a natural resource, perhaps the most valuable resource a society has. Although the raising of the child is entrusted to the family, the ultimate responsibility for the child's development belongs to the state.

As the children finished their breakfast, they wiped their mouths on their napkins, asked the nanny if they could be excused, thanked her, and went to the other side of the room to play. A few children stayed behind; it was their turn to help clear the table.

Teaching the children to take care of their own needs, and to help with the chores and with the younger children, is an important part of the "work training" portion of the nursery-school program. The children do not receive concrete rewards for their "work," but they are profusely praised when they do a good job.

"They should all work well," Mrs. Shvedova said. "But we know that there are individual differences and that one child is not as capable as another. We try to measure them all against their own achievement. We can't give a child a gold star when he breaks a plate, but we can say, 'Tolia did a very good job today. He tried very hard. He broke a dish, but he did it because he was trying so hard.'"

Surprising as it might seem to many Americans, Mrs. Shvedova's insistence on acknowledging individual differences and on judging the child against his own abilities is based on official ideology. The government-distributed manual for preschool teachers says that nursery schools should teach friendship and cooperation and also form individuality: the school's program of physical, intellectual, moral, work, and esthetic training should take into account the age and individual characteristics of each child.

Language Training

Later in the morning, a teacher took Preschool 67's three- and four-year-olds aside to read them a story. The children listened intently. When the teacher had finished, she asked them to retell parts of the story and to answer questions about it, gently correcting their mistakes and insisting on answers that were complete, grammatical sentences. One little girl was overeager: she shouted the right answer before a slower and shyer child could finish. The teacher restrained her gently and then encouraged the other child to answer by himself.

Teaching the children to speak Russian correctly and to express themselves fully is one of the major aims of the preschool program. Language training is a continuous process, carried on throughout the day by means of books, stories, and direct contact with adults.

In another room, the older children followed their teacher's story in books of their own. Before the teacher began to read, she asked the children several questions about books and how they are used. During the story, she stopped often to ask what letter or sound a word began or ended with. Later, she requested summaries of the plot and descriptions of the characters.

For five- and six-year-olds, who will soon start school, there is great emphasis on skills like these. The preschool is in close touch with the grade schools that the children will attend, and it teaches them the work habits and procedures that are used there. Reading and writing as such are not formally taught in nursery school, but reading and writing readiness are. The children learn to analyze the sounds they hear in the spoken language and to write the elements used in the letters of the Russian alphabet.

Elementary mathematical concepts are introduced gradually, through the use of concrete materials. The children learn to count to ten by eye, ear, touch, and movement; to answer questions of number, size, and position in space; and to subtract or add one or two to any number up to ten. It is only in the last year of nursery school, when the children are six years old, that they begin to work with written numbers and with the symbols +, −, and =.

Rest and Play

After lunch, we stood at the door of a dormitory crowded with high, white iron bedsteads and watched the children take their usual two-hour rest. They were supposed to be asleep, but they seemed determined not to succumb. Stripped to their underwear and covered with sheets, they tossed, turned, whispered, sucked their thumbs, asked the nanny for glasses of water, and requested permission to go to the potty—or reported that it was too late.

The nanny treated the bed-wetters and thumb-suckers matter-of-factly. If a child wet his bed, she changed his sheets and underwear with little fuss and no reprimands. She privately asked a few older children to take their thumbs out of their mouths, but when the thumbs were put back in a few moments she seemed not to notice.

After their naps, the children went outside to play. The yard was provided with swings, sandboxes, and little pools of water; there were also gazebos and arbors, tables and chairs, and bookcases full of games, toys, books, and arts-and-crafts materials.

One two-year-old boy, ignoring these enticements, began to wander off the nursery-school grounds. The nanny in charge, a motherly, middle-aged woman, ran after him and brought him back. She scolded him affectionately, threatening to punish him by making him sit still.

"He's such a little one," she said. "He really doesn't understand. It's impossible to really punish him."

Mrs. Shvedova told us later that punishment is meted out only if the children hurt someone or are very dis-

obedient. "The first time a child is bad, we don't do anything. We try to understand. But after a while we must punish, because of the other children. We try to suit the punishment to the child and the situation. We know the children well and we know what each one will consider a punishment." Corporal punishment is frowned on in the Soviet Union, and the usual method of discipline is the temporary withdrawal of affection and praise.

Creativity Training

During the play period, one group of girls five or six years old went to an arts-and-crafts area to color. They were eager to please and to show us their work, which was very neat. When one girl offered to draw us a picture to take home to our daughter, we requested a dog. "I can't," she said. "No one has taught me how."

In Soviet nursery schools, drawing is a lesson—something to be learned. There are exercises on how to draw straight lines, circles, and other forms, and simple figures. These exercises are not considered play, and the teacher keeps a little folder of each child's work to encourage a serious attitude toward it.

Looking through these folders, we found that the children's drawings were all the same. The teacher had shown them how to draw a house, a person, or whatever, and they had done it. Unlike most Americans, who believe that a child will be creative "naturally" if he is given the chance, the Soviets believe creativity is more than a matter of opportunity. It requires training. But they are quick to point out that the object of training is not stilted, narrow drawings like those in the folders at Preschool 67. How to teach creativity properly is a problem now being studied at the laboratory of esthetic education of the Institute of Preschool Education.

However, the development of creativity does not seem to be very high on Soviet preschools' list of priorities. When we asked Mrs. Shvedova what goals Preschool 67 had for its children, she replied, "We want them to be smart and honest. If they are honest, they will be fair. We want them to love beauty, to be real people. We don't want them to be all alike, but originality and creativity are not that important."

Sensory Training

One thing that *is* important is sensory training, which the Soviets define rather more broadly than we would. At the preschool one morning we watched a row of three-year-olds, seated on small benches under an arbor, receive a lesson in sensory training that was also a lesson in language. The teacher showed the children five vegetables and named them: an onion, a beet, a carrot, a cabbage, and a potato. Then she put the vegetables in a cloth sack and asked a child to draw one out and name it.

When each child and the teacher had named the vegetables several times and repeated the names in unison, the teacher told the children that the five objects together were called vegetables. The class said the word "vegetable" several times and was dismissed.

The four- and five-year-olds had a harder task. After they chose a vegetable from the sack they were asked, without looking at it, to name it and tell everything they knew about it—its color, its shape, how it grows, and how it is eaten. The rest of the children in the group corrected and helped them.

According to the Russians, perception is more than the physical reception of energy by the sense organs. It also involves the organization of perceptual signals—the way a person selects and systematizes certain characteristics of perceptible reality so that he can use them in such activities as speech, music, art, and work. For the Soviets, then, perception means not only "perception" as we usually think of it; it includes a number of cognitive functions as well. When a child learns to perceive, he learns to orient himself in the world of the senses.

The Russians will allow that this can occur spontaneously, as a by-product of normal activity. But they do not believe that spontaneous development is very efficient or very effective. As A. V. Zaporozhets, director of the Institute of Preschool Education, explained when we talked with him, "Our nursery schools differ from most of those in the West, where there is no special program of education and it is believed that, given the chance, a child will ask questions and learn through his own initiative."

Soviet psychologists, Zaporozhets continued, disagree with both Jean Piaget and Maria Montessori. According to Piaget, the kind of thinking a child is capable of depends on his age. If beans are poured from a short, fat jar into a tall, thin one, a child of four is likely to think the tall jar contains more beans, while a child of six or seven will not be fooled. Piaget attributes this to the fact that the older child understands the principle of conservation.

The Russians, Zaporozhets said, do not agree "that a child cannot do such and such until a certain age. We think that teaching plays a decisive role in learning, and that a child can do quite a bit more than we previously imagined he was capable of."

They do think it is *easier* to develop certain abilities at certain ages, although they are not sure which abilities are easiest to develop at which age. As a working policy, they try to develop intuition and sensory abilities in early childhood, leaving abstract thought for later on. "We believe that thought is a hierarchical structure. For a complete intellect, the entire system, from the most concrete to the most abstract, must exist. You don't have to rush to the third stage when you haven't gotten through the first."

Like Montessori, Zaporozhets said, the Soviets think sensory abilities should be developed during early childhood. But "Montessori believed that the child is born with all his sensory abilities and that training will simply strengthen them. We think this is incorrect."

As the handbook for nursery-school teachers written by Institute psychologists, *Sensory Training*, explains, the Russians find the Montessorian system of training too formal, too "pure," too far removed from the everyday world in which the child must use his senses. They believe it is not enough to acquaint the child with an endless variety of sensory data. He must be taught a generalized method of orientation and investigation—an approach to the world of the senses—that will efficiently give him the information he needs. This is best done informally, within the context of regular nursery-school activities such as making models, drawing, constructing things with sand or blocks, singing, dancing, and storytelling.

Abstract exercises in which the child discriminates triangles from circles in an unanalyzed way are thought to teach him very little. In the Russian nursery school, a child is taught not only that red is different from blue but that red is the color of apples and, indeed, that red apples are ripe apples and ripe apples are edible apples.

The child is taught to use his senses, and he is also taught what the things he perceives mean and what words he can use to describe his sensory experiences precisely. At the same time, he is encouraged to generalize and categorize on the basis of his immediate sensory experience—he is taught, for instance, that onion-beet-carrot-cabbage-potato equals vegetable.

Here is a typical elementary exercise in sensory training used with two- and three-year-olds. The object of the exercise, which is preliminary to developing the kind of perception the Soviets are talking about, is to teach the child to use his sensory apparatus to the fullest.

The teacher gives the child two cardboard circles (or triangles, or squares) that are the same size but different colors. She asks the child to put one circle on top of the other so that the edges are even, and to run his finger along the edges of the figures so that he can tell whether he has aligned them correctly or not. Then she gives the child a circle and a square of the same color—say, blue—and shows him a *red* square. His task is to find which of his figures has the same *shape* as hers. The child makes his choice and verifies it by placing it on the teacher's model. If it fits, the child is praised; if not, the teacher suggests he try the other figure.

As *Sensory Training* points out, the object of perceptual training is to prepare the child for future activity. In short, the Russian approach is highly pragmatic and task oriented. Perhaps for this reason, the schools make considerable use of construction exercises. Like drawing, building requires the child to perform a detailed visual examination of the form, size, and spatial arrangement of an object, but *Sensory Training* warns that there is an important distinction between construction and pictorial tasks. A picture always reflects the exterior characteristics of an object as it is visually perceived; construction serves a practical purpose. "Garages are built for cars, barns for animals, houses for dolls. Constructions are made by children to be used—acted with."

Thus a teacher might provide the children with bricks, have the children pile them up in different ways and test the stability of the piles, and then suggest the construction of a road. Or she might give the children beams of different lengths and ask them to build a corral. She would point out the various factors the children should consider if the corral is to serve its purpose—that it must be high enough to prevent the animals from jumping out, that the beams must be close enough together to keep the animals from squeezing through, and so forth.

Although the stress in exercises like these is on purpose and practicality, note that it is also on *activity*, and particularly on physical activity as an important way to develop perceptual skills. The child is an active agent in his own development. *He* places the geometric figures together and runs his fingers around the edges; *he* piles the bricks and builds the corral.

This emphasis on the role of active experience in the child's development has its counterpart in contemporary American developmental theory. Richard Held of MIT, for example, has shown that there is a close relation between motor experience and visual perception, especially when one must coordinate what one sees with what one does. In one well-known experiment, Held provided a man and a woman with special glasses that shifted their visual fields to the right. Then he had the woman sit in a wheelchair while the man pushed the chair around the campus. When the two were tested later, the man—who had had motor experience with the visual shift—was much better than the woman at correcting for the distortion that the glasses created.

In a similar experiment, Held placed two kittens in a circular box whose walls were painted with vertical stripes. One kitten sat in a cart; the other wore a yoke and walked around the box rather in the manner of a water buffalo, moving the cart around as he did so. Although the kitten who got the free ride saw the same

things as the walking kitten, the walking kitten seemed to learn more. When the two were tested later, the kitten that had the motor experience showed superior ability to perform a number of tasks that required visual-motor coordination.

The notion of the child as an active agent in his own development also occurs in the work of Jerome Bruner of Harvard. Just telling the child a set of facts, Bruner says, does not produce real learning. The child must operate on his environment in such a way that he discovers solutions to the problems it poses. As the child searches for solutions, his approach becomes more sophisticated and also more effective. For example, young children who have not learned how to gather information efficiently play Twenty Questions by asking about specific items: "Is it the dog?" "Is it Mommy?" Older children try to structure their questions so that each yields a maximum amount of information: "Is it a living American man?" Through a process of active searching, the older children have learned generalized techniques for gathering information.

Much of the research now being done by Zaporozhets and his colleagues at the Institute is based on this general premise that activity leads to learning. There are experiments, for example, on teaching cooperation and consideration of others through role-playing. Several children who are not friendly with each other are asked to perform a joint task—to tell a story together, or to put on a puppet show—in the hope that they will be friendlier after than they were before.

We arrived in the Soviet Union with a mental image of a monolithic preschool system, chiefly Pavlovian in theory, and rigid, regimented, and stifling in practice. Soviet psychology does include some Pavlovian concepts, and Soviet preschool programs do follow a common outline, but these are a much smaller part of the whole picture than we had supposed. In fact, the theoretical and empirical research conducted at the Institute would command the respect of developmental psychologists in Geneva or New York, and the care given the children of Preschool 67 could serve as a model anywhere—anywhere, that is, where children are treated as one of society's most valuable resources.

II
The Student in Transition

Emotional Barriers to Education
Richard E. Farson

Richard Farson here argues that the contemporary technological revolution in education need not turn students into Orwellian mechanical idiots but may indeed offer teachers and students the time and freedom to have real person-to-person relationships without the intrusion of the bureaucratic and clerical routines of today's pretechnological schools. One should note that Farson broadly defines technology to include not only educational hardware but also systems engineering, social technology, classroom simulation, and sensitivity-training groups.

How do Dr. Farson's ideas fit in with the technological advances being made in education, as discussed in Part VI?

Tomorrow's world, with the push-button machine replacing the button-down mind, will be automated, calibrated, and cybernated—and yet I believe that the ultimate in mechanization will make us more human. The lines will be clear—what man is for and what machines are for—and we will value each other for our humanness rather than because we are "useful" and "productive."

We all know that the twenty-first century will be technologically different from this one. We have been told about space exploration and sea farming, about computerized kitchens and waterless bathing. What we do *not* know is that people themselves will change, too. Their goals will be to develop uniquely human capacities to the fullest—capacities for love, creativity, joy, sensory and esthetic appreciation, and interpersonal skills for continuing growth along every dimension, not only the cognitive.

Our educational system, then, will face a new set of human values as well as a new technology. If it is to be ready, we must change not only our educational *methods*—that is hard enough—but our basic *concepts* of education. That is far more difficult.

The goals of education, the curriculum, and classroom instructional methods have not changed in any fundamental way for generations. Yet there are, in abundance, fresh, creative, and workable ideas that could revolutionize education almost overnight. Educators, behavioral scientists, teachers, and students already know a lot about how to create a favorable climate for learning. In part, we have been prevented by political, social, and economic obstacles from putting our knowledge to use. Equally frustrating are psychological barriers to change, which too often go unrecognized. Fortunately, though, psychological barriers sometimes topple when we do no more than point a finger at them. So I want first to discuss some of these psychological barriers, and then to talk about new ways for bringing about change.

Pointing the Finger

One of the most difficult barriers to overcome is the notion that education should be irksome. "You can't get something for nothing" is the motto that governs our view of learning. Somehow, we feel that if learning is exciting, fun, easy, then it can't be "educational."

Another barrier is what might be called our allegiance to the accustomed. We try to create conditions that are familiar to us, to change a strange situation until it resembles what we are used to. So no matter how wretched our school experience may have been, when we set about designing a learning environment for our children, we make it as similar as possible to what we knew. We may accept a new idea, but then we proceed to take the newness out of it. For example, we accept the idea that letter grades are bad, but we replace them with nothing more radical than their verbal equivalents—"satisfactory for grade level," "above grade level."

We feel the same way about the content of education. Education as we knew it was a dignified and formal process of transmitting information, imparting facts, stimulating the higher mental processes, and providing techniques for analyzing and solving intellectual puzzles. So today we apply the term "education" only to those activities that seem to involve "thinking." Developing the other dimensions of humanness—awakening the senses, recognizing feelings and emotions, deepening esthetic sensitivity, acquiring taste and judgment, and expanding skills in the vast area of human relations—seems to us only to be "doing what comes naturally" and therefore not within the province of education.

Pandora's Box

At present, noncognitive and nonverbal skills just are not considered academically respectable. They have not yet been formulated into a conceptual structure, and they seem imprecise, fuzzy, vague, and even threatening. We feel we must keep the lid tightly closed on Pandora's box, for we fear that it contains the irrational, the potentially explosive elements of human nature.

When emotionality or interpersonal relationships escape from the box, we flinch and take refuge in the dictum that only the qualified professional is capable of dealing with the layers of humanness below the rational. Old-fashioned psychiatry is largely responsible for the prevailing attitude that teachers should avoid tampering with children's psyches. This nonsense has so frightened teachers that they shun almost any engagement with the student as a person.

We treat each other as if we were very fragile, as if any hurt or penetration of our defenses would lead to a crumbling of the entire person; or we regard each other as a tenuously contrived set of social roles that serves to cover what might be the frightening reality—a vicious beast, or, at best, man's "animal nature."

There is no doubt that educating for humanness will call upon teachers and students to encounter each other in their totality as human beings, with all of the problems and possibilities, the hopes and fears, the angers and joys, that make up a person. To relate to each other in this way, we will have to learn to be less afraid of what people are like and to recognize that they are not likely to shatter when anyone engages them on an emotional level.

This fear of emotionality is in part, I think, responsible for our widespread fear of intimacy. We dare not reveal ourselves, share our feelings. We have developed an elaborate set of social devices that allows us to put distance between ourselves and others, that lubricates our relationships, and that gives us privacy in a crowded and complex society. Even to use such terms as "intimate" or "loving" disturbs most people. Popular belief and much professional opinion hold that the machinery of any social organization, and certainly of a school, will become clogged if people are concerned with each other instead of tending to business. Nevertheless, we have a deep need for moments of shared feeling, for they give us a sense of community and remind us of our membership in the human race.

"Don't Rock the Boat"

Increasingly in the last few years, most of us who are concerned with education have discoursed on ways of fostering creativity in the classroom. We talk as if it were difficult to identify creativity in people and even more difficult to liberate it. But it is just the other way around. The potential for creativity exists in almost everyone, and it is easy to liberate. The trouble is that, although we want creativity, we want it only in manageable amounts—because its offspring, innovation, rocks the boat. So the only creativity we tolerate in school is the kind that follows the rules, pleases teachers and parents, and isn't noisy.

Another barrier to change is that many of us secretly enjoy viewing with alarm. We *like* to be mad at something or somebody; it is exhilarating, a safety valve for our frustrations, perhaps. But unfortunately the expression of outrage is often sufficient. We do not really care whether the situation is rectified—indeed, we often are disappointed if it is.

One of the great paradoxes of change—and perhaps one of the most important reasons that organizations and institutions resist change—is that the inevitable consequence of improvement is discontent. When things get better, we ask, "Why stop here?" The higher we climb, the wider the vista before us; we see the discrepancy between what we have and what we now

see it might be possible to have. The urgent need for educational change is itself an illustration of this paradox. The enormous advances in technology, which so radically have improved the material aspects of American life, demand that the methods and goals of education be changed to meet newer and higher needs. As Abraham Maslow, president of the American Psychological Association, has put it, when our grumbles result in improved conditions, we get "meta-grumbles."

But social institutions do change, even if they fail to keep up with the changes in science and technology. How are the barriers overcome? In education, as in other fields, most innovation will be brought about by invasion from without and by rebellion from within.

Technology—Hardware

One wave of invasion already has begun: an overwhelming technological revolution is underway in the education industry. Its impact will be monumental, and I say this with all due respect for the ability of the educational enterprise to resist technological changes. It is significant that the greatest resistance comes less from parents than from teachers. One might suppose that teachers would welcome relief from routine tasks that can be better accomplished by machines, but this does not seem to be the case. No matter how serious the shortage of personnel, no teacher is immune to fear of being replaced by a machine. Seldom do teachers see the machine as an assistant, and perhaps they are right.

For although machines can relieve the teacher of burdensome detail, they will change enormously the teacher's role vis-à-vis the students. And very likely this new role will at first seem far more complex and demanding, though actually it may turn out to be simpler and far more joyful. Teachers have chafed under the record-keeping, evaluation-oriented tasks of present-day schools, but I suspect that most teachers would have mixed feelings about interacting with their students in real person-to-person relationships, unprotected by the buffer of these tasks and roles.

In the last few years, scores of major American business firms have moved into the great new "people" industries—health, education, welfare, recreation, and entertainment. This shift from the production of goods to the provision of services is significant for both public and private educational systems because it is these systems that will have to furnish the manpower for the people industry. The schools will have to educate for new qualities—they will have to produce people who are suited for human service. The task will be as different from the present one as educating graduates for the automobile industry is different from preparing people for the Peace Corps.

The human service industries are already big business; well over 150 major American firms recently have moved into the educational business. They and other organizations will invent, produce, and sell more sophisticated, effective devices for teaching, which inevitably will transform education. They plan only to *service* education. It may be that soon they will try to *replace* the present educational system with something quite different.

At present, only about a half billion dollars are spent by educational systems for discretionary purchases, so the market for educational services that might be provided by American industry is not very large. Industry might try to enlarge it by developing demand outside the schools—or by moving into school systems in somewhat the same way that certain large firms have taken over the organization, management, and operation of some Job Corps centers.

Technology—Social

The new technology does not consist solely of audio-visual aids, computers, and programmed instruction. One of the most important resources for change—perhaps the most important of all—is the new social technology, which enables us to use social processes to change a social system so that it becomes freer, more flexible, and more responsive to the needs and goals of all its members.

One of these new social technologies is known as "systems engineering." The most popular new word in education—as in almost every other field—is "systems." Its wide and often inappropriate usage may obscure the subtle revolution that is being put in motion by the application of systems engineering to education.

In its simplest terms, systems engineering is the application of common-sense analysis to a large and complex organization. It means looking at the overall picture, trying to understand the informal as well as the formal ways the organization functions, its implicit as well as its explicit goals. To understand the operation of an educational system, assessment of the physical facilities would be only the first step; one would need to analyze not only the activities and goals of students, teachers, administrators, parents, and school-board members, but the activities and goals of all the systems that articulate with the educational system, to see what bearing they have on its operation.

Systems analysis forces an organization to clarify its real goals; it studies what people really do and really need; and it provides the means for confronting people with rapid feedback on the effects of their action. Finally, it capitalizes on the fact that almost any well-intended disruption of a given system seems to produce a reintegration of the system at a somewhat higher level. Apparently, there are reliable forces toward growth and integration in any organization if some means can be found for releasing them.

Another social technology that is becoming increasingly familiar under a variety of names is the "intensive small group," "T-group," "sensitivity-training group" or "human-relation group." After a slow start, the use of the small group now is spreading with astonishing rapidity through all the institutions of society—schools, churches, industries, business organizations—to promote personal growth and organizational effectiveness.

At the Western Behavioral Sciences Institute, we have done research on such groups in a variety of settings. Currently, a parochial school system that embraces all levels of education from kindergarten through college is cooperating with Carl Rogers of WBSI, who explains that he wants to learn whether involving all members of the system in the intensive group experience will:

create a climate conducive to personal growth in which innovation is not frightening, in which the creative capacities of administrators, teachers, and students are nourished and expressed rather than stifled. [For] educators themselves must be open and flexible, effectively involved in the processes of change. They must be able both to conserve and convey the essential knowledge and values of the past, and to welcome eagerly the innovations which are necessary to prepare for the unknown future.

Still a third new social technology, which has been co-opted from the research laboratory to the classroom, is the simulation exercise, or "educational game." Classroom use of simulations has received a great deal of attention recently, not because simulations offer a better way of teaching subject matter—they may not—but because they alter the social structure of the classroom, that is, the relation between teachers and students. The teacher who uses simulations is released from his traditional role as evaluator, content specialist, disciplinarian, and record keeper because the rules of the simulation require that the students themselves perform those functions. Freed of routine chores, the teacher can deal with deeper, more interesting individual learning problems arising during and after the simulation exercise.

At WBSI, Hall Sprague has developed and tested a variety of simulation games in which students represent decision-makers in business and in national and international politics. On the basis of his experiences, Sprague says that simulations "may lead students to more sophisticated and relevant inquiry, may help them learn such nonacademic skills as decision-making, communication, and influence-resisting, and may integrate the subject matter and make it seem more realistic and relevant. They also may produce a more relaxed atmosphere between teacher and students later on."

Educational games now are being used to teach concepts of international relations, national politics, community leadership, business decision-making, home management, career planning, and the like, but there is no limit to the subjects that might be learned through simulation. We presently are developing a game that will confront a school system with probable changes in its future so that all the members of the system may simulate responses to these events. As a result of playing the game, they will be developing a long-range plan—inventing their future, if you will.

Rebellion from Within

It is almost impossible nowadays to pick up a magazine or a newspaper without encountering some reference to the "student revolt" or the revolt of youth embodied in the Hippie movement, the New Left, or the war- and draft-resisters. These rebellious young people are telling us, in the words of their own poet, Bob Dylan, that "The times, they are a-changin'." And these youths are, in effect, joining forces in an attempt to create a new kind of society that will fulfill a new set of demands— their right to be fully human, to be honest, to be themselves, to create their own experiences and to discover new experiences, and to control their own lives.

Perhaps on the whole, these young people know more than we adults do about what life in the twenty-first century will be like, because I think they are shaping it now. They are demanding the right to have a voice in the decisions that affect them. They take education more seriously than we do, for they are saying in countless ways, "We refuse an education that merely prepares us for a place in this impersonal machine that our society has become. We refuse to be 'taught' only what you think we ought or need to know; we demand the right to learn everything we can about the things that really matter."

In "New Schools" and "Free Universities," on and off the campus, they are re-creating, in a sense, the medieval university, in which the students decided what they wanted to learn, and hired and fired the scholars who taught them. And the young rebels are being joined by a few professors, teachers, parents, counselors, and even administrators who equally constitute a powerful force for change from within. We already are beginning to see major shifts in educational practices at the college and university level, where revolutionary experiments in student-oriented and student-determined education are being permitted.

"Underground" newspapers published by bright young high-school and even junior-high-school students are causing ripples in supervisory circles. One high-school "underground" editor reports spending half his time in the Vice Principal's office: "He wants to explain to me all the reasons for his decisions before they are announced to the students." This is hopeful. Last year, author Lyn Tornabene posed as a high-school student to research what she planned as a funny book. She got by successfully with her masquerade, but she found only miserable students in boring courses. Her book was *not* funny.

Education in the twenty-first century will be a life-long, richly rewarding experience, engaged in because it is fun, joyful, deeply involving. It will be designed to expand and enrich all aspects of human experience— sensory, emotional, and esthetic, as well as intellectual—and to liberate creativity in all these realms.

And people will be declaring, as they are today, that education isn't nearly as good as it could be, and that something will have to be done about it.

The Child
as a Moral Philosopher

Lawrence Kohlberg

If the student is going to acquire keener moral sensitivity in the present climate of social and value criticism, his teachers must prepare to help him move from one moral level to another and must engage in an ongoing moral examination of themselves. No matter what the subject—humanities, social sciences, natural sciences, or various skills—as we move toward a more humanistic culture with high emphasis on the pluralism of individual and group life styles, the ethical dimension of what is taught will increasingly occupy the attention of students.

Lawrence Kohlberg's penetrating analysis and corroborating study of the orderly development of ethical thought in children points to dimensions of the child's behavior that are frequently ignored in determining what is taught and tested and how. It might be an interesting exercise to review Kohlberg's moral levels and stages to determine the level of one's own ethical development.

How can one study morality? Current trends in the fields of ethics, linguistics, anthropology, and cognitive psychology have suggested a new approach that seems to avoid the morass of semantical confusions, value bias and cultural relativity in which the psychoanalytic and semantic approaches to morality have foundered. New scholarship in all these fields is now focusing upon structures, forms, and relationships that seem to be common to all societies and all languages rather than upon the features that make particular languages or cultures different.

For twelve years, my colleagues and I studied the same group of seventy-five boys, following their development at three-year intervals from early adolescence through young manhood. At the start of the study, the boys were aged ten to sixteen. We have now followed them through to ages twenty-two to twenty-eight. In addition, I have explored moral development in other cultures—Great Britain, Canada, Taiwan, Mexico, and Turkey.

Inspired by Jean Piaget's pioneering effort to apply a structural approach to moral development, I have gradually elaborated over the years of my study a typological scheme describing general structures and forms of moral thought that can be defined independently of the specific content of particular moral decisions or actions.

The typology contains three distinct levels of moral thinking, and within each of these levels distinguishes two related stages. These levels and stages may be considered separate moral philosophies, distinct views of the sociomoral world.

We can speak of the child as having his own morality or series of moralities. Adults seldom listen to children's moralizing. If a child throws back a few adult clichés and behaves himself, most parents—and many anthropologists and psychologists as well—think that the child has adopted or internalized the appropriate parental standards.

Actually, as soon as we talk with children about morality, we find that they have many ways of making judgments that are not "internalized" from the outside, and that do not come in any direct and obvious way from parents, teachers, or even peers.

Moral Levels

The *preconventional* level is the first of three levels of moral thinking; the second level is *conventional*, and the third *postconventional*, or autonomous. While the preconventional child is often "well behaved" and is responsive to cultural labels of good and bad, he interprets these labels in terms of their physical consequences (punishment, reward, exchange of favors) or in terms of the physical power of those who enunciate the rules and labels of good and bad.

This level is usually occupied by children aged four to ten, a fact long known to sensitive observers of children. The capacity of "properly behaved" children of this age to engage in cruel behavior when there are holes in the power structure is sometimes noted as tragic (*Lord of the Flies*, *High Wind in Jamaica*), sometimes as comic (Lucy in *Peanuts*).

The second, or conventional, level also can be described as conformist, but that is perhaps too smug a term. Maintaining the expectations and rules of the individual's family, group, or nation is perceived as valuable in its own right. There is a concern not only with *conforming* to the individual's social order but in *maintaining*, supporting, and justifying this order.

The postconventional level is characterized by a major thrust toward autonomous moral principles that have validity and application apart from authority of the groups or persons who hold them and apart from the individual's identification with those persons or groups.

Moral Stages

Within each of these three levels there are two discernible stages. At the preconventional level we have:

Stage 1: Orientation toward punishment and unquestioning deference to superior power. The physical consequences of action, regardless of their human meaning or value, determine its goodness or badness.

Stage 2: Right action consists of that which instrumentally satisfies one's own needs and occasionally the needs of others. Human relations are viewed in terms like those of the marketplace. Elements of fairness, of reciprocity, and equal sharing are present, but they are always interpreted in a physical, pragmatic way. Reciprocity is a matter of "you scratch my back and I'll scratch yours" not of loyalty, gratitude, or justice.

And at the conventional level we have:

Stage 3: Good-boy—good-girl orientation. Good behavior is that which pleases or helps others and is approved by them. There is much conformity to stereotypical images of what is majority or "natural" behavior. Behavior is often judged by intention; "he means well" becomes important for the first time, and is overused, as by Charlie Brown in *Peanuts*. One seeks approval by being "nice."

Stage 4: Orientation toward authority, fixed rules, and the maintenance of the social order. Right behavior consists of doing one's duty, showing respect for authority, and maintaining the given social order for its own sake. One earns respect by performing dutifully.

At the postconventional level, we have:

Stage 5: A social-contract orientation, generally with legalistic and utilitarian overtones. Right action tends to be defined in terms of general rights and in terms of standards that have been critically examined and agreed upon by the whole society. There is a clear awareness of the relativism of personal values and opinions and a corresponding emphasis upon procedural rules for reaching consensus. Aside from what is constitutionally and democratically agreed upon, right or wrong is a matter of personal "values" and "opinion." The result is an emphasis upon the "legal point of view," but with an emphasis upon the possibility of *changing* law in terms of rational considerations of social utility, rather than freezing it in the terms of Stage 4 "law and order." Outside the legal realm, free agreement and contract are the binding elements of obligation. This is the "official" morality of American government and finds its ground in the thought of the writers of the Constitution.

Stage 6: Orientation toward the decisions of conscience and toward self-chosen *ethical principles* appealing to logical comprehensiveness, universality, and consistency. These principles are abstract and ethical (the Golden Rule, the categorical imperative); they are not concrete moral rules like the Ten Commandments. Instead, they are universal principles of justice, of the reciprocity and equality of human rights, and of respect for the dignity of human beings as individual persons.

Up to Now

In the past, when psychologists tried to answer the question asked of Socrates by Meno, "Is virtue something that can be taught (by rational discussion), or does it come by practice, or is it a natural inborn attitude?" their answers usually have been dictated not by research findings on children's moral character but by their general theoretical convictions.

Behavior theorists have said that virtue is behavior acquired according to their favorite general principles of learning. Freudians have claimed that virtue is superego identification with parents, generated by a proper balance of love and authority in family relations.

The American psychologists who have actually studied children's morality have tried to start with a set of labels—the "virtues" and "vices," the "traits" of good and bad character found in ordinary language. The earliest major psychological study of moral character, that of Hugh Hartshorne and Mark May in 1928–1930, focused on a bag of virtues including honesty, service (altruism or generosity), and self-control. To their dismay, they found that there were *no* character traits, psychological dispositions, or entities that corresponded to words like honesty, service, or self-control.

Regarding honesty, for instance, they found that almost everyone cheats some of the time, and that if a person cheats in one situation, it does not mean that he *will* or *won't* in another. In other words, it is not an identifiable character trait, *dishonesty*, that makes a child cheat in a given situation. These early researchers also found that people who cheat express as much or even more moral disapproval of cheating as those who do not cheat.

What Hartshorne and May found out about their bag of virtues is equally upsetting to the somewhat more psychological-sounding names introduced by psychoanalytic psychology: "superego strength," "resistance to temptation," "strength of conscience," and the like. When contemporary researchers have attempted to measure such traits in individuals, they have been forced to use Hartshorne and May's old tests of honesty and self-control, and they get exactly the same results— "superego strength" in one situation predicts little about "superego strength" in another. That is, virtue words like honesty (or superego strength) point to certain behaviors with approval but give us no guide to understanding them.

So far as one can extract some generalized personality factor from children's performance on tests of honesty or resistance to temptation, it is a factor of ego strength or ego control, which always involves nonmoral capacities like the capacity to maintain attention, intelligent-task performance, and the ability to delay response. "Ego strength" (called "will" in earlier days) has something to do with moral action, but it does not take us to the core of morality or to the definition of virtue. Obviously enough, many of the greatest evil-doers in history have been men of strong wills, men strongly pursuing immoral goals.

Moral Reasons

In our research, we have found definite and universal levels of development in moral thought. In our study of seventy-five American boys from early adolescence on, these youths were presented with hypothetical moral dilemmas, all deliberately philosophical, some of them found in medieval works of casuistry.

On the basis of their reasoning about these dilemmas at a given age, each boy's stage of thought could be determined for each of twenty-five basic moral concepts or aspects. One such aspect, for instance, is "motive given for rule obedience or moral action." In this instance, the six stages look like this:

1. Obey rules to avoid punishment.
2. Conform to obtain rewards, have favors returned, and so on.
3. Conform to avoid disapproval, dislike by others.
4. Conform to avoid censure by legitimate authorities and resultant guilt.
5. Conform to maintain the respect of the impartial spectator judging in terms of community welfare.
6. Conform to avoid self-condemnation.

In another of these twenty-five moral aspects, "the value of human life," the six stages can be defined thus:

1. The value of a human life is confused with the value of physical objects and is based on the social status or physical attributes of its possessor.
2. The value of a human life is seen as instrumental to the satisfaction of the needs of its possessor or of other persons.
3. The value of a human life is based on the empathy and affection of family members and others toward its possessor.
4. Life is conceived as sacred in terms of its place in a categorical moral or religious order of rights and duties.
5. Life is valued both in terms of its relation to community welfare and in terms of life being a universal human right.
6. Belief in the sacredness of human life as representing a universal human value of respect for the individual.

I have called this scheme a typology. This is because about 50 percent of most people's thinking will be at a single stage, regardless of the moral dilemma involved. We call our types stages because they seem to represent an *invariant developmental sequence*. "True" stages come one at a time and always in the same order.

All movement is forward in sequence, and does not skip steps. Children may move through these stages at varying speeds, of course, and may be found half in and half out of a particular stage. An individual may stop at any given stage and at any age, but if he continues to move, he must move in accord with these steps. Moral reasoning of the conventional, or Stage 3–4, kind never occurs before the preconventional Stage 1 and Stage 2 thought has taken place. No adult in Stage 4 has gone through Stage 6, but all Stage 6 adults have gone at least through 4.

While the evidence is not complete, my study strongly suggests that moral change fits the stage pattern just described. (The major uncertainty is whether all people at Stage 6 go through Stage 5 or whether these are two alternate mature orientations.)

How Values Change

As a single example of our findings of stage sequence, take the progress of two boys on the aspect "the value of human life." The first boy, Tommy, is asked "Is it better to save the life of one important person or a lot of unimportant people?" At age ten, he answers "all the people that aren't important because one man just has one house, maybe a lot of furniture, but a whole bunch of people have an awful lot of furniture and some of these poor people might have a lot of money and it doesn't look it."

Clearly Tommy is Stage 1: he confuses the value of a human being with the value of the property he possesses. Three years later (age thirteen) Tommy's conceptions of life's value are most clearly elicited by the question, "Should the doctor 'mercy kill' a fatally ill woman requesting death because of her pain?" He answers, "Maybe it would be good to put her out of her pain, she'd be better off that way. But the husband wouldn't want it, it's not like an animal. If a pet dies you can get along without it—it isn't something you really need. Well, you can get a new wife, but it's not really the same."

Here his answer is Stage 2: the value of the woman's life is partly contingent on its hedonistic value to the wife herself but even more contingent on its instrumental value to her husband, who can't replace her as easily as he can a pet.

Three years later (age sixteen) Tommy's conception of life's value is elicited by the same question, to which he replies: "It might be best for her, but her husband—it's a human life—not like an animal; it just doesn't have the same relationship that a human being does to a family. You can become attached to a dog, but nothing like a human you know."

Now Tommy has moved from a Stage 2 instrumental view of the woman's value to a Stage 3 view based on the husband's distinctively human empathy and love for someone in his family. Equally clearly, it lacks any basis for a universal human value of the woman's life, which would hold if she had no husband or if her husband didn't love her. Tommy, then, has moved step by step through three stages during the ages ten through sixteen. Tommy, though bright (IQ 120), is a slow developer in moral judgment. Let us take another boy, Richard, to show us sequential movement through the remaining three steps.

At age thirteen, Richard said about the mercy killing, "If she requests it, it's really up to her. She is in such terrible pain, just the same as people are always putting animals out of their pain," and in general showed a mixture of Stage 2 and Stage 3 responses concerning the value of life. At sixteen, he said:

I don't know. In one way, it's murder, it's not a right or privilege of man to decide who shall live and who should die. God put life into everybody on earth and you're taking away something from that person that came directly from God, and you're destroying something that is very sacred, it's in a way part of God and it's almost destroying a part of God when you kill a person. There's something of God in everyone.

Here Richard clearly displays a Stage 4 concept of life as sacred in terms of its place in a categorical moral or religious order. The value of human life is universal, it is true for all humans. It is still, however, dependent on something else, upon respect for God and God's authority; it is not an autonomous human value. Presumably if God told Richard to murder, as God commanded Abraham to murder Isaac, he would do so.

At age twenty, Richard said to the same question:

There are more and more people in the medical profession who think it is a hardship on everyone, the person, the family, when you know they are going to die. When a person is kept alive by an artificial lung or kidney it's more like being a vegetable than being a human. If it's her own choice, I think there are certain rights and privileges that go along with being a human being. I am a human being and have certain desires for life and I think everybody else does too. You have a world of which you are the center, and everybody else does too and in that sense we're all equal.

Richard's response is clearly Stage 5, in that the value of life is defined in terms of equal and universal human rights in a context of relativity ("You have a world of which you are the center and in that sense we're all equal"), and of concern for utility or welfare consequences.

The Final Step

At twenty-four, Richard says:

A human life takes precedence over any other moral or legal value, whoever it is. A human life has inherent value whether or not it is valued by a particular individual. The worth of the individual human being is central where the principles of justice and love are normative for all human relationships.

This young man is at Stage 6 in seeing the value of human life as absolute in representing a universal and equal respect for the human as an individual. He has moved step by step through a sequence culminating in a definition of human life as centrally valuable rather than derived from or dependent on social or divine authority.

In a genuine and culturally universal sense, these steps lead toward an increased *morality* of value judgment, where morality is considered as a form of judging, as it has been in a philosophic tradition running from the analyses of Kant to those of the modern analytic or "ordinary language" philosophers. The person at Stage 6 has disentangled his judgments of—or language about—human life from status and property values (Stage 1), from its uses to others (Stage 2), from interpersonal affection (Stage 3), and so on; he has a means of moral judgment that is universal and impersonal. The Stage 6 person's answers use moral words like "duty" or "morally right," and he uses them in a way implying universality, ideals, impersonality: He thinks and speaks in phrases like "regardless of who it was," or "I would do it in spite of punishment."

Across Cultures

When I first decided to explore moral development in other cultures, I was told by anthropologist friends that

I would have to throw away my culture-bound moral concepts and stories and start from scratch learning a whole new set of values for each new culture. My first try consisted of a brace of villages, one Atayal (Malaysian aboriginal) and the other Taiwanese.

My guide was a young Chinese ethnographer who had written an account of the moral and religious patterns of the Atayal and Taiwanese villages. Taiwanese boys in the ten to thirteen age group were asked about a story involving theft of food. A man's wife is starving to death, but the store owner won't give the man any food unless he can pay, which he can't. Should he break in and steal some food? Why? Many of the boys said, "He should steal the food for his wife because if she dies he'll have to pay for her funeral and that costs a lot."

My guide was amused by these responses, but I was relieved: they were, of course, "classic" Stage 2 responses. In the Atayal village, funerals weren't such a big thing, so the Stage 2 boys would say, "He should steal the food because he needs his wife to cook for him."

This means that we need to consult our anthropologists to know what content a Stage 2 child will include in his instrumental exchange calculations, or what a Stage 4 adult will identify as the proper social order. But one certainly does not have to start from scratch. What made my guide laugh was the difference in form between the children's Stage 2 thought and his own, a difference definable independently of particular cultures.

Figure 1 indicates the cultural universality of the sequence of stages that we have found. Figure 1a presents the age trends for middle-class urban boys in the United States, Taiwan, and Mexico. At age ten in each country, the order of use of each stage is the same as the order of its difficulty or maturity.

In the United States, by age sixteen the order is the reverse, from the highest to the lowest, except that Stage 6 is still little-used. At age thirteen, the good-boy, middle stage (Stage 3) is not used.

The results in Mexico and Taiwan are the same, except that development is a little slower. The most conspicuous feature is that at the age of sixteen, Stage 5 thinking is much more salient in the United States than in Mexico or Taiwan. Nevertheless, it is present in the other countries, so we know that this is not purely an American democratic construct.

Figure 1b shows strikingly similar results from two isolated villages, one in Yucatan, one in Turkey. While conventional moral thought increases steadily from ages ten to sixteen, it still has not achieved a clear ascendency over preconventional thought.

Trends for lower-class urban groups are intermediate in the rate of development between those for the middle-class and those for the village boys. In the three divergent cultures that I studied, middle-class children were found to be more advanced in moral judgment than matched lower-class children. This was not due to the fact that the middle-class children heavily favored some one type of thought that could be seen as corresponding to the prevailing middle-class pattern. Instead, middle-class and working-class children move through the same sequences, but the middle-class children move faster and further.

This sequence is not dependent upon a particular religion, or any religion at all in the usual sense. I found no important differences in the development of moral thinking among Catholics, Protestants, Jews, Buddhists, Moslems, or atheists. Religious values seem to go through the same stages as all other values.

Trading Up

In summary, the nature of our sequence is not significantly affected by widely varying social, cultural, or religious conditions. The only thing that is affected is the *rate* at which individuals progress through this sequence.

Why should there be such a universal invariant sequence of development? In answering this question, we need first to analyze these developing social concepts in terms of their internal logical structure. At each stage, the same basic moral concept or aspect is defined, but at each higher stage this definition is more differentiated, more integrated, and more general or universal. When one's concept of human life moves from Stage 1 to Stage 2, the value of life becomes more differentiated from the value of property, more integrated (the value of life enters an organizational hierarchy where it is "higher" than property so that one steals property in order to save life), and more universalized (the life of any sentient being is valuable regardless of status or property). The same advance is true at each stage in the hierarchy. Each step of development, then, is a better cognitive organization than the one before it, one that takes account of everything present in the previous stage but makes new distinctions and organizes them into a more comprehensive or more equilibrated structure. The fact that this is the case has been demonstrated by a series of studies indicating that children and adolescents comprehend all stages up to their own, but not more than one stage beyond their own. And importantly, *they prefer this next stage.*

We have conducted experimental moral discussion classes that show that the child at an earlier stage of development tends to move forward when confronted by the views of a child one stage further along. In an argument between a Stage 3 and a Stage 4 child, the child in the third stage tends to move toward or into Stage 4, while the Stage 4 child understands but does not accept the arguments of the Stage 3 child.

Moral thought, then, seems to behave like all other kinds of thought. Progress through the moral levels and stages is characterized by increasing differentiation and increasing integration, and hence is the same kind of progress that scientific theory represents. Like accept-

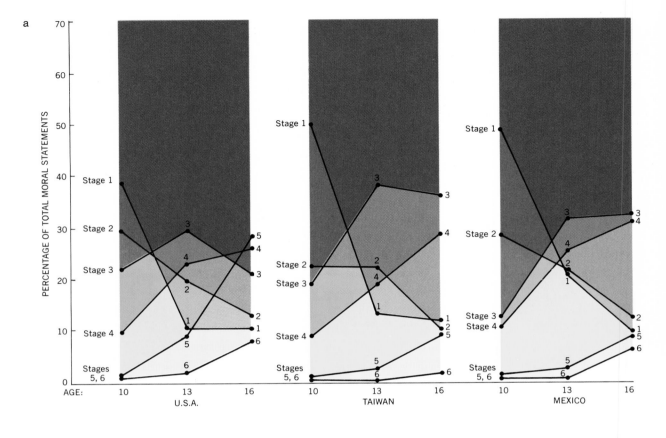

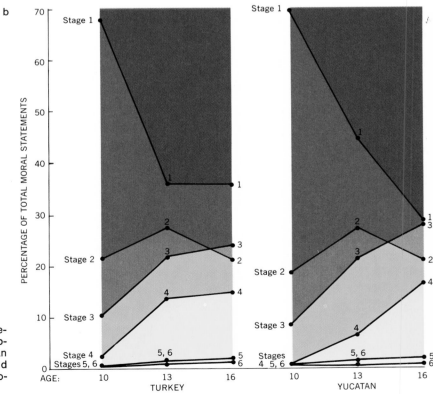

Figure 1. Cultural universality of the sequence of stages in moral development. (a) Stages for middle-class urban boys in the United States, Taiwan, and Mexico. (b) Stages for boys from isolated villages in Turkey and Yucatan.

able scientific theory—or like *any* theory or structure of knowledge—moral thought may be considered to partially generate its own data as it goes along, or at least to expand so as to contain in a balanced, self-consistent way a wider and wider experiential field. The raw data in the case of our ethical philosophies may be considered as conflicts between roles, or values, or as the social order in which men live.

The Role of Society

The social worlds of all men seem to contain the same basic structures. All the societies we have studied have the same basic institutions—family, economy, law, government. In addition, however, all societies are alike because they *are* societies—systems of defined complementary roles. In order to play a social role in the family, school, or society, the child must implicitly take the role of others toward himself and toward others in the group. These role-taking tendencies form the basis of all social institutions. They represent various patternings of shared or complementary expectations.

In the preconventional and conventional levels (Stages 1–4), moral content or value is largely accidental or culture bound. Anything from "honesty" to "courage in battle" can be the central value. But in the higher postconventional levels, Socrates, Lincoln, Thoreau, and Martin Luther King tend to speak without confusion of tongues, as it were. This is because the ideal principles of any social structure are basically alike, if only because there simply are not that many principles that are articulate, comprehensive, and integrated enough to be satisfying to the human intellect. And most of these principles have gone by the name of justice.

Behavioristic psychology and psychoanalysis have always upheld the Philistine view that fine moral words are one thing and moral deeds another. Morally mature reasoning is quite a different matter, and does not really depend on "fine words." The man who understands justice is more likely to practice it.

In our studies, we have found that youths who understand justice act more justly, and the man who understands justice helps create a moral climate that goes far beyond his immediate and personal acts. The universal society is the beneficiary.

Student Activists: Result, Not Revolt

Richard Flacks

In his studies of politically active youth of the mid-1960s, Richard Flacks identifies a new breed of student who will dominate the school scene. A product of parents who reject middle-class values and endorse social action, the activist student now belongs to a humanistic subculture, which stresses "autonomous and authentic behavior freely initiated by the individual and expressing his feelings and ideas." He is romantic, intellectual, and committed to social action.

Consider how these students differ from the student you are or were and from students you know and have known. What changes will the new generation make in what happens in our classrooms and schools? Does the thesis of this article conflict with the ideas offered by Richard Farson?

The scene might have been written by Genet; it was worthy of filming by Fellini. A young man, well clothed and well groomed but with his shirt collar open now, and his tie pulled down, shouted to the audience like an old-fashioned revivalist.

"Come up," he cried, "come up and confess. Put some money in the pot and be saved!"

And they came. The first youth, clutching the green pieces of paper in his hand, recited for all to hear: "My father is a newspaper editor. I give twenty-five dollars." His penitence brought cheers from the assembly. The sin of the next young man was a father who was assistant director of a government bureau. He gave forty dollars. "My dad is dean of a law school," confessed another, as he proffered fifty dollars for indulgence.

The occasion was not a rehearsal for the theater of the absurd but a convention of Students for a Democratic Society. The "sins" that the students confessed were the occupations or the social classes of their fathers. Their origins placed these students in the elite, the high-status group of any community, and yet here they were, exuberantly adopting a political stance and a style of life that they believed to be the very antithesis of those origins.

Why this should be so, frankly puzzled me and led to research that has confirmed and refined my earliest impression of the social make-up of today's youth in dissent. They are of the middle- and upper-middle class. They are the core of the student movement. They are the dissenters.

That the activist student movement is a small minority of the student population cannot be denied. But it is of great significance—partly because of the movement's social composition, partly because this movement is a phenomenon that was unforeseen by professional social scientists, and *mostly* because many of the themes and ideals of the movement are concurred in by a wide cross section of students.

Are students really in revolt? The simple fact may be that, on the contrary, today's students are tuned in to a developing cultural tradition in the United States, a tradition that has grown all but undetected because certain of our lingering assumptions about American society no longer prevail.

The phenomenon that has come to be called the student movement began in the late 1950s, when Northern white students responded to efforts by Southern Negro students to break down the barriers of segregation. However, as the protest has grown, it has broadened beyond the fight for civil liberties. Now, of course, it includes such issues as nuclear testing, the arms race, campus democracy, the educational quality of the university, and above all the undeclared war in Vietnam.

This evolution to active protest, and to action itself, began even as sociologists and social psychologists were despairing of political commitment among the young. University students of the 1950s were termed "the quiet generation," and experts predicted a button-down-minded generation. Polls showed that students were unconcerned with deep values; they were also complacent, status-oriented, and uncommitted. Conformity was much discussed, as were grey flannel suits, organization men, suburbia, status symbols, and security.

Then, suddenly, young people of the 1960s surprised everyone—they questioned everything and they protested most of the things that they questioned. Theorists were nonplussed, and conventional wisdom about the sources of radical action got a slap in the face.

We are not confronted with youths who are attracted to radicalism because they are economically deprived, or because their opportunities for mobility—or for anything else—are blocked. These highly advantaged youths are indifferent to, or repelled by, the best opportunities for high status and income. Yet these young people cannot be explained and understood as a generation in revolt. This is no effort to break free of the constricting, tradition-oriented, or obsolete values of parents. The parents of student protestors share with their offspring an unusual divergence from conventional religious, political, and social attitudes.

Most activists are recruited from a very special kind of middle- and upper middle-class family. In most of these families both mother and father are highly educated, the father is a professional, and the mother very often has a career as well. Many of these families are Jewish, but regardless of their denominational allegiance, both parents and children tend to be political liberals—there are very few Republicans among them. Activists say that their parents have been permissive and democratic, and the parents' description of themselves agrees.

Our studies indicate that activism, as well as other expressions of youth disaffection, are symptoms of the declining power of those values and goals that traditionally have given direction and meaning to the lives of the American middle class and direction to the American dream. Both students who are attracted to new radical politics and youths who experiment with new styles of Bohemianism—no matter how they may differ in personal history, personality, or perspective—repudiate mainstream middle-class values.

Moving parallel to the line of conventional middle-class values and the families that carry them, there appears to be emerging an alternative value system embodied in certain types of families. These variant families, intentionally or not, create dispositions in their children toward radical social action. This is a *result*, not *revolt*.

Dominant Values

There is a sociological consensus about the substance of middle-class values that derives from Weber's famous analysis of the Protestant ethic. Central in American life remains the value placed on achievement in an occupation.

This emphasis upon career demands a conception of self in terms of occupational status, so that the meaning of one's life centers around activity and achievement in a chosen profession. Thus, experience must be organized in terms of career patterns that demand a strongly future-oriented psychology—present experience is shaped to career requirements. And finally, in this conception, one's full potential for occupational achievement can be realized only to the extent that the emotional life is regulated and rationalized.

To the Weberian emphasis on achievement and self-control may be added the observation of Alexis de Tocqueville: Middle-class Americans are strongly concerned with the opinions of their peers. Increasingly, according to David Riesman and others, efforts to achieve group acceptance depend on one's skills as a consumer. Furthermore, according to Kenneth Keniston, absorption in consumption of material goods within the context of the family provides a much-needed balance to the discipline required in one's occupation.

Humanistic Values

Student activists and their parents are strongly characterized by humanistic values, whereas student nonactivists and their parents are characterized by dominant values. Two clusters of values can be identified within the humanistic subcultures. The first is a basic concern with individual development and self-expression, with a spontaneous response to the world. The free expression of emotions and feelings is viewed as essential to the development and integrity of the individual. Humanistic parents thus raise their children in an environment relatively free of constraints and favorable to experimentation, expressiveness, and spontaneity. They also stress the significance of autonomous and authentic behavior freely initiated by the individual and expressing his feelings and ideas.

Concern with self-development and expression also is reflected in this group's attitude toward aesthetic and intellectual capacities. Creativity in these areas is prized and encouraged in children, who also are given a feeling for their capacity for personal development.

The second group of values within the humanistic subcultures might be called ethical humanism. There is a sincere concern for the social condition of others. This strong humanitarian outlook results in socially and politically aware and active parents, who tend to share their views with their children.

Self-Expression Versus Self-Control

Humanistic values like aestheticism and intellectualism do not appear to be at odds with such dominant middle-class values as career achievement or materialism, but a basic conflict between the humanistic and the dominant attitudes can be seen in the contrast between self-expression and self-control.

In the dominant culture, behavior follows relatively fixed rules of conduct that represent objective authority and that secure the individual against unpredictable and possibly destructive impulses. The humanist, however, rejects such fixed rules. He is more flexible, and he sees the spontaneous flow of feelings and ideas as intrinsically good and necessary for personal growth.

Thus humanistic students are raised in a permissive and egalitarian family environment by parents who encourage them to be expressive and fill them with a sense of their own capacity for self-development. At school and at college these students first discover that the society at large expects them to be centrally motivated around goals and values that they cannot accept. Pursuit of status goals to them means hypocrisy and sacrifice of personal integrity.

In the eyes of humanistic youths, the public world is dominated by large authoritarian organizations, which severely regiment the individual. Subjection to impersonal authority is incompatible with their attitudes toward autonomy and authority. Many of these youths, suspecting that the policy of most organizations does not reflect their own ideals and principles, feel threatened.

Constraints on expression that exist in the world of work threaten youths who have been relatively unconstrained by parents. And they see the university as becoming just another impersonal institution—a big computer. Since so many plan university careers, they want to stop this trend.

Our original study of student activists and their parents, which led to the discovery of the humanistic subcultures, was made in 1965. The activist sample was matched with a control sample by type of college attended, neighborhood of parents' residence, sex, and religion. The interviews with both students and parents averaged about two hours and concerned political attitudes, broader values, and family life.

Parent and student values were not measured identically, although the definitions of values were the same

in both cases. The aspirations that parents have for their children frequently were used to ascertain parent values. In most cases, the parents of activist students scored significantly higher on the values we have identified as part of the humanistic subcultures than did the parents of nonactivists. Parents of activists also scored much lower on most of the values we have identified as belonging to the dominant culture.

The values of activist and nonactivist students are very different. Youths active in the student movement have rejected the traditional middle-class values, which still direct the goals of the nonactivist students.

Romanticism, a humanistic value, was identified as a concern with beauty and a sensitivity toward the realm of feelings and emotions. The high romantic was likely to want to become a poet, musician, or artist. He frequently expressed a desire for experience and a love of wandering, an aversion to settling down, and a need to find a liberating social environment in which institutional constraints would be lessened. These themes are traditionally associated with Bohemianism, rather than with radical social action, but our study found them significantly related to student activism.

Parents of activists generally scored higher in romanticism than did parents of nonactivists—none in the latter group could be considered high romantics. Parents who were high romantics were vitally interested in the arts—and hoped their children would be, too. Only a few parents were professional artists; most of them were leisure-time aesthetes.

Intellectualism is high on the list of humanistic values. While romanticism and intellectualism often have been considered mutually incompatible, our data suggest that there is a strong positive relationship between them. Most of the students who scored highest in intellectualism expected to teach and write within a university. They read extensively, particularly in philosophy, the humanities, and the social sciences. The empirical relationship between intellectualism and activism proved to be very strong, as did the link between parent intellectualism and child participation in the student movement.

Parents who were highest scorers talked repeatedly about the importance of books in their own lives and how they had interested their children in books. Their reading interests were the same as their activist youths', and many reported a shared interest with their children in ideas, books, and intellectual discussions.

Authenticity was measured as acute sensitivity to hypocrisy, a wish for self-knowledge and understanding, concern that one's own personal potentialities—as well as those of others—be realized, rejection of imposed standards of behavior, and acceptance of situational ethics.

In appraising the American culture, students who scored highest in authenticity were critical of the political, social, moral, and religious hypocrisies characteristic of middle-class life. Our statistics clearly demonstrate that authenticity is strongly connected with activism and that scores of the children and their parents were closely related.

Parents who scored high on this value viewed their children as autonomous individuals who must have the chance to realize their potentialities. Children of these parents always had been encouraged to make their own decisions, even if they violated parental standards of morality. Like the students, but not to the same degree, these parents were sensitive to hypocrisy.

In student interviews, interpersonal intimacy was explored in terms of both friendship and love. Losing one's self in love and caring deeply were stressed by the highest scorers in this area. The idea of the I-thou relationship as developed by Martin Buber is the most fully elaborated expression of the possibilities felt to be inherent in depth relationships.

The range of interpersonal intimacy correlated less strongly with activism than any of the other humanistic values. But when this area was broken into the separate categories of love and friendship, it was found that concern with deep love was concentrated almost exclusively among the activist students; those concerned with continuous contact with friends were slightly more likely to be nonactivist students. Parents of activist students in turn were slightly more concerned than were nonactivist parents about open and frequent interaction with friends.

Humanitarianism is grounded in a compassion and sympathy for the suffering of others and an outrage at institutions that deprive individuals or groups at any level. In order to separate humanitarianism from activism, we excluded attitudes and actions that related specifically to political ideology or to organized political projects. (This area showed the strongest empirical relationship to activism.) The relationship between parent humanitarianism and activism of children was especially high in the case of fathers.

Occupational Success and Materialism

Occupational success is held up as a major value for boys in the dominant culture, yet difference between the two groups was not nearly as marked as one might expect. And the difference between activist and non-activist girls is even less pronounced.

Activist and nonactivist males do aspire toward different kinds of careers, however. Nonactivists strive for careers in industry, law, or medicine, while activists lean toward politics, the arts, or the academic life. Only one activist male manifested a strong concern with success in a profession—a Harvard student whose goal is the Nobel prize in physics.

Activist parents consider career just as important as nonactivist parents do. Activist sons, however, tend to be a bit less concerned about a profession than non-activist young men. Unlike their children, many parents believe it is necessary to realize the dominant value of career in public life if one hopes to realize humanistic values in private life. The new generation either has not met the necessity for compromise, or *will* not.

Moralism and self-control were measured by studying implicit systems of morality, especially in the area of sexual and other forms of personal expression. Students who scored highest in this category indicated an adherence to a control-dominated moralism and an inflexible personal approach to morality centered around absolute right and wrong. The low-scoring end was for students who rejected conventional morality and who believed in free expression of impulses and emotions. Scores of nonactivist students, obviously, were much higher than those of the activists.

Parents who scored highest were deeply concerned lest the Protestant ethic break down through the weakening of discipline and authority in the institutional world. Low-scoring parents were convinced that traditional morality systems were hypocritical and repressive, and they supported a morality emphasizing expressiveness.

This rating is powerfully related to activism in students and appears to be at the core of value differences between the parents of activists and those of nonactivists. The strong correlation validates our thesis that the central conflict between dominant and humanistic cultures is the opposition between self-control and self-expression (see Figure 1).

In dealing with materialism and status, we explored the concern with making money and the enjoyment of a high level of material consumption, as well as the attainment of social prestige. Those who aspired toward material success included social prestige as an important goal, while those who rejected materialistic considerations were even more emphatic in their rejection of social status. The empirical relationship between materialism-status and student activism was a strongly negative one.

Although parents of student activists score somewhat lower on this scale than do the parents of nonactivist students, the relationship between the parents' material values and the students' activism is not statistically significant. Rather, this is often the major area of disagreement in the families of many students of both sorts. Students view their parents as rooted in an empty and ostentatious suburban life, and parents do not understand their children's rejection of comfort and advantages. Flagrant unorthodoxy in dress and personal appearance particularly disturbs parents. The haircut problem is acute.

Impact of Existentialism

As we tabulated the responses to our interviews, the possibility that existentialism has had a significant impact on the thinking of student activists became more pronounced. The writers who are important to students who scored highest on intellectualism were Dostoevsky,

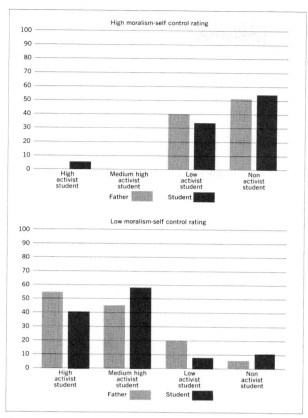

Figure 1. Correlation of activist and nonactivist students' and parents' ratings in terms of conventional morality and self-control versus free expression. The measurements were derived from the study of implicit systems of morality.

Nietzsche, Camus, and Sartre. An existential concern with authentic choice and action showed strongly on the authenticity rating.

In an attempt to discover whether activist students consciously identify with humanism and existentialism, we interviewed a second sample of student activists and again contrasted the sample with a control group. As a part of this interview, we gave students a list of twenty-two "isms" and asked them to list the three items with which they most identified (see Table 1).

The core of the current student movement consists of youths who are searching for an alternative to established middle-class values. And those who are engaged in this search come from families who are skeptical of conventional values. This tradition of skepticism and humanism is growing, and the families that identify with it are likely to increase rapidly in number.

Despite the apparent family roots of humanism and activism in the current student generation, it would be

an error to say that there is a one-to-one correspondence between parental and student values. It would be as great an error to say that parental influence is the sole factor in predisposing youth to radical politics. Children raised in the humanistic subcultures are potential recruits to a wide variety of student deviant, Bohemian, and drug subcultures.

Parental status, values, and practices indicate a predisposition toward humanist values and activist participation by students, but the degree or intensity of their involvement seems to depend on factors that are independent of family background. The college the student attends, the friends and teachers he meets in college, even the dormitory to which he is assigned his freshman year may affect his selection. Other strong influences include the impact of groups and organizations, of books and journeys, of historical events and how the individual experiences them, and of personal experiences such as long illnesses, living and working abroad, or time spent in jail.

The humanist family tradition has contributed a huge share of the initiators of the student movement, and a very large proportion of the most active participants continues to be recruited from middle-class humanistic subcultures.

TABLE 1

Impact of Humanism and Existentialism—Survey Results

Group	First choice (%)		Second choice (%)		Third choice (%)	
	Human.	Existen.	Human.	Existen.	Human.	Existen.
Activists (N = 61)	30	23	22	15	12	15
Nonactivists (N = 55)	16	11	16	5	11	4

Our parent-student research indicates strongly that the movement has a dynamic of its own, which is shaping student attitudes and their commitments. Our data show that the recent protest groups are made up, in part, of a central core of activists who come from humanistic subcultures and have a long history of active protest, and, in part, of a larger group of newly recruited students. Fascinatingly or alarmingly, depending on one's viewpoint, recent recruits more closely resemble the general student population. They come from widely diverse backgrounds, even from conservative and conventional parents. Protest appeals to an increasingly broader spectrum of students. The movement is spreading to the dominant culture.

The Roots of Development

The Young Monkeys
Harry and Margaret Harlow

The vast and strong appeal that the Harlows' research on the development of filial and peer affection in newborn monkeys has had for a generation of students in educational psychology is clearly a reflection of at least a tacit belief in the emotional basis for student learning and life style. Also, research on monkeys, like an Aesop fable, provides a buffer between knowledge about the various effects of child rearing and child teaching and the traditional, rigid practices still engaged in.

For two decades now the Harlows' research has told parents and teachers that shelter and nutrition, which the laboratory, like the suburban home, adequately provides, are not enough, and that children, like monkeys, require the emotional bond of parents, peers, and teachers in order to become relaxed and satisfied adults.

When we watch a newborn rhesus monkey with its mother, the infant seems to display signs of affection almost at once, clinging to the mother's body and climbing into her arms. The slightly older infant cries piteously when separated from its mother. Still later, as the maternal bond weakens, the young monkey reaches out to others its own age for companionship and, finally, for sexual satisfaction.

These examples illustrate the three basic social responses of primates—affection, fear, and social aggression. In fact, the responses usually emerge in that order as the infant monkey matures.

Affection, the reaction to cuddling, warmth, and food, comes first in these broadly based and sometimes even overlapping categories. Then comes fear, as the infant begins to explore a sometimes dangerous world. And finally, there is social aggression when the monkey is older, more exploratory, and better able to handle itself.

These responses obviously are not the simple component behavior patterns that B. F. Skinner has described, nor are they like Pavlovian reflex reactions. Rather, they are highly complicated and built-in patterns of behavior that can be modified by learning. Under certain circumstances, normal development can be blocked, and the patterns disrupted. When this is done under experimental conditions, we can learn more about the sensitive, vital process of socialization.

Certainly monkeys are not people, but they are the next highest form of animal life, and we can perform complex experiments with them, manipulating their environment with a freedom not possible when using people as subjects. For example, we can put monkeys into isolation as they develop, we can add to or take away from their basic emotional needs. And as we learn more about the basic emotions of monkeys, we can profit from this knowledge in our ever-active search to find out more about ourselves in the world.

The Beginnings of Affection

The first sign of affection by the newborn rhesus monkey is a reflex action that facilitates nursing. The infant grasps its mother's fur and moves upward on her body until restrained by her arms. This brings the baby monkey's face close to the mother's breast, and the infant begins to nurse. Throughout the first two or three weeks of life, the response of infant to mother continues to be based on reflexes, although the baby gradually gains voluntary control of its motor behavior. But even after the young monkey is skilled enough to walk, run, and climb by itself, it continues to cling to its mother. The bond of affection between infant and mother continues to grow stronger instead of weaker during the next few months.

The mother monkey warmly returns her infant's affection, and this reciprocal affection operates in a way that helps prepare the young monkey for participation in a more complex social environment. The mother shows her fondness by cradling, grooming, caressing, and protecting her baby. At first, this affection is primarily reflex behavior and is stimulated by the touch, sound, and sight of the baby. Interestingly, the baby need not be the female monkey's own, for preadolescent, adolescent, and adult females are attracted to all the infants in their group. Given the opportunity, even females who have not recently borne young will adopt infants, and this indicates that hormonal changes associated with parturition are not essential to the establishment of maternal affection.

Fear

Fear responses show themselves after the young rhesus has matured intellectually and has had enough experience to recognize objects that are strange and dangerous. In its first two months a young rhesus shows little or no fear. But by the third or fourth month of life, unfamiliar places, persons, and objects as well as loud or unusual noises make the infant screech and cling to its mother. Young monkeys separated from their mothers will cry frequently and clasp themselves. An infant that has previously known only its mother can be frightened by other monkeys, but if the young rhesus has previously been part of a group, it will be afraid of other monkeys only when threatened by them, or actually hurt.

Making Friends

By the time they are two months old, young monkeys that have been allowed to live in groups show an interest in other monkeys, especially infants. First contacts are usually brief, beginning with physical exploration, which can be one-sided or mutual. From these early experiences come more complex play behavior and the development of affection for other young monkeys. Emotional attachment to monkeys of the same age usually appears before the emergence of fear. However, if such attachments are not permitted to develop—if, for instance, the young monkey is kept apart from his peers—there is some possibility that this friendly emotion will not emerge at all. Nevertheless, the infant that has received a good deal of maternal affection can sometimes make friends even when the normal age for doing so has passed.

Emotional bonds among those of the same age usually grow stronger as the maternal relationship begins to ebb. The infant's first emotional experience, the attachment to its mother, is quite distinct from later emotional ties. For example, the peer relationship originates in and develops through play. Young monkeys that have not been permitted to establish relationships with other infants are wary of their playmates when finally allowed to be with them, and these deprived monkeys often fail to develop strong bonds of affection. Yet monkeys that have been deprived of mother love but provided with early contacts *can* develop ties with their peers that seem comparable to the bonds formed by mother-reared infants.

Affection of age mates for one another is universal within the entire primate kingdom. It starts early in all species of monkeys and apes, and it is evident throughout the life span. The beginnings of human sociability, however, are more variable because children's opportunities to contact their age mates differ from family to family and from culture to culture. Four decades ago, research by Charlotte Buhler and her associates in Vienna showed that human infants in their first year of life generally are responsive to one another. This can be confirmed informally by anyone who looks in on a pediatrician's waiting room where healthy young children contact one another quickly. If held, they strain toward one another, and if close together, they reach out to one another. They smile at each other, and they laugh together.

Sex Roles

In early infancy, the child's sex is relatively unimportant in social interactions: Human boys and girls, like male and female monkeys, play together indiscriminately at first. Though this continues for several years in humans, behavioral differences begin to appear in monkeys by the third or fourth month and increase steadily until the animal is mature.

Male monkeys become increasingly forceful, while the females become progressively more passive. A male will threaten other males and females alike, whereas females rarely are aggressive toward males. During periods of play, males are the pursuers, and the females retreat. As they grow older, increasing separation of the sexes becomes evident in friendship and in play.

During their juvenile period, one to two years of age, and even after, rhesus monkeys as a rule form pairs and clusters of friends of the same sex. Only in maturity when the female is in heat does the pattern change, and then only temporarily. Male-female pairs dominate until the mating period ends. And then the partners return to their own sex groups. With humans, too, friendships with those of the same sex predominate in childhood, adolescence, and maturity. Even when men and women attend the same social event, men often cluster together with other men, while women form groups by themselves. Clubs for men only, or for women only, further demonstrate this sexual split.

At both the human and subhuman levels, this separation is undoubtedly based on common interests, which in turn are based on anatomical and physical differences between the sexes. For example, male primates of most species are larger and stronger than the females and better equipped physiologically for feats of strength and physical endurance. This probably leads the male to more large-muscle activities. Culture influences do not create differences in behavior between the sexes, but they do mold, maintain, and exaggerate the natural differences. Thus boys, not girls, are encouraged to become athletes, and women boxers and shot-putters are generally regarded as oddities.

The importance of peer relationships in monkeys cannot be overemphasized. All primates that live in groups achieve much of their communal cohesiveness and adult sexual social behavior through affectionate relationships with others of the same age. Monkeys learn their sex roles through play. By the third or fourth month of life, male and female sexual behavior are beginning to be different. By the time they are a year old, most monkeys who have been reared in groups display mature and specialized sexual behavior, except that male intromission and ejaculation do not occur until puberty, at about four years of age.

Social Aggression

Sexual differentiation usually is learned by monkeys before social aggression appears. After numerous and varied studies at the University of Wisconsin, we have concluded that unless peer affection precedes social aggression, monkeys do not adjust; either they become unreasonably aggressive or they develop into passive scapegoats for their group.

Rhesus monkeys begin to make playful attacks on one another almost as soon as they are old enough for actual contact, and their aggression increases steadily throughout the first year of life. The young monkeys wrestle and roll, pretend to bite one another, and make threatening gestures. But they do not hurt each other, even though their teeth are sharp enough to pierce a playmate's skin.

If the young rhesus has had normal group contact during infancy, it will show restraint toward both friends and strangers. Only if threatened, or to protect weaker members of its group, will it fight.

While in the group the young try to find a place in the hierarchy, and as dominance is established, a relative peace ensues. In contrast, monkeys who have been socially deprived may seriously injure one another when placed together at this stage.

Isolation Breeds Fear

One experimental rearing condition that throws much light on the problems of aggression and peer affection is total social isolation. At birth, the monkey is enclosed in a stainless steel chamber where light is diffused, temperature controlled, air flow regulated, and environmental sounds filtered. Food and water are provided, and the cage is cleaned by remote control. During its isolation, the animal sees no living creature, not even a human hand. After three, six, or twelve months, the monkey is removed from the chamber and placed in an individual cage in the laboratory. Several days later it is exposed for the first time to peers—another monkey who has been reared in isolation and two who have been raised in an open cage with others. The four are put in a playroom equipped with toys and other apparatus designed to stimulate activity and play (see Figure 1); they spend usually half an hour a day in the room five days a week, and these sessions go on for six months.

Fear is the overwhelming response in all monkeys raised in isolation. Although the animals are physically healthy, they crouch and appear terror-stricken by their new environment. Young that have been isolated for only three months soon recover and become active in playroom life; by the end of a month they are almost indistinguishable from their control age mates. But the young monkeys that had been isolated for six months adapt poorly to each other and to the control animals. They cringe when approached and fail at first to join in any of the play. During six months of play sessions, they never progress beyond minimal play behavior, such as playing by themselves with toys. What little social activity they do have is exclusively with the other *isolate* in the group. When the other animals become aggressive, the isolates accept their abuse without making any effort to defend themselves. For these animals, social opportunities have come too late. Fear prevents them from engaging in social interaction and consequently from developing ties of affection.

Monkeys that have been isolated for twelve months are very seriously affected. Although they have reached the age at which true aggression is normally present, and they can observe it in their playmates, they show no signs of aggression themselves. Even primitive and simple play activity is almost nonexistent. With these isolated animals, no social play is observed and aggressive behavior is never demonstrated. Their behavior is a pitiful combination of apathy and terror as they crouch at the sides of the room, meekly accepting the attacks of the more healthy control monkeys. We have been unable to test them in the playroom beyond a ten-week period because they are in danger of being seriously injured or even killed by the others.

Our tests have indicated that this social failure is not a consequence of intellectual arrest. In the course of thirty-five years of experimentation with and observation of monkeys, we have developed tests of learning that successfully discriminate between species, between ages within species, and between monkeys with surgically-produced brain damage and their normal peers. The tests have demonstrated that the isolated animals are as intellectually able as are monkeys of the same age raised in open cages. The only difference is that the isolates require more time to adjust to the learning apparatus. All monkeys must be adapted to testing, but those coming from total isolation are more fearful, and so it takes longer for them to adjust to the situation.

From Apathy to Aggression

We continued the testing of the same six- and twelve-month isolates for a period of several years. The results were startling. The monkeys raised in isolation now began to attack the other monkeys viciously, whereas before they had cowered in fright. We tested the isolates with three types of strangers: large and powerful adults, normal monkeys of their age, and normal one-year-olds. The monkeys that had been raised in the steel isolation cages for their first six months now were three years old. They were still terrified by all strangers, even the physically helpless juveniles. But in spite of their terror, they engaged in uncontrolled aggression, often launching suicidal attacks upon the large adult males and even attacking the juveniles—an act almost never seen in normal monkeys of their age. The passage of time had only exaggerated their asocial and antisocial behavior.

In those monkeys, positive social action was not initiated, play was nonexistent, grooming did not occur, and sexual behavior either was not present at all or was totally inadequate. In human terms, these monkeys, who had lived unloved and in isolation, were totally unloving, distressed, disturbed, and delinquent.

Sexual Inadequacy

We have found that social deprivation has another long-term effect that is particularly destructive—inadequate sexual behavior. This is found in all males and most females reared in total or semi-isolation. Whereas some of the females that had been in semi-isolation still show a certain amount of sexual responsiveness, this is probably due to their easier role in copulation. The separate actions required for copulation begin to appear in young infants, but these actions are not organized into effective patterns unless early social play—particularly of a heterosexual nature—is allowed. Monkeys that fail to develop adult sexual patterns by the time they are twelve to eighteen months old are poor risks for breeding when they are mature.

For example, we found in one study that semi-isolated females that are placed with breeding males avoid social proximity and do not groom themselves. They often engage in threats, aggression, and autistic be-

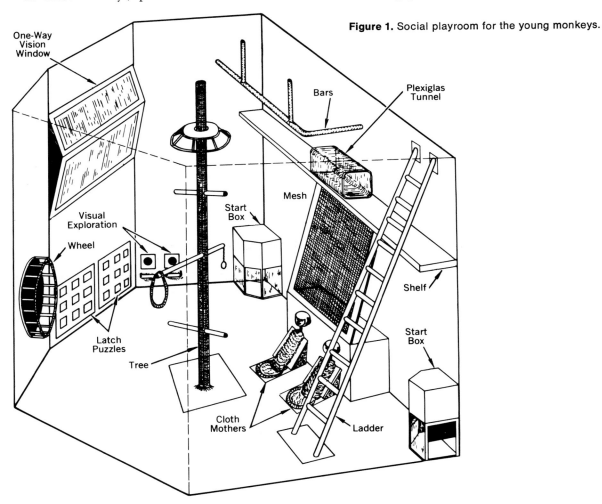

Figure 1. Social playroom for the young monkeys.

One-Way Vision Window

Bars

Plexiglas Tunnel

Mesh

Visual Exploration

Wheel

Start Box

Latch Puzzles

Tree

Shelf

Start Box

Cloth Mothers

Ladder

havior such as clutching and biting themselves, and they frequently fail to support the male when mounting occurs. In contrast, normal females seldom threaten males, are not aggressive, and do not engage in autistic behavior; they maintain social proximity, groom themselves, and provide adequate support for the mounting male.

Parallel tests with males show that socially deprived males are even more inadequate than their female counterparts. Compared to the normal males, they groomed less, threatened more, were more aggressive, rarely initiated any sexual contact, engaged in unusual and abnormal sexual responses, and—with one exception—never achieved intromission.

The sexual inadequacies of the socially deprived monkeys did not come from a loss of biological sex drive. High arousal was often seen, but it led to inappropriate responses—autistic behavior, masturbation, and violent aggression—all in a frenetic sequence lasting only a few seconds.

Monkeys Without Mothers

In another series of experiments on the emotional bases of social development in monkeys, we raised some infants with continuous peer experience and no mothers. Two, four, and six monkeys were reared together in groups. The groups of two tended to cling together in the first few weeks, chest to chest, and this behavior persisted long after normally raised infants would have stopped clinging to their mothers. The two young monkeys moved about like Siamese twins joined at the chest. When some external force turned up to break the two apart, or one rhesus attempted to explore an object, the other quickly tried to resume the clinging posture. This immature behavior continued until the animals were put in separate cages, although we found that it could be drastically reduced if the pairs were reared together for a fixed period of time, separated for another specified time, and then subjected to alternate togetherness and separation.

We also found that four or six infant monkeys living together in one cage tend very soon to form a line in which one rhesus leans forward and the others get behind him in a single file, each clinging to the back of the animal in front of him. If the first monkey moves without breaking loose, the whole group usually moves in unison with it, but if the lead rhesus frees itself, the pattern breaks up, to be re-formed shortly.

While monkeys reared in pairs play very infrequently —the tight clasp they have on one another restricts movement—the infants raised in larger groups play extensively. In one respect, the monkeys that have been raised in the larger groups are quite precocious: Their sexual behavior is perfected at an early age and as adults they breed readily. This is in sharp contrast with the absence or insufficiency of sexual activity in male and female isolates.

Throughout our studies, we have been increasingly impressed by the alternative routes monkeys may take to reach adequate social behavior, which by our criteria includes affection toward peers, controlled fear and aggression, and normal sexual behavior. In protected laboratory conditions, social interaction between peers and between mother and child appear to be in large part interchangeable in their effect on the infant's development. A rhesus can surmount the absence of its mother if it can associate with its peers, and it can surmount a lack of socialization with peers if its mother provides affection. Being raised with several age mates appears to compensate adequately for a lack of mothering, although it is likely that animals reared in this way would be at a disadvantage if confronted by monkeys that had had a mother and early experience with others their age as well.

From an evolutionary point of view, there is an advantage to the animal in having two independent sources of affection—mother and peers. Each in part compensates for the deficiencies of the other. Mothers vary considerably in the depth and type of their attachment to their children. A rhesus mother denied normal affection in her early life may be so detached from her infant and, in many cases, may be so brutal that the effects could be devastating for her infant unless there were companions available for play. Human mothers may also exhibit detachment and physical abuse, which pediatricians refer to as the "battered baby" syndrome —a much more prevalent phenomenon than police and court records indicate.

Isolation studies that begin at birth and continue until some specified age provide a powerful technique for the analysis of maturational processes without interference from an overlay of learning. Indeed, the isolation experiment is one of the few methods by which it is possible to measure the development of complex behavior patterns in any pure or relatively pure form. While it is commonly thought that learning shapes preestablished, unlearned response patterns, this is barely half the picture, at least as far as social learning is concerned.

One of the most important functions of social learning in primates—and perhaps in all mammals and many other classes of animals as well—is the development of social patterns that will restrain and check potentially asocial behavior. These positive, learned social patterns must be established before negative, unlearned patterns emerge. In this sense, social learning is an anticipation of later learning: The inappropriate exercise of negative behavior can be checked within the social group while the same behavior is permitted toward intruders threatening from without.

Monkeying with the Mother Myth
Gordon D. Jensen and Ruth A. Bobbitt

The Harlows' research has enthroned mother love, even though it provides evidence of the value of surrogate mother love in the form of peer affiliation. Gordon Jensen and Ruth Bobbitt have found, however, that there are some limitations of mother love. They have discovered, for example, that the monkey mother shortly after the infant's birth substitutes punishment for love, that mothers rarely love strange infants, and that deprived early environments, that is, where the mother-infant pair were together but where the infant had no peers or playthings, slowed down considerably the development of normally independent and aggressive male and female infants.

There can be too much of a good thing, and maternal love and protection are not exceptions. What would be the appropriate limits of teacher-student intimacy in a school that removes the existing formal interpersonal barriers?

The special bond between mother and child has been extolled since the Byzantine days of Christianity and before. In the 1950s practicing psychologists and psychiatrists held a strong conviction that mother was the most important figure in a child's life. To both psychoanalyst and behaviorist the relationship between mother and child was the heart of child development. When a child lost its family, finding a substitute mother was the chief concern. This emphasis on the *primacy* of mother-child interaction in early development was so great that the other environmental factors were neglected. In the 1960s attention began to turn toward enriching the social and material environments of children. Although the notion of mother primacy continues to predominate, it is coming under more critical study. Mother is still on her pedestal, but other factors are likely to share this place of respect with her.

We recognize that the interacting variables affecting human social behavior are difficult to analyze scientifically. We also realize that it is unethical to control these variables in humans; the separation of a mother and her child for experimental purposes is unacceptable. So we turned to the study of animals that most resemble the human in anatomy, function, and social behavior—apes and monkeys. These fellow primates offer a convenient foreshortening of the childhood development period. A four-year-old child, a two-year-old chimpanzee and a one-year-old monkey are at about the same level of behavioral development. For these reasons primates are the best models for controlled experiments on certain aspects of child development. Even though we cannot apply results of monkey studies directly to humans, they often suggest previously unsuspected interactions between infant and mother, and between infant and environment, which then can be investigated in humans. Results of most primate studies to date suggest that there is a need to reassess some of our preconceptions about child development.

Outline of the Experiment

To achieve as much objectivity as possible, we developed an original systematic method for observing the interaction of pig-tailed monkeys (*Macaca nemestrina*). Our studies required soundproof rooms large enough to maintain social groups of monkeys, which we found at the Regional Primate Research Center at the University of Washington. This center was the second of seven built and supported by the Division of Research Facilities and Resources, National Institutes of Health, in various areas of the United States. All are devoted to research on nonhuman primates. By means of letter codes, we identified items or units of behavior such as mother grooming infant or infant climbing on a toy. With the letter codes, observers could easily list the continuous flow of behavioral events into a tape recorder, producing a kind of verbal motion picture. In short, we collected data continuously rather than by the usual checklist, time-interval technique. Computer programs then identified and analyzed the developmental trends and interactive patterns.

To assure that a number of infants would be born within a period of one month we conducted a precisely timed breeding program. Monkeys are generally born at night. We artificially reversed their days and nights by controlling the light-dark and feeding periods, and by providing sound to simulate daytime noises (a radio tuned to an all-night disc jockey program). In this way we encouraged monkeys in our "delivery room" to have their blessed event at our convenience, allowing us to observe the delivery during the normal human working day and to begin our experiments from the moment of delivery.

Early primate studies by Harry and Margaret Harlow at the Wisconsin Regional Primate Research Center inspired our study of the normal mother-infant relationship. In an ingenious series of experiments designed to isolate variables of mother love, Harlow found that with mother surrogates (wire or terry-cloth-covered cylinders), the infants preferred the cloth-covered surrogates, even though the nursing bottle was available only on the wire "mothers." However, despite surrogate contact, these motherless-raised infants always showed bizarre, stereotyped behaviors such as rocking and body-clasping. They frequently sat frozen in positions resembling those assumed by emotionally disturbed or psychotic children. In contrast, mother-raised monkeys do not develop these autistic behaviors, according to other laboratory studies.

The Harlows' most recent studies at the Wisconsin laboratories, in which infant monkeys were raised together from birth without mothers, showed that monkeys may take alternative routes to achieve adequate social behavior. These investigators believe that infants raised *without* mothers but in a group of monkeys of the same age—as well as infants raised with *both* mothers and companions—can develop essentially normal social behavior (see preceding article). Although Harlow's studies demonstrated that playmates were essential for adequate social development, they also indicated the importance of the mother. Future studies may pinpoint the critical times in the infant's development for maternal and peer-group experiences, and may specify more precisely the extent to which they may compensate for each other.

Normal Mothers and Infants

In contrast to the isolation conditions employed by Harlow and his associates, our initial approach was to study the *mother-infant relationship* in both normal and abnormal situations. It seemed to us essential to first determine the general characteristics of the normal maternal behavior of a monkey, particularly how she provides her infant with basic security early in life. It is equally important to know what role the mother plays in giving her infants experience in social interaction and in instigating the development of their independence. Our empirical observations corroborated the importance of the mother's role in all these capacities. At the infant's birth, the mother is protective and affectionate. But what may be more significant is that very early in the infant's life, the mother begins to direct less of her attention toward her infant and more toward the environment. During this time, her behavior toward the infant becomes increasingly punitive.

It is the mothers, not the infants, who actively initiate separation. All our measures show a continuous developmental process directed toward the goal of mutual independence. We became interested in the dynamics of this development and in the effects of external factors on it.

A number of the elements that produce normal or deviate maternal behavior are known. Personal factors and life history of the mother may be significant, for example, whether or not she had herself been "mothered." Harlow found that motherless female monkeys generally rejected or were indifferent to their firstborn, although they showed improved maternal response with later infants. These findings have not yet been substantiated in other studies, but our and other investigations show that *normal* mothers are unaffected by number of previous deliveries. The type of delivery, however, may affect maternal behavior. In one study, Caesarean delivery did not affect the maternal response of jungle-raised monkeys, but it did lessen the maternal response of laboratory-reared mothers.

By forcibly separating mother monkeys from their infants, we were able to observe the power of the mother-infant bond. Both mothers and infants make violent vocal and physical protests during the separation procedures. When the infants are returned to their mothers, a period of intensified closeness and affection follows.

When an infant monkey is removed from its mother but left so that the mother still can see and hear it, the agitation of the mother decreases. If a newborn infant is removed, the mother will display less agitation if she can see and hear another infant monkey—even a strange one. But by the time an infant is four days old, the sight of a substitute infant no longer calms the mother, indicating that mother monkeys recognize their own infants by sight and sound at a very early stage.

Most monkey mothers are quite punitive toward a strange infant when it is placed in her cage along with her own infant. But one of our mothers, Brunie, showed unusual acceptance of strange infants. Her "adopting" behavior was particularly interesting because most mother monkeys in the laboratory show great reluctance to care for other infants, whether or not their own infants are allowed to remain.

Brunie permitted a strange infant to sit near her, and she dealt out little punishment. When her own infant was removed, Brunie allowed the substitute to come closer and eventually to nurse. When Brunie's infant was returned to her, both infants demanded to nurse simultaneously and were allowed to do so by this exceptional monkey mother. As a further challenge to Brunie's maternal capacity, a second strange infant was offered for adoption after the previous stranger and her own infant were removed from the cage. The same sequence of events occurred, and in the end Brunie accepted all three infants even though only two at a time could nurse. Thus Brunie earned the title of "Supermother." We can only assume that some factors in Brunie's life history were responsible for her unusual maternal qualities, although the possibility of genetic influences should not be neglected.

Environmental Effects

One of our goals was to determine how isolation of naturally mothered infants would affect their development. We wanted to know if isolated, mother-raised infants without playmates, or with later contact with playmates, would develop normally. We arranged a study of mothered monkey infants according to the amount of contact with playmates of the same age, ranging from none at all, through visual and auditory contact only, to full and free association. If we could understand the importance in humans of contact with companions of the same age, we could devise improved child-rearing guides for parents and programs for optimal institutional and foster care of children.

We constructed three types of environments. In the privation environment, the mother-infant pair lived in a four-foot-square cage in a soundproof room, with no sight or sound of other animals or people. The delayed enriched environment involved placing the mother and her newborn infant in a privation environment for four months followed by normal contact with playmates and toys for two months before any testing. The rich environment provided the mother-infant pair with a changing variety of objects to play with and to manipulate. The cage was located in a large open laboratory where the subjects could hear and see other monkeys and people. At four months of age these infant monkeys were separated from their mothers and became the playmates for the infants from the delayed enriched environment.

We asked ourselves how these environments might affect the growth of independence between the mother and infant. We found that the privation environment produced prolonged physical closeness between mother and infant, or what could be called a retardation of the mutual independence process.

To measure one aspect of independence, we defined four mother-infant physical positions. Position 1 is the closest, the mother and infant are situated front-to-front, with the infant grasping the mother with his arms and legs. In position 2, the infant is still within the mother's lap area, but not necessarily clinging. In position 3, the animals are in contact, but the infant is outside the mother's lap area. In position 4, the two

animals are completely separated, with visible space between them.

We reasoned that deprivation of environmental stimuli would retard the onset of independence. Statistical analysis of our data showed clearly that infants and mothers from the privation environment were slower to use the most independent position and used it less frequently than did those from the rich environment (see Figure 1). The rich environment provided both infant

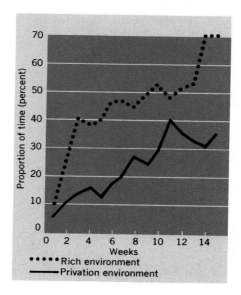

Figure 1. The proportion of time monkey mothers from the two environments spent physically separated from their infants (position 4).

and mother with diversion or stimuli for activity away from each other. In the privation environment, the infant and mother turned to each other for most of their reinforcements. This situation is analogous to the overprotective human mother and her child, or to families living in very isolated and severely deprived conditions.

We have already observed that normal monkey mothers are the initiators of separation. We determined this by counting the number of times one animal left the other. We found that mothers are almost exclusively "leavers" while infants are predominantly "approachers." This was true irrespective of rearing environments. These and other findings led us to conclude that there is a basic process in the development of mutual independence in laboratory monkeys. The process is continuous and begins in the first weeks of life rather than at a particular stage, such as at weaning or later. A rich environment does not affect the nature of this process; it merely produces an earlier elaboration of the infant's behavior toward independence.

In order to test the effects of privation, delayed enriched, and rich environments on mother-raised infant monkeys we compared the social adequacy of infants from the three environments. The infant monkeys from the various environments were removed and placed in individual cages for two weeks. Then the infants were paired to determine relative dominance or "pecking order" by tabulating the aggressive-submissive interactions.

The infants from the three different environments were tested in all possible paired combinations. It was evident that the richer the early environment, the greater the infant's social development. Infants from the rich environment dominated infants from the privation environment even when the deprived infant was male and the other a female. Animals from the rich environment usually dominated and were never dominated by monkeys from the delayed enriched environment even though the privileged infant had to cope with a seemingly more difficult situation. Each privileged infant monkey was separated from its mother earlier, and placed in the delayed enriched environment with a strange mother-infant pair. This was a somewhat hostile situation for him since the substitute mother tended to reject the intruder and sometimes was overly punitive. That the rich environment infant did so well emphasizes the advantage provided by his rich environment in the earliest months of life. Conversely, the retardation in social and motor development shown by deprived infants in the earliest weeks of life later manifested itself in the poor showing of deprived infants in social and competitive situations.

These studies, by showing the effects of environment on the mother-infant relationship and on infant development, indicate the potential value of human environmental enrichment programs such as Head Start and antipoverty programs that provide educational and cultural enrichment for deprived school-age children.

We wondered how normal our laboratory-born and raised infants were compared to monkeys reared in a natural or free-ranging environment. Accordingly, we simulated a natural environment for a captive group of monkeys. The group was structured to resemble a natural monkey band in terms of sex and adult-juvenile ratios. Infants reared by their mothers in the restricted laboratory settings were compared with those raised by their mothers in the tribal group, and we found the same basic pattern of mother-infant interaction. For example, as in the laboratory pairs, mothers were leavers and infants were approachers. Finding the same basic results in this group gave us greater confidence in the general validity of our more controlled and restricted studies.

The differences between restricted and group-living infants are very few. One difference of particular interest is that nipple contact (nursing) is greater for the group-reared infants. This type of mother contact may provide the security necessary in a group environment, where there are more challenges to adjustment than are found in a bare cage environment.

Little mention has been made of the father's role. It must be kept in mind that monkeys do not enjoy the same monogamous family structure popularly ascribed to humans. However, field studies indicate that males play important roles in the social organization and defense of the group. Undoubtedly, they have a significant effect on young monkeys' learning to behave as group members. The subject of father-infant and of leader-infant relationships in monkeys has still to be investigated.

Inferences for Human Behavior

Differences in interactions between mother monkeys and male or female infants may provide another important insight to human behavior. Human mothers are often convinced that boys behave differently from girls right from the start, even *in utero*. We looked to our experiments to see what behavioral differences between male and female monkey infants existed and to what variables they could be attributed. We found that from the first weeks of life, male monkey babies do indeed develop behavior patterns different from those of female monkey babies. Males quickly surpass the female infants in the rate of achieving independence from their mothers, as well as in their general activity level. Mothers play an active role in the instigation of the greater independence of the male by punishing the males more, holding and carrying them less, and paying less attention to them. Failure of human mothers to "let go" is often postulated as a cause of homosexual deviation in males.

Males in all three test environments did relatively more biting of their mothers as well as other punitive actions such as hitting, pushing, shoving, yanking, jerking, and grabbing. This was especially true of the male infants in the privation environment. The deprived male infants did more thumb-sucking and genital manipulation than did females in the same environment. We feel that these data support a general hypothesis that males and females in a privation environment will show early behavioral differences, and that the differences will be in a deviant and pronounced form. This finding may well parallel the observations of humans that males need many more outlets (environmental stimuli) than do females. This is exemplified in public school playgrounds that cater almost exclusively to male-oriented sports.

The experiments being carried out with monkeys show how early maternal, environmental, and social factors affect the later social behavior of infants. These studies of primate behavior have challenging implications for theories of emotional disturbance in human beings. For example, the finding that playmates or companions are important may modify the tendency to overemphasize the importance of the mother-infant relationship. Also, the role played by peers may have practical application in devising programs for optimal institutional and foster-home care of infants. Primate studies of the early environment of infants support the belief that enhanced environments will enrich the behavioral development of children.

The results of primate studies to date lead us away from thinking in terms of the exclusive importance of mother, peers, or the environment in early life. With all due respect to contemporary literature, television, films, and funnies that satirize and spoof mother, it appears that although mothers are important, their role has been oversold. Experiments support the idea that playmates and environmental factors are important too. In time, although mothers may get less credit for man's success, they may also receive less blame for his failure.

Up from Helplessness

Jerome Bruner

Jerome Bruner's research and writing now distinguish a decade of American education that shifted its focus from personal and social development to the intellectual development of the student. In his more recent work Bruner has studied primate and infant development as almost an anthropological odyssey through civilization.

The appeal of his present article lies mainly in the interesting parallels he has found in the development of physical coordination, attention, and language. His theme seems to be that the child gradually organizes his freedom in all three areas from states of random movement, diffuse attention, and incoherent babbling to states of skilled operation, concentration, and thematic development. How may this principle of development be employed by the teacher in the selection and presentation of subject matter?

It is a working premise of mine that infant development cannot be understood without considering what it proceeds from and what it moves toward. The human infant has behind him a long process of primate evolution, which has endowed him with certain biological capacities. In front of him, in adulthood, lie not only the behavior man shares with other primates but the use of a culture that is uniquely human. Human culture, as Claude Lévi-Strauss pointed out, is based on three types of exchange, carried out through language, kinship arrangements, and economies. They are used by all men and by men alone.

From his evolutionary inheritance, then, the newborn child develops the capacity to use a culture that is exclusively human. This is not to say that evolution or culture *causes* infants to develop as they do, but merely to point out the central position that the infant in fact occupies.

It may seem that this view of infant development places a large burden on a very small pair of shoulders. The equipment and the actions at a child's disposal when he begins his enormous task look, at first glance,

rudimentary. To illustrate, the research I am about to describe focuses on sucking and looking, reaching and grasping, and prelinguistic communication—little acorns indeed.

Through these activities, however, the infant develops four abilities that are crucial to the use of human culture. He develops, first, voluntary control of his behavior, a highly complex matter that requires the anticipation of an outcome, the choice of a means to achieve it, and the ability to start and sustain a chosen series of acts. Second, he gains internal control of his attention, so that he can direct it toward solutions to problems instead of following the dictates of external stimuli. Third, he learns to carry out several lines of action simultaneously. Fourth, he establishes reciprocal codes that pave the way for speech and other forms of human exchange.

Before I discuss how these abilities develop, I should point out that there are certain inequities in the young child's situation. For example, the infant's sensory equipment provides him with more information than his motor system can use: he can look at a toy well before he can reach out his hand to take it. Similarly, his motor system has more slack, more degrees of freedom for movement, than he can control. He begins to learn by cutting down drastically on his available neuromuscular freedom, developing that form of clumsiness so characteristic of human infancy. Initial learning, then, may be learning to reduce the complexity of response in order to gain control.

Sucking and Looking

The human infant is notorious for his helplessness, but one thing he can do from birth is suck. Sucking begins as a reflex action, and the infant uses it for several functions apparently preordained by evolution: nutrition, discomfort reduction, and exploration. Even on the first day of life, however, the child has some control over his sucking and can adapt it to changes in the environment. If milk is delivered to a day-old child in response to only a little pressure on the nipple, the baby will almost immediately reduce the amount of pressure he exerts.

Another thing the child can do almost as soon as he is born is look, but he cannot look and suck at the same time. The newborn infant sucks with his eyes tight shut. If he begins to look at something, he stops sucking. By two or three months of age, when a burst-and-pause sucking pattern has become established, the baby will suck in bursts and look during the pauses between. At four months, he seems able to suck and look simultaneously, but this turns out to be not quite true. Though suctioning stops when the baby looks, a mouthing of the nipple continues. This phenomenon is called place-holding. By maintaining one feature of an ongoing activity, the infant seems to remind himself to resume that activity after he has carried out a different one. His ability to suck-(look)-suck is probably part of a general decrease in the extent to which one activity preempts all others.

One way to test an infant's voluntary control is to see whether he will use an action as a means to some new end. Infants as young as one or two months old show considerable ability to use sucking for a novel purpose. They can learn to suck on pacifiers in order to bring about visual clarity—to increase the illumination of a picture in a darkened room (as in E. R. Siqueland's experiment at Brown University)—or to bring the picture into focus (as in one by Kalnins in our laboratory at Harvard).

Watching infants do this has taught us something about how they learn to coordinate the two ordinarily independent activities, sucking and looking. A six-week-old baby will suck the picture into focus, but then he starts looking and stops sucking, so that the picture drifts back out of focus again. He may try to resolve this dilemma by sucking without looking until the picture is in focus and then looking and sucking together for a brief period. As soon as he stops sucking, and the picture starts to blur, he averts his gaze. Gradually, the amount of time he can spend both sucking and looking increases. What the child seems to be learning here is not so much a specific response as a sequentially organized, adaptive *strategy* of responses.

Reaching and Grasping

Grasping, like sucking, is one of the infant's very early reflexes. By the time he is four weeks old, he automatically catches and holds an object that touches his hand. What role this reflex plays in the development of *voluntary* grasping is a matter of considerable controversy. Some psychologists see a very close relation between the two: they say that voluntary grasping develops from reflexive grasping through a purely internal process of maturational unfolding. Others see little or no relation; they say that a voluntary grasp develops only through interaction with the environment.

In my opinion, both views are false. The existence of prepared reflex machinery clearly facilitates the acquisition of voluntary motor control. For one thing, as T. E. Twitchell of Tufts Medical School has observed, voluntary control often starts with the self-evocation of a reflex, much as in the recovery pattern of hemiplegics. But to leave the matter at that ignores one crucial aspect of voluntary control: intention. Much of the infant's earliest voluntary activity is characterized by the *absence* of aid from prepared reflex mechanisms. Instead, it begins with diffuse activity that bears less resemblance to organized reflex responses than to athetoid behavior (the wormlike movements of fingers, toes, hands, and feet seen in certain brain-damaged children). Even when a reflex pattern does precede voluntary control, there is a period of diffuse, athetoid activity before voluntary control begins.

Once it has begun, how does it proceed? As I mentioned earlier, the infant has much more freedom of movement than he can control. His strategy for increasing his control is to impose severe restrictions on his freedom—to keep his elbow locked as he reaches for something, for instance—and to reduce the restrictions as he consolidates his skill within them.

The child uses this strategy as he learns to reach. If an object crosses the visual field of a month-old child, he will move his head in pursuit. As the object approaches him, he changes his level of activity, becoming quieter if he was active or more active if quiet before. Tension in the child's trunk increases. In a six-week-old, this tension takes the form of an attempt to lift the shoulders and arms, even though the child has had no experience reaching for or retrieving objects. By ten or twelve weeks, the approach of the object makes the infant pump his arms, shoulders, and head, staring at the object and working his mouth at the same time. From this position, he may launch swiping movements toward the object, keeping his hand clenched in a fist. I have seen babies blink in surprise as they execute the

The Many Faces of Response

Jerome Kagan

Jerome Kagan here reports research on the development of attention and makes interesting comparisons between younger and older infants, boys and girls, various social-class levels, and American and Mayan Indian children. The level of attention is usually measured by the amount of time the infant will study an object. The objects of attention, in this case, are ordinary and disarranged masks of human faces.

Kagan concludes that fixation times are related to different factors at different ages. Some of these factors are: (1) the infant's richness of association, (2) the amount of facial distortion, (3) sex differences, (4) social-class differences, and (5) cultural differences.

Each generation of psychologists seems to discover a fresh set of phenomena and a sparkling new object to study. The favorite of the academic psychologist during the opening years of this century was the adult trained to report sensations of color, light, and weight. Then, as psychology decided that learned habits and biological drives were more critical than feelings and sensations—and easier to objectify—the white rat captured the stage. The current star is the human infant, and the theme centers on his emerging mental life.

The human child has become a favorite subject for many reasons. Historical explanation always has been basic to American psychology. The belief that early learning governs later behavior stems in part from our recently strong commitment to behaviorism, and from our hope that bad habits learned early in life can be unlearned, or at least that good habits can be taught to the next generation.

The work of Harry Harlow and his colleagues with monkeys and terry-cloth mothers has intensified psychologists' concern with the effects of early experience on later behavior, as has the heavy stress that psychoanalytic theory places on the first five years of life.

Interest in the young child clearly rests on more than one base. But a major catalyst for experimentation with the infant was the work of Robert Fantz of Western Reserve University, which showed that by remarkably simple methods one could determine what a baby was looking at. To everyone's surprise, the infant turned out not to be perceptually innocent. The hope that we might be able to determine what a baby perceives led us to believe that we might begin to probe his mind.

Moreover, some psychologists believe that the infant provides a simple prototype of adult processes. After all, important discoveries about heredity in man were made by biologists who studied generations of fruit flies. The maxim that the easiest way to discover basic principles is through the study of simple forms has become a part of scientific catechism. Thus, many hope that the infant will yield some of nature's basic truths about psychological functioning.

Three primary questions currently motivate infant watching. Observation of the baby may lead to a better understanding of the laws of perceptual processing and the principles of learning. In addition, the belief—which derives from the overwhelming differences among day-old babies—that variations among young infants preview the psychological structure and behavior in the older child requires validation.

Finally, there is the "early learning" hypothesis. How

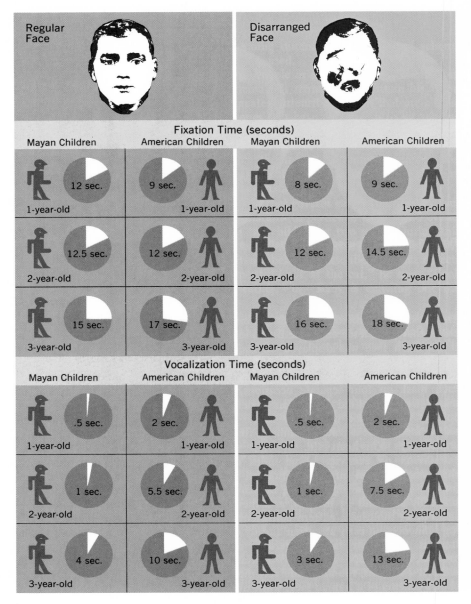

Figure 2. Differences between Mayan and American children's responses to paintings of regular and disarranged human faces.

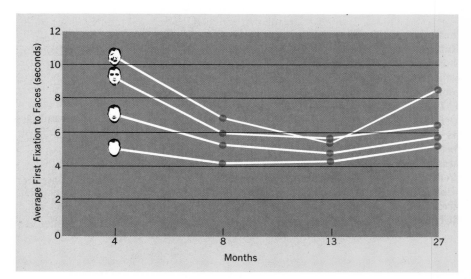

Figure 3. Changes in length of fixation time with infants' age. The different spans correspond to known influences on early attention.

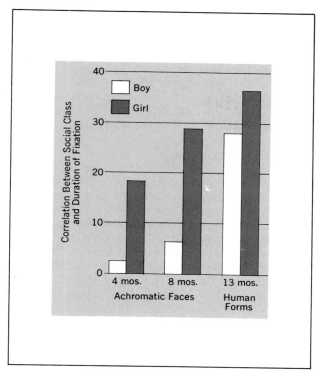

Figure 4. Correlation between social class and attentiveness for girls and boys.

Figure 5. The natural and disarranged human forms used to test the attention of 13-month-olds of different social-class backgrounds.

a more consistent relation in girls between specific experiences that are presumed to promote attention and subsequent attentive behavior.

Consider the following analogy: Two hands are placed separately on two pieces of clay, each piece of clay representing an infant. One piece of clay is of uniform softness and pliability; the other is lumpy, and varies in pliability. If the two hands come down on the two pieces of clay with the same force, each makes a different impression. The homogeneous clay reflects more faithfully the force that was imposed on it than does the clay with variable pliability.

An alternative interpretation is not inconsistent with the first, but it requires no biological assumptions. It assumes instead that social class has a stronger influence on the way mothers treat their daughters than on the way they treat their sons. Observation of some of our 4-month-old children in their homes supports this idea. Middle-class mothers talked substantially more to their daughters than lower-class mothers did; this difference was not present between lower- and middle-class mothers of sons. The longer fixation times at 8 and 13 months by the daughters of well-educated mothers may be a function, in part, of the greater face-to-face stimulation that the child may receive. Longer face-to-face contact may cause the child to show longer fixation times not only to interesting facial stimuli but perhaps to all classes of interesting events.

A study by Judith Rubenstein, of the National Institute of Mental Health, supports this argument. On two occasions she visited the homes of 44 Caucasian babies 5 months old and observed the behavior of their mothers. The mothers were classified as high-attentive, medium-attentive, or low-attentive, depending upon the number of times they looked at, touched, held, or talked to their babies.

The babies with highly attentive mothers spent longer times studying and manipulating a novel stimulus than did babies of least attentive mothers. It was as if the close reciprocal play experienced by the babies with highly attentive mothers established their interest in long explorations of interesting events.

Attention and Heart Deceleration

The use of a decrease in heart rate to assess processes related to attention has a short but interesting history. One reason cardiac deceleration was not used earlier to measure attentional reactions can be traced to general arousal theory. This theory implies that when an organism is "tense" about anything—fear, sexual passion, or intense attention—it will show autonomic reaction patterns that reflect internal arousal. That is, among other things, it should show an *increase* in heart rate. Thus investigators did not search for *decreases* in heart rate in response to episodes that involved attention, and they often did not know how to interpret them when such did appear.

IV
Cognition and Thought

Understanding Children's Art

Rhoda Kellogg

The esthetic development of the child, as represented in his early scribbles and graphic shapes, is an interesting bridge between his primitive emotional and his sophisticated conceptual states. Art links feeling and thought and thereby becomes the highest synthesis human beings achieve. Rhoda Kellogg's study of children's self-taught (or preschool) art is particularly provocative because it catches the child young enough to be close to his feelings and old enough to engage in an abstract portrayal of them.

In a novel interpretation of her findings, Miss Kellogg concludes that the child does not accommodate his scribbles to real objects but rather has a basic esthetic, which exists even in his scribbles, that he comes to shape to the real world: If an adult says that one of his designs looks like a house, he will graciously call it a house, but he made the drawing to satisfy his own esthetic—not to depict a house. She says that adults should avoid imposing a conventionalized pictorial depiction of the world on the budding esthetic sensibilities of young children and thus allow them to go their own artistic directions.

During the last hundred years, there has been increasing interest in children's drawings and paintings. Adults flock to gallery or museum shows of children's art, delighting in its freshness and originality and in the glimpse it offers of the child's world. Moreover, ever since Freud drew attention to the ways by which repressed psychological material is overtly expressed, psychologists have used children's drawings as a means of understanding child development in general, and the problems of individual disturbed children. And for many years the ability of the child to copy simple forms or to "draw a man" has been widely used as a test of intelligence for preschool children.

My study of children's art began more than twenty years ago, primarily out of a desire to understand very young children, my favorite people. I had already read many books on psychoanalysis, among them the works of Carl Jung, who believed that mandalas, or designs based on a crossed circle, were of great human and psychological significance. When I first noticed that three-year-olds were drawing crossed circles, my interest in child art was intensified and I wanted to know what kinds of drawings preceded the crossed circle, and what kinds followed it. Thereafter, no scribblings made in the nursery schools operated by the Golden Gate Kindergarten Association in San Francisco landed in the wastebasket. Each child's dated drawings were filed, and I began to sort a few hundred scribblings into look-alike groups.

Since then, I have seen more than a million pieces of children's art, half produced by children below the age of six and the rest by grade-school children. About a third of these works are now housed as the Rhoda Kellogg Child Art Collection at the Phoebe A. Hearst Preschool Learning Center in San Francisco, and the rest are still in storage elsewhere. More works by some 300 children between the ages of two and twelve who attend the nursery school, or the child art classes at the Center, are being collected.

To most people, "child art" calls to mind the stick figures that children draw as representations of people. Contrary to popular belief, however, the stick man is not a spontaneous product of child art. It is a figure children learn after the age of five from adults or from other children. Because there are such important differences between the work done by preschoolers and that done later, I call the former *self-taught child art*. This article will emphasize the early art, which children under six teach themselves before adults start showing them "how to draw."

For generations, adults have viewed children's scribblings as no more than the natural products of random motor activity. Most adults rate a child's drawing according to how well it represents a person or a familiar

Figure 1. Child's painting of a human figure.

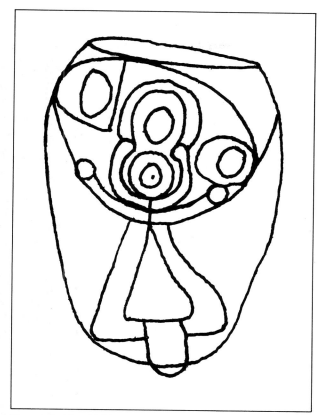

Figure 2. The hidden abstract design in the painting in Figure 1.

object. This representational approach has prevented adults from appreciating the wealth of structured, non-pictorial work that children teach themselves to produce before they begin to pictorialize.

Because most adults consider the ability to draw representationally to be an exceptional talent possessed by only a few individuals, and because almost every child possesses the capacity for scribbling, it is very difficult for us as adults to see that early scribblings can be valuable documents for understanding the origins of art. Some parents may save their children's pictorial drawings, but few save their children's scribblings. From my recent analysis of these nonpictorial, early works produced before age three, I have concluded that early scribblings are essential to understanding all forms of graphic art as well as child art.

As I studied the self-taught art work of children from all over the world, the main sequential stages of child development in art became evident. In 1955 I reported my findings for the work of three- and four-year-olds in a book, *What Children Scribble and Why*. Not until 1965, however, did I understand the work of two-year-olds; therefore the *why* of scribbling is much better explained in my new book, *Analyzing Children's Art*, published in 1969.

At this point you may ask: By what criteria can the term "art" be applied to the scribblings of two-year-olds? I answer that graphic art of whatever kind is produced by the human hand moving over a surface with a marking instrument. Any number of descriptive labels can be applied to these markings—scribblings, designs, gestalts, motifs, charts, symbols, signs, compositions, abstractions, representations, or pictures. The label depends upon who does the labeling and in what context the work is viewed.

Basic Scribbles

Every form of graphic art, no matter how complex, contains the lines found in children's work, which I call the *twenty basic scribbles*: vertical, horizontal, diagonal, circular, curving, waving or zig-zag lines, and dots (see Figure 3a). Basic scribbles can be made whether or not the eye controls the movement of the hand, for scribbles are the product of a variety of directional muscular movements that human beings make even before the age of two. Basic scribbles are not learned from adults—they are spontaneous human "events" that take place when a finger or marking instrument moves over a surface and leaves a record of the movement. Not until I had studied child art for many years did I realize that though these early scribblings are visually meaningless to adults, they are visually significant to the child who makes them.

The basic scribbles are the building blocks out of which all graphic art, pictorial and nonpictorial, is constructed. And when the child looks at his scribblings, he sees them as visual wholes or entities.

Before young children can draw the figures called a "man," a "horse," a "dog," and so forth, they will not only have scribbled, but will have constructed many abstract components and designs. I now know that children's first pictorial drawings are not early attempts to draw specific objects as the sight of those objects registers in the mind. Instead, children gradually realize that certain objects resemble their own designs and observe that adults call some of these designs "houses," "boats," "people," "flowers." Thus children learn which drawings are pictorial and which are not. Drawing "from life" comes at a much later time. All children spontaneously scribble and make designs, but adults must teach them how to "copy nature."

It is difficult for adults to appreciate and understand self-taught art because the minds of children and of adults are so different. Through years of living, adults have accumulated a store of rich associations, which children have yet to acquire. For example, when a child looks at an O he has drawn, he sees only a round form, or gestalt, but the adult may see this as a scribble, a letter, a circle, an ornament, a symbol, a sign, a wheel, a ring. . . . The famous psychologist Arnold Gesell once said that our knowledge of the child is about as reliable as a fifteenth-century map of the world. The scribblings of children can help adults gain a more reliable map.

Sequential Development in Self-taught Art

As children progress from scribbling to picture making, they go through four distinguishable stages: the Placement Stage, the Shape Stage, the Design Stage, and the Pictorial Stage.

| PLACEMENT STAGE | Even the very earliest scribblings are not placed on the paper by happenstance. Instead, most of them are spontaneously drawn on the paper in *placement patterns,* that is, with an awareness of figure and ground relationships. I have detected seventeen different placement patterns. The Spaced Border Pattern is shown below, left, and six others are shown in Figure 3b. The seventeen patterns appear by the age of two, and once developed are never lost.

| SHAPE STAGE | Placement patterns produce overall gestalts, or forms, which result from the location of the scribblings on the page. These gestalts contain implicit shapes. For example, the spaced border pattern below, right, usually implies a rectangular shape:

By age three, most children can draw these implied shapes as single-line outline forms, called *diagrams,* and have reached the Shape Stage. There are six diagrams: circles (and ovals), squares (and rectangles), triangles, crosses, Xs, and odd forms.

| DESIGN STAGE | As soon as children can draw diagrams, they almost immediately proceed to the Design Stage, in which they put these simple forms together to make structured designs. When two diagrams are united, the resulting design is called a *combine:*

and when three or more are united, the design is called an *aggregate:*

$$X + \square + + \rightarrow \boxtimes$$

| PICTORIAL STAGE | Between the ages of four and five, most children arrive at the Pictorial Stage, in which their structured designs begin to look like objects that adults can recognize. The Pictorial Stage can be divided into two phases: the first contains *early pictorial* drawings, and the second contains *later pictorial* drawings.

The early pictorial drawings differ from the gestalts of the Design Stage in that they are suggestive of "human figures," "houses," "animals," "trees," and the like. The later pictorial drawings are more clearly defined and are easily recognized as familiar objects by adults. The later pictorial drawings do not necessarily represent a more advanced stage of artistic develop-

ment; they are merely those pictorial drawings that adults recognize and approve of.

In his pictorial drawings, the child is not necessarily trying to draw representationally but is more concerned with creating esthetically satisfying structures. For example, a multiple-loop scribble (smoke) might appear more pleasing to him if it circles around a square aggregate (a house). Logical consistency does not become his concern until adults restrict his expression along lines considered to be "proper."

From Humans to Rockets

The child's first drawings of the human figure look very odd to adults; the figure is round like a ball and the arms come out of the head. The reason for this lack of likeness is that the child is not drawing persons as seen, but is modifying the mandalas and suns of the late Design Stage in order to give his familiar gestalts a new look.

Mandala is a Sanskrit word denoting a "magic circle," though crossed squares and concentric circles or squares are also mandalas. The distinguishing characteristic of a mandala is its perfect balance, and mandala balance is dominant in self-taught art. The child's mandalas are prominent in the combines and aggre-

Figure 3. The lines found in children's art. (a) The twenty basic scribbles; (b) Placement patterns; (c) Diagrams; (d) Combines; (e) Aggregates; (f) Early and late pictorial.

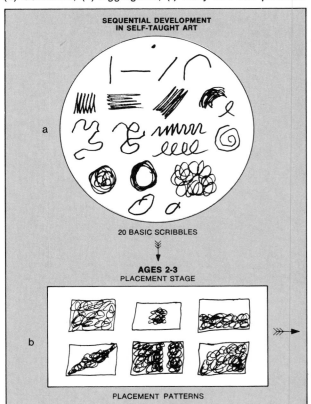

gates, and are a departure point for proceeding to draw suns, radials, and human figures. The mandala gestalt (1) suggests the sun gestalt (2), and the two of them evolve into the first human figure (3). In the first drawings of humans, the arms are attached to the head and there are markings on top to balance the legs. Later the child omits arms from his drawings, perhaps in the effort to relieve the monotony of mandala balance. But

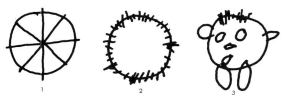

actually almost all drawings of humans that children create before age six do fit nicely into an implied circular or oval shape, no matter what distortions of anatomy are required. This leads me to conclude that the child is not at all concerned with trying to draw his "humans" so that they look like people; he is striving for variety within a set of esthetic formulas.

Drawings of human figures are followed by drawings of animals that are only modified gestalts of humans. For example, when the ears are on top of the head, the human becomes what adults call an animal (compare drawings in top row of Figure 4).

In the same way, the "buildings" that children spontaneously draw are not attempts to depict real houses. Instead, these gestalts are interesting variations on designs made up of squares and rectangles. This applies to drawings of boats, cars, trees, airplanes, and rockets.

Before age five there are no differences between art gestalts produced by boys and girls. From then on, however, cultural influences lead them to draw different subject matter.

Is Picasso Right About Child Art?

The child's production of art gestalts collides head-on with the conception of art that adults have learned after age six and have passed on from one generation to another, according to the approved formulas of the local culture. Adults who coach children to draw real-life objects are not really being helpful; they may even be causing harm. The child's purpose is not that of drawing what he sees around him; rather, he is probably a very experienced master of self-taught art, concerned primarily with the production of esthetic combinations that are often the envy of adult artists. In fact, Picasso

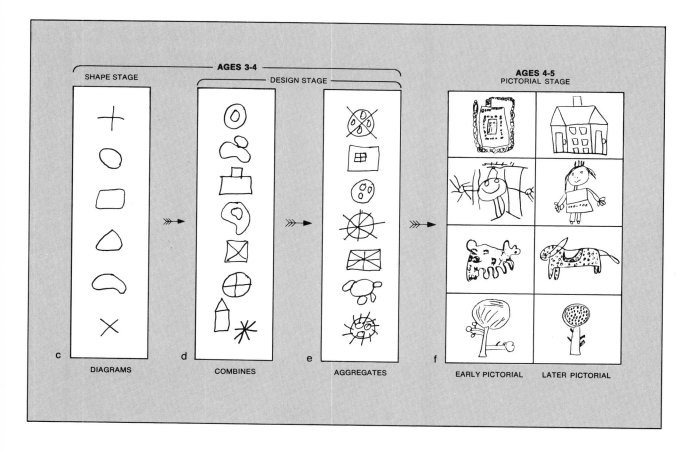

says that adults should not teach children to draw but should learn from them.

It is very difficult to convince adults that art is not essentially a matter of portraying reality. A deep appreciation of art derives from an appreciation of both the explicit and the hidden esthetic gestalts present in all art; the pictorial aspect of art is important, but it is not the ingredient that separates mundane art from great art.

Children left alone to draw what they like, without the interference of adult "guidance," usually develop a store of gestalts that enables them to reach the culminating stage of self-taught art. From there, if they are especially gifted, they may develop into great artists, unspoiled by the stenciled minds of well-meaning adults. Few children, however, are given this opportunity, and most relinquish art after the first few years in school.

Child Art and Learning to Read

Failure to allow self-taught art to take its natural course of development after age six causes confusion in the child mind and misunderstandings between children and adults, both of which interfere with learning and discipline in school. The child whose ability to create art gestalts has been developed usually learns to read quickly and well. Since neither parents nor educators know the value of scribbling, they fail to provide a place, under proper supervision, for the very young to scribble. This is unfortunate, because scribbling and

Figure 4. Progressive changes of mandalas from scribbles to representation.

drawing develop the child's ability to perceive abstract gestalts, an ability so necessary for learning to read. The teaching of reading and writing has never been based on any awareness of the child's interest in abstract expression. Children who have been free to experiment with and produce abstract esthetic forms have already developed the mental set required for learning symbolic language.

As the child learns to read, he is expected to comprehend difficult systems of gestalt-making, each with its own order and rules: (1) the written and printed language system of the culture; (2) the simple art gestalts that teachers and parents make and that the child is supposed to copy; (3) adult art used as illustrations in books; (4) gestalts as they appear in photographs, movies, and television; and (5) gestalts as they appear in charts, graphs, diagrams, and maps.

Reading and writing primarily involve visual skills, yet prevalent teaching methods emphasize association of the spoken word with the graphic symbols for those words. I believe that teaching the alphabet and stressing phonetics may be the wrong approach. Reading can better be taught by recognizing the importance of the child's inherent gestalt-making system as it is developed in self-taught art, and then by building upon it. Allowing a child to draw what he likes for at least thirty minutes every day in school might very well free him to continue developing his capacity to perceive abstract gestalts. This would lay the groundwork for improving his reading and would improve his writing ability also, because scribbling and drawing develop the fine muscle skills required for making precise markings on paper.

Using Child Art to Test Intelligence

In our country today, drawing is widely used as the basis for measuring general intelligence in young children. These "intelligence" tests can be categorized according to the kinds of drawing abilities that they emphasize. In the Goodenough test, the child is rated by his ability to draw a man; in the Bender test, he is rated by his proficiency in copying visual gestalts; and in the Lantz test, his spontaneous art is subjectively judged by an "expert." Because we fail to understand the nature of child art, these tests are imperfect instruments of measurement.

For example, the Goodenough Draw-a-Man test, devised in 1926 and recently revised by Dale Harris, is based on such erroneous conceptions of the child mind and of child art that its use today is pure psychological ritual with no scientific validity. Scientific statistical treatment has been given to data so meager and so highly selected as to be absurd, but the human mind finds ritual comforting where knowledge is lacking. For the last forty years the intelligence of many American four-year-olds has been measured by the Goodenough test, which is "standardized" on only 119 drawings of children of that age. The test itself was devised on the

basis of but 2,306 drawings, made for the most part by children of various ages who lived on the wrong side of the tracks in Perth Amboy, New Jersey. In revising the test, Harris standardized 3,000 more drawings, but his conceptions of how children should draw the parts of the body—that is, the 71 features to be scored—resemble neither anatomy nor natural child art. The use Goodenough and Harris made of child art cannot be justified on rational grounds because both of them refused to consider the esthetic components of children's drawings as being relevant.

Before a child can learn to draw from the stimulus of an adult's drawing—that is, learn to copy—he must have developed certain skills of hand-eye-brain coordination. Gesell found that few three-year-olds could copy perfect circles and squares, and he claimed that children could not draw the mandala below, left, until the age of seven. (Yet five-year-olds will commonly draw this mandala in non-test situations.) The Bender Motor Gestalt test consists of a set of tricky gestalts that the child is asked to copy but that no one would ever draw outside of a test situation. Few children or adults can complete the test perfectly. The Bender test is not a good test because it fails to take into consideration the natural development of child art. The gestalt below, center, would look wrong to any child, for the figure below, right, is the natural way to combine a square and a circle. Another gestalt might look to a child somewhat

like an awkward diagonal cross, for which a substituted graceful cross is a "failure."

Still another test based on art is the Lantz Easel Age Scale, which is standardized on 3,000 paintings of such subject matter as houses and boats—because drawings of the human figure are too complicated to rate. The test is "satisfactorily correlated" with the Goodenough test and has been given the usual statistical treatment so that it looks scientific. The ratings on the test are based on an Easel Age Score, which is said not only to measure intelligence but to measure it quantitatively. I do not see how this is possible when even adults, whose intelligence has been proved by their functioning, are not able to "draw a man," make paintings of houses, or copy designs perfectly in the Bender test. Another flaw in the test arises from the fact that children who persist in painting abstract works, called "Q" paintings, are said to be in need of help of a special psychological or medical nature. This discourages the natural development of artistic expression and may send perfectly healthy children into unnecessary clinical treatment.

A Proposed Child Art Test

I am not sure that we need more tests for children, but if we must have them they should be as accurate and as harmless as possible. A child's artistic creations could be used as the basis for assessing more general mental functioning if the usual drawbacks associated with the testing situation were eliminated. Since any child's file of drawings shows that he can waver between scribbles and suns from one day to the next (see Figure 5), it is unreasonable to suppose that the child's "intelligence" can be assessed on the basis of his performance during a short test period. Spontaneous drawings done over a period of several weeks should be examined for the presence or absence of certain gestalts considered to be "normal" at certain age levels.

In order to set up the standard against which the child's performance would be evaluated, a large number of children's works would have to be studied to determine the age range for the first appearance of particular gestalts. A frequency distribution of selected aggregates, mandalas, suns, and human figures could then be plotted as a function of age level. Any child's stage of artistic development could then be compared with the norm to determine his relative performance.

This test would be particularly useful for diagnosing mental retardation—and pseudoretardation. Often I

have been able to convince the parents of a supposedly retarded child that their child was perfectly normal in his art development and hence probably perfectly normal in intelligence.

Universals and Universities

Parents, educators, and psychologists are not the only adults who fail to understand the significance of the origins of art in childhood. Art historians, anthropologists, and archeologists, who encounter the motifs of self-taught art in their studies of primitive and past cultures, usually view these gestalts as products of the adult mind, rich in symbolic meaning and characteristic of local cultures. For example, Giedion, the noted art

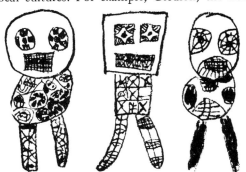

Figure 5. Each pair of drawings compares one child's "best" and "poorest" representations of a human, both done within the same week.

historian, interprets triangular diagrams as vulvas and fertility symbols; and Margaret Mead believes that "art comes from art"—that each generation teaches its favorite gestalts to the next generation. A better understanding of these ancient gestalts could be achieved through a greater knowledge of the universal nature of self-taught child art.

Human beings throughout the world, from Paleolithic times to the present, have used some of these basic motifs of child art. Pictorial drawings made by children in many lands are remarkably similar because they are the outgrowths of earlier scribblings and designs (see Figure 6). Since this early art is so uniform in expression from country to country, culture to culture, past to present, I conclude that the child's early abstractions (as well as later, derivative, pictorial drawings) are the products of innate patterns of neurological growth and human development.

Indeed, Max Knoll has discovered that the phosphenes, or light patterns that adults experience when the cortex is electrically stimulated, are similar to children's scribblings. This suggests that there are some inherent neurological mechanisms that enable us to produce and to perceive the basic line gestalts out of

which art forms are produced. Several studies have shown that infants only a few weeks old can respond with movement of their eye muscles to the stimulus of abstract patterns, and it is now generally agreed that the mind at birth is not a blank, nor is it a "blooming buzzing confusion," as William James suggested.

Live Art Scribbles

Children's scribblings and drawings contain a voluminous written message, a message that has not yet been completely deciphered. It may turn out that "live art scribbles" are as important as the Dead Sea Scrolls.

I believe that the hidden message in child art, when properly understood, will free us to recapture the un-*adult*erated esthetic vision of the child. Perhaps the day will come when adult and child can enjoy self-taught art together, not as "cute" or "remarkable" products of the childish mind but as the groundwork of all art. Then adults will not make stencils for children to fill in, nor will they patronizingly laugh at what they do not understand.

Children are happy when they can draw objects to fit into implied esthetic shapes. What the great artist struggles to achieve, the child creates naturally.

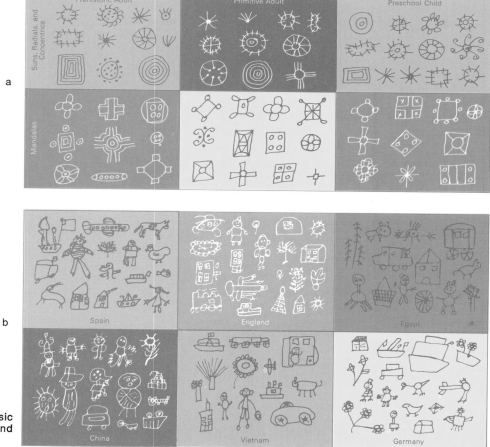

Figure 6. Universality of basic art motifs (a) across time and (b) across cultures.

The Mystery of the Prelogical Child

Joachim F. Wohlwill

The theoretical influence of Jean Piaget in cognitive development equals the influence of B. F. Skinner in learning psychology and Freud in personality theory and psychotherapy. Piaget emphasizes the innate and biological over learning and environmental factors. According to Piaget, cognitive development is an orderly progression through stages that more or less correspond to age levels.

The thrust of American research on cognitive development is to test how well ages and stages correspond and also how much development can be accelerated by specific types of teaching interventions. Although Joachim Wohlwill believes the present evidence is still shaky, he contends that teaching can hasten the development of logical thinking. Knowledge of the student's logical capacities, even as they are portrayed by Piaget, can help to guide the teacher's selection of cognitive tasks.

A five-year-old girl, Mary, has been taken out of her kindergarten class to participate in a psychological experiment. She is seated in front of a table on which two brightly colored necklaces lie side by side; they are of equal length, and their ends are neatly aligned. "Let's pretend that the blue one is yours," the psychologist tells her, "and the red one is mine. Who do you think has the longer necklace, you or me?" Mary, slightly puzzled, replies with conviction, "We both do!"—her way of asserting that the two lengths are equal. "That's right, but watch carefully," says the experimenter as she picks up her own necklace and forms a circle out of it. "Now tell me, Mary, whose necklace is longer, or is mine still just as long as yours?" Mary stretches out her arms to illustrate length and beams: "Mine is longest! You made yours into a ring, and mine is all *this* long."

In schools, psychological laboratories, and child-study centers across the country and throughout the world, children are participating in such experiments in our attempts to answer one of the most difficult and puzzling questions about child development: How does the uniquely human capacity for logical thought develop? How does the child's thinking evolve from a prelogical stage to one defined by the rules of adult logic? Children are being asked questions about lengths, weights, amounts, and numbers, and about space, time, and probability to see if they use a type of reasoning qualitatively different from that used by adults, or if children—naive realists that they are—place undue trust in appearances.

By the time she is six or seven, Mary will know that the length of a string of beads is conserved—that is, that its length will not change even if its longness disappears when both ends are joined in a circle. How does she gain the concept of length as a dimension so that she ignores the perceptual cues presented by changes in shape? Does understanding of dimension, class, probability, and the like come from a natural process of maturation or from extensive teaching and experience? A generation ago the child mind was pictured either as an empty shell that gradually fills with knowledge picked up piece by piece from the environment, or as an adult-mind-in-miniature that grows to its full size as the child develops. Today, many psychologists believe that neither view is correct. Instead, they see a structured mind, internally consistent yet externally illogical—a kind of Alice-in-Wonderland world where lengths, weights, and distances have as much constancy as the shape of Silly Putty.

This new picture has aroused widespread and vigorous debate not only among child psychologists but also among educators because it raises a host of questions about our understanding of mental processes in general and about child development in particular. Do we develop in specific stages on our way to adult reasoning? Is this development "preset," as is a child's physical growth, or can it be speeded up by teaching and experience? If so, by what methods of teaching and by what kinds of experiences? Since what we call intelligence involves to a large extent conceptual thinking, our inquiry holds important implications for our understanding of this much-debated subject.

Jean Piaget—Explorer of a New World

The current concern with the conceptual world of childhood and with the child's mode of reasoning has been inspired very largely by the work of Jean Piaget at the Institut Jean-Jacques Rousseau in Geneva, Switzerland. During the past thirty years, Piaget and his collaborators have mapped out, step by step and book by book, the dimensions of the curious and fascinating world that exists in the child's mind.

Let us sit in on one of Piaget's experiments. On the table in front of Johnny, a typical five-year-old, are two glasses identical in size and shape. Piaget's glass is half full of orange soda and Johnny's glass is half full of lemonade. Piaget puts a tall, thin glass on the table and

pours Johnny's lemonade into it. "Now who has more to drink, you or me?" the famous experimenter asks the five-year-old. "I have," Johnny says. "There's more lemonade in mine because it's higher in the glass." The five-year-old is convinced that he has more lemonade in his new glass even when he is asked: "Are you sure it just doesn't look as though there is more?" Piaget points out that his own glass is wider than Johnny's new glass, but the child replies, "Yes, but this one goes way up to *here*, so there's more." Pointing to the original lemonade container, the experimenter then asks: "Suppose we pour your lemonade back into the glass it came from—then what?" Johnny remains firm: "There would still be more lemonade."

The responses of Lonny, a typical six-year-old, are interestingly different. When the lemonade is poured into the taller, narrower glass and Piaget asks, "Do we both have the same amount to drink?" Lonny, on thinking it over, says, "Well, no." Asked to explain why, he says, "Your glass is bigger." But he becomes confused when the experimenter points out that the new glass is taller: "I guess there's more lemonade in the tall glass." Piaget asks, "Suppose we poured your lemonade back into the glass it came from?" Shades of Alice in Wonderland, the answer is, "Then we'd have the same amount to drink."

But now here is Ronny, a year older than Lonny. When the lemonade is poured into the narrow glass, Ronny is sure that there is still the same amount of lemonade as there was before. The conversation goes this way:

"How do you know it is still the same?"
"Well, it was the same before."
"But isn't this new glass higher?"
"Yes, but the old glass is wider."

What do these three tests tell us? Five-year-old Johnny's insistence that there is more to drink in the tall, narrow glass comes from his preoccupation with the most salient fact about the liquids—the difference in their heights. He blithely ignores the difference in the widths of the two glasses. Six-year-old Lonny shows some confusion. He seems to recognize that both the height of the liquid and the width of the glasses must be taken into account, but he can focus only on one aspect of the situation at a time. He recognizes, however, that if the lemonade is poured back into its original container, equality will be restored. But seven-year-old Ronny has no doubts. He *knows* the amount of liquid remains the same because he understands the compensatory relationship between height and width; he understands the concept of conservation of amount.

The Idea of Logical Necessity

Ronny's *understanding* is the critical point for Piaget. It is not merely that Ronny, at seven, can simultaneously perceive both the height and the width of the con-

tainers, but also that he can understand the inverse relationship between the two dimensions and can thus recognize that conservation of amount is a logical necessity. Some children may express this recognition without referring to dimensions at all: "You only poured my lemonade into that glass; it's still just as much." Or, "Well, it's the same as it was before; you haven't given me any more lemonade."

The conservation of amount—which Ronny understands at seven—is but one of a set of dimensions for which children acquire the concept of conservation at different ages. The more important of the "conservations" and the ages at which children, on the average, first show understanding of them, are the following:

Conservation of number (6–7 years): The number of elements in a collection remains unchanged, regardless of how the elements are displaced or spatially rearranged.
Conservation of substance (7–8 years): The amount of a deformable substance such as dough, soft clay, or liquid remains unchanged, regardless of how its shape is altered (as in transforming a ball of clay into a long, narrow snake).
Conservation of length (7–8 years): The length of a line or an object remains unchanged, regardless of how it is displaced in space or how its shape is altered.
Conservation of area (8–9 years): The total amount of surface covered by a set of plane figures (such as small squares) remains unchanged, in spite of rearranging positions of the figures.
Conservation of weight (9–10 years): The weight of an object remains unchanged, regardless of how its shape is altered.
Conservation of volume (14–15 years): The volume of an object (in terms of the water it displaces) remains unchanged, regardless of changes in its shape.

It must be emphasized that the ages given above are only gross averages: first, because children vary considerably in the rate at which their thinking develops, and second, because their recognition of the concept depends to a certain extent on the way the problem is presented. For example, children may recognize that the number of checkers in a row remains unchanged when the length of the row is expanded but fail to recognize it when the checkers are stacked in a pile.

The Stage of Concrete Operations

The responses of young children to tests such as those I have described give us a fascinating glimpse into processes that we, as adults, take so much for granted that they scarcely seem to involve thinking at all. But what is the significance of the conservation problem for an understanding of mental development? Piaget holds that the attainment of conservation points to the formation of a new stage in the child's mental development, the stage of concrete operations. This stage is manifested by conservation, and in a variety of other ways that attest to a new mode of reasoning.

For example, if children who have not yet reached the stage of concrete operations are presented with a set of pictures comprised of seven dogs and three horses and are asked, "How many animals are there?" they will readily answer, "Ten." They are quite able to recognize that both the subsets—dogs and horses—are part of a total set—animals. But if asked, "Are there more dogs or more animals?" these "preoperational" children will maintain there are more dogs. They translate the question into one involving a comparison of majority to minority subsets and have difficulty in comparing the elements of a single subset with those of the total set.

For Piaget this indicates that these children as yet lack mental structure corresponding to the logical operation of adding classes—or to use modern jargon, they are not "programmed" to carry out this operation.

The various manifestations of the stage of concrete operations do not necessarily appear at the same time. As we saw, concepts of conservation are attained for various dimensions at different age levels, and one concept may consistently lag behind another closely related concept. Suppose we present a child with two balls of modeling clay, identical in appearance and weight. Let us flatten one of the balls and roll it out into the form of a sausage. Now we will ask the conservation question for two different dimensions, *substance*—"Is there still as much clay in the ball as in the sausage?"—and *weight*—"Does the ball still weigh as much as the sausage?" The same child often will give opposite answers to these questions, and in such cases the child almost invariably asserts conservation for substance while denying it for weight. Thus it appears that the mode of reasoning involved in recognizing conservation of substance precedes that for weight.

The Young Child: Prelogical or Merely Naive?

Piaget holds, first, that these phenomena represent qualitative developmental changes in the child's mode of thinking, and second, that they are largely spontaneous and occur independently of teaching or of specific experiences. His views have aroused controversy as vigorous and at times as heated as did the views of Freud. Piaget's descriptions of the phenomena themselves—the diverse ways in which children respond to conceptual tasks—have been on the whole verified and accepted as essentially correct. The controversy rages over the explanation for them. Can the young child's lack of conservation be explained as resulting from a qualitatively different mode of reasoning, characteristic of the preoperational stage? Or is it merely the result of a naive trust in perceptual cues, combined with a strong tendency to respond to the most obvious, or perceptually salient, aspect of a situation?

For example, the sight of liquid rising in a narrow glass to a height well above that of the shorter, wider glass from which it came conveys a compelling impression of difference in quantity. It is easy to lose sight of the compensating difference in the width of the two glasses. Moreover, in the child's everyday life, glasses tend to be fairly similar in size; thus the height of liquid in a glass is a reasonably reliable index to its amount. There is indeed some evidence to support naiveté as an explanation. Studies carried out at Harvard suggest that children who initially lack the notion of conservation can recognize it if the misleading perceptual cues are screened out—that is, if the child cannot see the level of liquid as it is poured into the new container. It must be said, however, that other investigators who replicated this experiment did not obtain similar results.

Martin Braine of Walter Reed Medical Center conducted experiments using the ring-segmented illusion (see Figure 1) that showed that children can learn to resist perceptual cues when they are induced to differentiate between appearance and fact. Two shapes, A and B, are first superimposed so that the child can see that B is bigger. A is then placed above B; the child now will assert that A both looks bigger and really is bigger. As a result of a series of such problems in which the experimenter corrects all erroneous responses, the child will learn to pick B as really bigger than A, in the face of the contrary evidence of the senses.

Figure 1. The ring-segmented illusion.

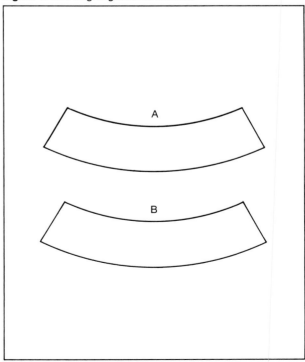

These experiments suggest that the child is inclined to respond naively to perceptual clues, but is this really the whole truth? In collaboration with a student, Michael Katz, I recently carried out the following experiment on the class-inclusion (set-subset) problem described earlier. Instead of presenting pictures of animals, we asked five- and six-year-old children, "Suppose that on a farm there are seven dogs and three horses. Are there more dogs or more animals?" Lo and behold, when the problem was presented in purely verbal form, avoiding perceptual cues, many of the children did consistently better than they did when asked to solve the problem on the basis of pictures.

On the face of it, this finding is the reverse of what might be expected. It is generally considered that at this age children's thinking is highly concrete, making it difficult for them to deal with purely hypothetical situations. However, it may be that the children did better when the problem was presented verbally because the pictures offered perceptual cues that strongly impelled the children to compare the two subsets. This explanation is in line with the view that children have difficulty with such tasks not because their reasoning is faulty but simply because they focus on the compelling aspects of appearance.

Nevertheless, further data uncovered in our studies seem to show that the interpretation is at best a gross oversimplification of the situation. When we tabulated the results for each child and compared scores on the verbal and the picture tests, we found the following: Among the large number of children who did not give any correct answers at all on the picture test, almost half also failed to give any correct answers in the verbal test. But of those who did give at least one correct answer to the picture test, 90 percent scored higher on the verbal test.

Eliminating the perceptual factor did *not* guarantee that a child could relate the subsets to the total set. These children seemed quite incapable of recognizing that an object can belong to two classes at once. Improved performance on the verbal test seems to indicate that there is an intermediary phase in the establishment of the class-inclusion concept. During this phase the perceptual cues are still dominant enough to bias the child's recognition of the concept.

Moreover, it is difficult to interpret the results of Piaget's experiment with the two balls of clay on the basis of perceptual cues alone. Why should the change in shape from sphere to sausage, with length becoming salient, bias the child toward thinking that the *weight* has changed and yet not bias the same child with respect to the *amount of substance*? The question becomes even more significant when we ask ourselves why one concept precedes another.

If we assume that conservation concepts are acquired primarily through experience, we would be led to the conclusion that weight conservation should be acquired first. The weight of an object, or more particularly the difference in weight between two objects, can be verified directly by weighing an object in one's hand; experiencing differences in the weight of objects begins in infancy. On the other hand, how does one *know* that amount of substance is conserved with change in shape? Yet the child recognizes that this "unexperienced" abstraction, amount of clay, is conserved and recognizes it well before he agrees that the readily defined, often-experienced entity, *weight*, is conserved.

Conceptual Development—Taught or Spontaneous?

The problems just discussed raise a more general question. Let us return to the types of reasoning displayed by Johnny, Lonny, and Ronny. I did not choose these names just to create a nursery-rhyme effect; I intended to suggest that the three boys could very well have been the same child at five, six, and seven years old. For, in the normal course of events, we expect Johnny to come to think as Lonny did, and Lonny, as he matures, to reason as Ronny did. Yet these changes usually occur spontaneously. In the course of play activities and everyday experience, children pour liquid from one container to another, roll balls of modeling clay into snakes, form rings with strings of beads. But five- and six-year-olds rarely ask themselves questions—or are asked questions by others—that lead them to ponder about things like the conservation of length. They are even less likely to be given direct information about questions involving conservation.

Somehow, therefore, these logical notions must be acquired indirectly, by the back door, as it were. The question is, where *is* the back door? If we assume that these seemingly spontaneous changes in mode of thinking do not occur in a vacuum, what sorts of experiences or activities can we postulate that may mediate them? What facets of his experience play a role in the child's acquisition of logical principles? It is this question that has been the subject of a great deal of concentrated discussion and research the world over.

Can such rules be taught before the child has discovered them for himself? A great deal of ingenuity has been expended to devise approaches aimed at teaching children "the logical facts of life," especially the conservations. Many such attempts have met with indifferent success, although recent studies have been more encouraging. Nevertheless, even where the zealous psychologist has succeeded in demonstrating the beneficial effect of this or that type of training, the results have been quite limited. That is, the learning has rarely been shown to have much transfer, even to similar concepts or tasks.

There is a real question, then, whether such restricted, short-term training offers sufficient conditions for establishing the basic rules of thought, which, according to Piaget, are "of the essence" in the child's mental development. At least equally important, however, is the question—do such experiences represent *necessary* conditions for the development of logical thought?

If we look at what children actually do during the years in which changes in their mode of thinking take place, the answers to our questions may not be quite so difficult to find. For example, children do gain considerable experience in counting objects, and so it does not seem unreasonable to suggest that the child comes to realize—quite implicitly—that *number* is a dimension totally independent of the perceptual aspects of a situation. But doesn't this directly contradict the suggestion that such concepts are not established through knowledge gained from experience? What I am suggesting is this: Through his experience in measuring, counting, and the like, the child may develop a *conceptual attitude* toward dimension in general. Then, confronted with a conservation-type question, he is able to ignore the perceptual cues that had previously been predominant and can respond to those aspects that, as a result of his experience, have now become dominant. Thus for Johnny, at five, the situation was dominated by a single perceptual cue—height of liquid in the glass. By the time he is seven, Ronny has, one might say, become an operationist; his concept of quantity is determined by the criteria he utilizes in measuring—for instance, as with the number of glasses of equal size that could be filled with the contents of a jar.

Ronny has developed a concept of quantity, furthermore, that may be of sufficient generality to encompass related dimensions that cannot be directly measured. This is particularly true if the dimension that is difficult to measure—for example, amount of substance—is assimilated to one that is easily measured—for example, quantity of liquid. Indeed, conservation for substance and liquid do appear at about the same time! It is interesting to note that the conservation-promoting attitude can go astray by dint of overgeneralization—a square and a circle made from the same piece of string do not have the same areas, counter to what even many adults assume.

Counting, Measuring, Ordering, Classifying

This interpretation of the way young children form logical concepts suggests that we may better understand their development by looking at activities such as counting, measuring, and ordering or seriating, for these are clearly relevant to concepts of quantitative attributes like weight, length, area, and the like. In a similar vein, classifying or sorting are relevant to understanding class and subclass relationships.

Counting, measuring, sorting, and the like are usually part of children's spontaneous, unprogrammed, everyday experience along with the more formal instruction they may receive in school. In research currently underway at Clark University, we are focusing on an intensive study of these activities and on their possible relationships to concepts like conservation and class-inclusion.

For instance, we want to see the extent to which children will arrange spontaneously a set of stimuli according to some plan or order. Children are offered a set of nine blocks with different pictures on each face, representing six classes of pictured objects—houses, birds, flowers, vehicles, stars, and dolls. Each class is subdivided according to size, color, and type; for example, there are three kinds of flowers, each pictured in one of three colors. The child is given a board divided into nine compartments in a three-by-three layout, into which he can place the blocks in whatever way he thinks they should go, though he is asked to do so in successively different ways.

We are interested in seeing how many categories the child constructs and how much internal order is displayed in each arrangement. In addition, we want to see how actively and systematically he handles the blocks (for example, in searching for a particular face). Not surprisingly, there is a close relationship between the two aspects of a child's performance: Children who receive high scores for recognition of categories and internal order generally go about their task in a much more systematic manner and manipulate the blocks more actively than the low scorers.

A perfectly consistent arrangement, showing three rows and three columns filled with pictures belonging to the same category, would earn a score of six. The five- to seven-year-olds we have studied thus far tend to be relatively unsystematic in their handling of the blocks, and lacking in consistency and order. On any one trial the median number of rows or columns filled with pictures in the same category is only 0.6. In one study carried out with a group of lower-class children from a day-care center, we found, however, that their scores could be substantially raised by intensive experience in responding to dimensions of order and to relationships of identity and difference in a set of stimuli.

Thus far, we have not found an unequivocal correlation between these measures of block-sorting behavior and conservation. However, we did find that of those children who were very poor in ordering the blocks, only 25 percent showed number conservation, whereas among the children who did somewhat better at ordering the blocks, 64 percent did show number conservation. The relation between block-sorting scores and performance on the class-inclusion task is much closer, as would be expected, since the two tasks are similar.

In other experiments we looked at children's approach to comparing and measuring lengths, heights, and distances. In general, almost no kindergartners and few first-graders showed awareness of the function of a unit of distance or a reference object. They failed to make use of a plastic ruler to measure distance. In many instances they did not even think of placing two objects side by side to see which was longer. In other words, since they had as yet no real understanding of length as a dimension, it is not surprising that many lacked conservation.

Other interesting insights were provided by experiments with the dowel board. When children are given a set of red dowels of different lengths and asked to put them any way they like into the holes of the accompanying wooden base, a majority come up with an ordered series. They are then given an identical set of blue dowels, but the holes in the accompanying base vary in depth, matching the variations in the lengths of the dowels. Thus, if they like, the children can arrange the blue dowels in a series identical to that of the red dowels or, by matching the lengths of the dowels with the depth of the holes, they can produce a series of equal height. Many children find this "problem" highly puzzling. Their behavior often becomes so disorganized and erratic that they produce no sort of order whatsoever. Of the thirty-five children we tested, twenty-five were unsuccessful. Again, comparing this kind of ordering ability with conservation-of-number ability, we found that, of the twenty-five unsuccessful children,

sixteen lacked number conservation, whereas among the ten successful children, only two lacked conservation of number.

Though our research is still in its early stages, the results thus far obtained encourage us to believe that our approach may help solve the mystery of the prelogical child and tell us something about how the conservations and other concepts manifested in the stage of concrete operations come into existence.

Our finding that children's scores could be raised by intensive experience suggests a profitable focus for instruction in the primary grades, where little attention is generally given to cultivating the child's measuring and classifying skills. Our guess is that concerted efforts to encourage and guide children's activities in this area might well pay handsome dividends. Beyond merely speeding the development of the skills themselves, an imaginative approach should provide children with a sounder, more broadly based foundation on which subsequent learning of mathematical and scientific concepts can be built.

Pay Attention

Tom Trabasso

*Perhaps the most hallowed exhortation in the teacher's verbal repertory is the phrase "Pay attention."
It is the anguished plea of the teacher whose student finds more interesting stimuli to compete with
her voice, and it is the earnest request of the teacher identifying the crucial and salient aspects of
material and skills that the student is acquiring: Unless the student pays attention he cannot learn.*

*Trabasso defines attention as "stimulus selection" and shows how it is a necessary precondition for
concept learning. Trabasso provides evidence that teachers must simplify the learning environment by
eliminating distracting stimuli. Environmental enrichment, in the perceptual sense, requires the appropriate stimulus selection rather than a carnival atmosphere of audio-visual cacophony and material
superabundance.*

People have been saying that everyone knows what
attention is, at least since William James brought out
his *Principles of Psychology*. In James' time, "attention"
was generally understood to mean the process or act of
admitting into the conscious mind a mere dribble of
the oceans of stimuli around us—the focusing on some
event, idea, or object and the simultaneous exclusion of
millions of others. Attention is so understood in our
own time as well, although some of us probably would be
happier with a term like "stimulus selection" or something of the sort.

Although attention was a thing or concept accorded
textbook status in the late nineteenth century, it was
excluded as a subject of study or even comment by all
the major schools that followed. For some thirty years,
the dominant (behaviorist) theories of learning had
nothing at all to say about attention because "everybody
knows what it is."

We are now, however, witnessing a revival of interest
in the operation of attentional processes in learning, a
revival generated by pressures both from within and
from outside of learning research. (This in itself is a
fascinating tale of the *Zeitgeist*.)

Rosslyn G. Suchman (now at the University of California at Berkeley) and I tested nursery-school children
for their "preference" for color and form as attention-
getting stimuli. Then we had the children learn to sort
cards into bins on the basis of color and form. If we
made color the relevant stimulus feature (the one that
led to the right answer), those children who preferred
color as a stimulus learned very rapidly; if color was of
no use in solving, learning was very slow. That is, the
ease or difficulty of learning seemed to depend on the
probability that a child would attend to and use the
relevant stimulus feature.

In another series of experiments, Gordon Bower (of
Stanford University) and I presented college students
with a problem in which they had to learn to sort out
red triangles and blue circles. Color and form both were
relevant; either one or the other, or both, could be used
to solve. After the students had (speedily) solved the
problem, we tested them for what they had learned.
Clear evidence of selective attention was found. Many
students had not learned triangles versus circles, or red
triangles versus blue circles, but only redness versus
blueness.

Thus we can say that one's preference for or attentional interest in form versus color stimuli sometimes

can block or impede learning. One practical upshot of this is a warning not to use distracting colors with letters in the teaching of reading. Another is that there is some danger in enriching a learning environment—perhaps we might do better as teachers to impoverish the environment by displaying only those objects, words, or relationships that are to be learned.

From Stimulus to Concept

It has been commonly assumed that learning consists fundamentally of the association between stimulus and response. But in order for such associations to occur, it is necessary for the learner to detect a stimulus and to discriminate it from other stimuli. It is also essential that he be able to deal with similar stimuli in some generalized way. Differences and similarities among environmental events may be conveniently described in terms of simple stimulus dimensions or attributes like form (round or square) and color (red or blue). When similarities are perceived and generalized in terms of more abstract attributes, we speak of a concept—roundness, squareness, redness, and so on.

The learning of elementary concepts may be conveniently studied. A child is given a simple two-choice problem in which he is asked to find a trinket or a piece of candy under round as opposed to square objects. In such a problem, we have made form relevant; if the child is successful in making rewarded choices all the time, we say that he has demonstrated a grasp of the concept of form. To complicate matters, we can color each form red or green, producing four patterns: a red ball, a green ball, a red square, and a green square. If we make the color uncorrelated with reward, we say that color is irrelevant: the child cannot use it to solve the problem and therefore must disregard it in making his choices.

When performance on such discrimination tasks is analyzed, the data are usually reported in terms of learning curves that represent the average performance of a group of children. The typical group learning curve is a smooth arc and is negatively accelerated; that is, gains in learning become smaller as the number of trials or amount of time spent learning increases (see Figure 1a). Most investigators have tended to interpret this group curve as characteristic of the individual learner.

But Betty House and David Zeaman, of the University of Connecticut, conducted analyses that were more sensitive to the character of the *individual* learning process, and thus were among the first researchers to show the importance of attentional factors in learning. They took a group of retarded children and segregated them in terms of which day the children reached a learning goal. This amounted to separating the children into divisions of fast, moderate, and slow learners (see Figure 1b). *Backward* learning curves were then constructed for each of these groups.

A backward learning curve begins with the trial on which each child makes his last error. In Figure 1c each child thus "starts" his criterion of learning in the upper right-hand corner. His proportion of successes on trials approaching the criterion is then plotted downward to the left. The result is therefore a curve that may be read backward to examine the rate at which subjects in a relatively homogeneous grouping approach the criterion of learning, in this case zero errors.

In the analysis of the backward and grouped curves for fast, moderate, and slow learners an interesting picture emerged. All of the backward curves showed two distinct portions: an initial phase that was quite flat with performance near a chance level of success, and a second phase that showed a sharp rise from chance responding to nearly perfect performance. These phases of chance successes and a sudden shift to perfect learning were identified as two subprocesses: an *attention* phase, where the learner is viewed as searching among several possible features of the stimulus patterns until he attends to those features that are relevant, and an *association* phase, where the learner attaches correct responses to those features he has selected as relevant.

The main difference between the fast and slow learners was in the length of the initial attention phase; the association phases for both fast and slow learners were approximately the same, as is indicated by nearly identical slopes in the backward curves.

House and Zeaman's identification of two phases of learning implied that deficits in learning by children, normal or otherwise, might lie not in their intellectual inability to form associations or to solve problems but in their inability to attend to the critical features of the task. This conjecture was supported by further analyses of backward learning curves for bright and dull children, both normal and retarded. Those children in each group with higher mental age scores showed faster overall learning, but their initial phases of chance responding were short; those children of lower mental age showed considerably longer initial phases. The slopes of the association sectors of the curves, however, were virtually identical for all groups and were steep-rising.

Cues and Learning Rates

In subsequent studies, it was found that the attention phase of the learning curves (but *not* the association phase) could be shortened by many stimulus factors that are known to affect the salience of a cue.

A clear demonstration of the relationship between stimulus salience and learning speed was made by Brian Shepp of Brown University, in collaboration with Zeaman. These investigators picked, as the relevant stimulus feature in a learning problem, a difference in the size of two blocks. For one group of learners, the size difference was small; for another it was very large. When the larger size difference was used, the overall learning rate was found to be very much faster and the initial (attention) portion of the backward curve much

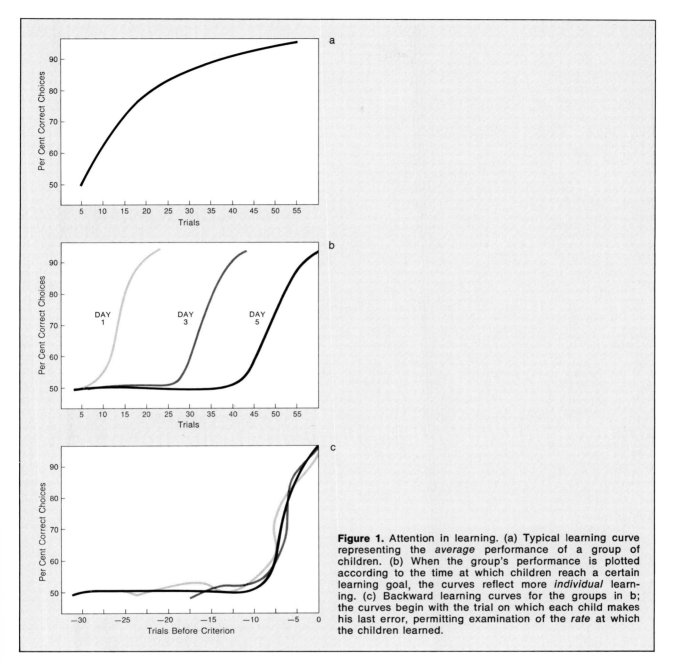

Figure 1. Attention in learning. (a) Typical learning curve representing the *average* performance of a group of children. (b) When the group's performance is plotted according to the time at which children reach a certain learning goal, the curves reflect more *individual* learning. (c) Backward learning curves for the groups in b; the curves begin with the trial on which each child makes his last error, permitting examination of the *rate* at which the children learned.

shorter. However, the slope of the association phase was not materially affected by changes in the saliency of the size difference.

Gordon Bower and I have obtained similar results with college students who learn simple classification problems involving geometric patterns. In two-choice concept-identification tasks, where the subject must learn to base his responses on a single attribute such as the color of the patterns, we have frequently found evidence for one-trial learning. The backward learning curves show long, flat initial phases at the chance level

of responding while the association phase occurs in one trial.

The reason for one-trial learning is that the associations required are trivial from the point of view of an adult; all that is needed is a single association such as: "Red patterns are alphas." Most of the "learning" in these tasks appears to consist of a search process whereby the subject selects and tries hypotheses based upon different stimulus attributes until he finally hits upon the relevant one and then solves immediately.

The overall learning rate of these problems seems to

depend upon the ease with which the subject comes to attend to and use whatever attribute the experimenter has chosen to be relevant. We can directly influence the length of the attention phase by manipulating the obviousness of the relevant features or cues. For example, we have facilitated learning by using markers, arrows, or underlined letters that direct the learners' attention to attributes; we have also slowed discovery by embedding the relevant features among several varying and irrelevant attributes.

The role that attention plays in the conceptual development of the child has been dramatically demonstrated in a recent doctoral thesis by Rochel Gelman at the University of California at Los Angeles (now at the University of Pennsylvania). Gelman was particularly interested in the development of certain abstract and logical concepts known as "conservation." To understand conservation means that one can appreciate the fact that a substance preserves certain kinds of identity despite some transformation.

We may illustrate a standard test for conservation with the familiar water-beaker problem. Here a child is first shown two beakers of water that are identical in all respects: they are of the same height and width and are filled with water to identical levels. The child is asked: "Do the jars contain the same amount of water?" After the age of three or so, the typical answer is "Yes." Then the experimenter pours the water from one jar into another jar that is taller and narrower than the first and again asks if the jars hold the same amount of water. If the child says "Yes" and gives a reasonable explanation such as, "You just changed the jars but the water is the same," then he is judged to have the concept of conservation of volume. If, however, he answers, "No, they are different because one is taller," then he "fails" to conserve. The child who does not conserve is said not to appreciate that the amount of water is invariant despite changes in the shapes of the containers. Most children under age seven fail this test and therefore do not seem to demonstrate true conservation behavior. Their erroneous explanations are typically based upon the salient perceptual changes in the jars' height and width.

Does a failure to pass these tests mean that the child is at that point incapable of understanding the concept of conservation? Do we wish to conclude, like the great Jean Piaget, for instance, that conceptual development is dependent upon a number of stages, that each stage is related to the next, and that the child must pass through each stage in turn before he shows true conservation? Piaget has insisted that the child must possess certain cognitive structures or schemata before he is able to perform the formal, logical operations involved in conservation behavior.

In analyzing the tasks used to test conservation, Gelman reasoned that perhaps children who do not conserve by these tests fail as a result of some perceptual fixation—*not* because they cannot understand. Perhaps

when children err, they do so because their attention—and hence their resulting decisions—are based upon perceptual changes in the width, height, or thickness of the beaker. Could one devise a procedure that would train the child to ignore irrelevant changes and to pay attention to quantities that do not change?

Gelman's experimental design was quite simple. A number of children were first given standard conservation tests on length, number, mass, and volume. All children *who failed all tests* were then given training in one or two main conditions. In an experimental group, the child learned a series of short "oddity" discriminations, where he was shown three objects, two of which were identical; his task was to choose either two that were the same or two that were different. After each choice, the child was told whether or not his choices were correct. This "reinforcement" informed the child that certain attributes of the stimuli were relevant (for example, quantity) and others (such as changes in color, size, and shape) were irrelevant. Over a two-day period, the children in the experimental group learned thirty-two six-trial problems; half of these problems involved *length* as the relevant concept and the other half involved *number*. Features like size, shape, color, proximity, arrangement, and the like were varied so that they could not be consistently used as a solution for any of the problems.

A control group underwent exactly the same training experience with one exception: no feedback as to the correctness of their responses was given. Thus the only difference between the groups was in terms of an opportunity to learn which features of the stimuli were actually relevant to the problems. After training was completed, both groups of children were given identical tests. Half the tests were for specific transfer on standard conservation tests of length and number, while the other half tested for generalization on mass and volume. It will be noted that the mass and volume concepts were not involved in the training session. Recall that before training, similar tests had shown *no* correct responding by any of the children.

After training, the children in the experimental group responded correctly to 94 percent of the length and number conservation tests while the control subjects gave 25 percent correct answers. Of greater significance was the finding that the experimental group answered correctly 62 percent of the conservation tests on mass and volume. The control group showed about 7 percent generalization to these tests. Retention tests two weeks later gave nearly identical results.

On the basis of these impressive findings, one is forced to reconsider what is meant when one says that a child lacks the metaphysical underpinnings for a certain concept, or for that matter, what one means by learning per se. In the case of conservation concepts, the usual testing procedures seem to hide or baffle rather than demonstrate a cognitive ability, and one has merely to offset perceptual interference in order to show what ability the child actually has.

The Learning Environment

A final word or two about attention and the learning environment. A series of experiments similar to those I mentioned at the beginning of this article have shown that you can pare down the initial, or attention, phase and hence speed up the overall learning rate by increasing (1) the *number* and (2) the *vividness* or saliency of relevant stimulus cues. These same experiments have shown, however, that this accelerated learning can be inefficient or eccentric. If more stimulus patterns or cues are provided than are needed to solve, they will not all be used or learned. Furthermore, what *is* learned may be learned in odd, sometimes undesirable ways. A child who distinguishes Ts from Fs because "Ts are purple," has really only learned an unfortunate association, which sooner or later will impede his reading progress.

Thus it appears that more efficient engineering of the learning environment will require the seemingly para-doxical effort to impoverish the environment by eliminating potentially distracting and irrelevant material, while at the same time enriching it by using attention-getting cues having maximum vividness and interest. As early as 1912, Montessori advocated the use of three-dimensional cutouts in the teaching of form-and-number discriminations, a technique whose efficacy has only been recognized experimentally since World War II. On the other hand, brain-injured children seem to learn to read better and faster when, for instance, the windows of their room are covered, and when the children sit before a blank wall and are exposed to a small portion of reading material through a small opening in a screen—poverty of stimuli with almost a vengeance, it would seem.

It appears certain that many of the keys to successful teaching or training will be found in the close study of the attention planes or phases of the learning process. Such study may enable us to build a more productive learning environment and perhaps allow us finally to deal more cleverly with hoary old classroom menaces like the "slow" reader.

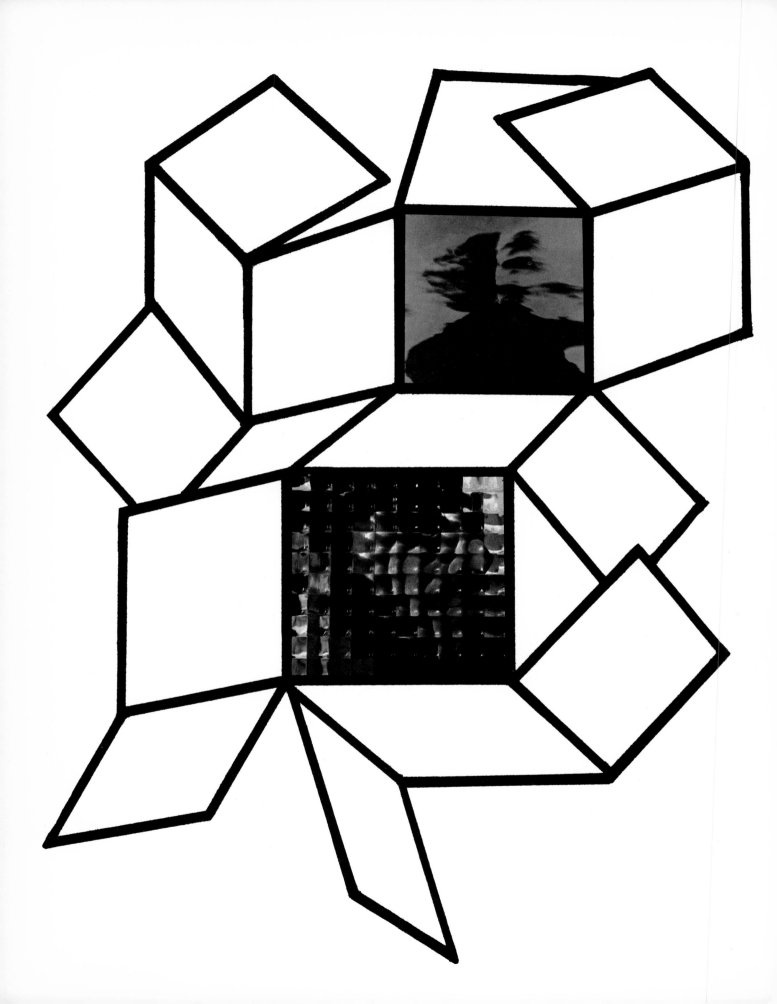

Are IQ Tests Intelligent?

Raymond Bernard Cattell

IQ tests have recently come under attack by leaders of the poor, minority ethnic groups, and alienated youth. Despite some rather brilliant empirical defenses of their reliability and validity as an intelligence measure, traditional IQ tests have never been able to free themselves of the suspicion of middle-class bias and of favoring "school intelligence" over other types of intelligence.

Dr. Cattell's distinction between fluid and crystallized intelligence enables us to reenter this controversy with new theoretical and empirical support as social needs and values are questioned by a new generation of youth. First try to understand Cattell's two intelligence types, then speculate as to what their respective values may be in this period of rapid political, social, and educational change.

The dilemma of the Mensa Society dramatizes the current upheaval in intelligence testing. Roughly three out of four of the prospective members selected on one kind of intelligence test failed to be selected by a second test, and three out of four of those chosen by the second type could not meet the standards of the first test. This international society, which limits entry to those at the 98th percentile or above in intelligence, was forced to make a policy decision on *which* kind of intelligence the society would consider.

Present controversy on the meaning of intelligence and of intelligence testing has erupted only in the past decade. It centers on whether there is a single factor of general intelligence and on the adequacy of present tests to measure it. My research indicates that there are two kinds of intelligence, fluid and crystallized, and that the former, which is independent of culture, can be measured as accurately as the latter.

To grasp what we now know of intelligence and the devices that attempt to measure it, one first must understand the background of the current dispute. In the first decade of this century Charles Spearman brought to a field crowded with untutored, arbitrary, and generally naive definitions of intelligence, the theory of the *g factor*, a unitary, objectively defined, general-intelligence factor. For fifty years Spearman's g factor has remained the only firm basis for the objective determination and measurement of intelligence.

This factor was defined by weights applied to different kinds of intellectual performances, and its existence was proved by the peculiar form of correlation coefficients that appeared in correlations of ability measurement. If correlation coefficients show that four abilities, a, c, e, and g, are mutually positively related when measured over a group of 300 people, whereas the correlations are essentially zero on the abilities b, d, and f, we can assume some underlying unity behind a, c, e, and g.

There is no reason that there could not be two, three, or more such correlation clusters in a large group of abilities. But Spearman argued that the squared table of all possible correlations among a widely sampled set of abilities had a uniform slope that pointed to the existence of only one factor. To support this argument, he went beyond correlation clusters and developed factor analysis—a means of discovering the influences behind clusters.

Factor Analysis

Factor analysis is a method of calculating—from the various correlation coefficients of measured individual performances—the number and the general natures of the influences that account for observed relations. Through such an analysis, Spearman found the tests that bore most heavily on his general intelligence factor were those that had to do with reasoning and judgment.

He therefore defined this factor as the capacity to educe relations and correlates.

Factor analysis also tells us how much of the individual variation in some particular performance is accounted for by each of the several factors that combine to produce that kind of behavior. Spearman concluded that g had about a 9:1 ratio to special abilities in determining mathematical learning rate; about 7:1 in accounting for the size of one's properly used vocabulary; about 2:1 in determining musical ability; and about 1:4 in judging drawing ability.

Decades later, Louis Thurstone developed a multiple-factor analysis. This improvement over Spearman's methods led to Thurstone's discovery and definition of a dozen primary abilities, among them verbal comprehension, word fluency, number, space, and reasoning. Neither g nor the IQ were invalidated by Thurstone's work. On the contrary, advances in factor analysis rectified the only known statistical and structural flaw in Spearman's work. General intelligence now emerged from multiple-factor analysis as a single *second-order factor*, based on the intercorrelation among primary factors. The general intelligence concept was strengthened, for the pyramids of primary factors provided a far more reliable base than did the grains of innumerable small variables.

The question of how Thurstone's primary abilities grew out of Spearman's general ability remained unanswered, but researchers tended to neglect its importance. Instead of investigating the natural structure of abilities, the experts devised tests to fill the holes in a subjective framework. And so, for thirty years, there has been only trivial consolidation in this field, with a consequent hardening of attitudes and custom among professional intelligence testers.

As one who investigated with both Spearman and Thurstone, I at first was as much disturbed as intrigued when I thought I saw flaws in their monolithic structure. The first signs appeared in data on the second-order analysis of primary abilities. There was evidence that *two* general factors rather than one were involved. On rather slender evidence, I put forward in 1940 the theory of two g's. Those original disquieting conceptions have since been strengthened by the accumulation of evidence.

The breadth of a factor and the number of factors depend upon what tests an experimenter uses to gather his data. From the twenty primary abilities surveyed by John French, John Horn obtained some four or five broad abilities, such as fluid intelligence, crystallized intelligence, speed, and visualization. But the broadest of all such abilities, and the ones with a semantic claim to the label "intelligence," are fluid and crystallized.

Crystallized general ability, g_c, shows itself in judgmental skills that have been acquired by cultural experience: vocabulary, good use of synonyms, numerical skills, mechanical knowledge, a well-stocked memory, and even habits of logical reasoning; g_c is high on the subtests that traditionally have been built into intelligence tests: vocabulary size, analogies, and classifications involving cultural knowledge of objects in the problem. Crystallized ability stretches across the whole range of cultural acquisitions. Mechanical knowledge—which is negligible or even negative on fluid ability—has a measurable effect on crystallized ability.

Differences in Ability Types

Tests of fluid ability, g_f, have little relation to a well-stocked memory. They are culture fair perceptual and performance tests and those specially developed tests of judgment and reasoning that have been considered relatively culture free. They involve solutions to tests of classifications, analogies, matrices, topology, and problems that do not involve much educational acquisition. Fluid ability does have a role in numerical reasoning and even in verbal skills. It is fairly powerful in spatial reasoning and very powerful in inductive reasoning (see Figure 1).

The difference between fluid and crystallized general abilities becomes apparent when the intellectual responses of two persons who contrast in them are described. To find a person high in fluid ability but low in crystallized, we should have to take someone who accidentally has missed schooling. I have measured deck hands and farmers who scored much higher than average professors in fluid ability but who acquired no comparable level of crystallized ability because they had not systematically applied their fluid intelligence to what is usually called culture. Such men will astonish you in a game of chess, or by solving a wire puzzle with which you have struggled in vain, or in swift insights into men and motives. But their vocabularies may be arrested at a colloquial level, their knowledge of history negligible, and they may never have encountered algebra or geometry. These men often excel at the strategy of games, and one suspects they are naturally good soldiers. Lord Fisher, who designed the Dreadnought battleship, said, "In war you need surprise." Surprise bursts from situations in which crystallized intelligence is useless. Napoleon claimed that he would make his despairing opponents "burn their books on tactics." The characteristic of fluid intelligence is that it leads to perception of complex relationships in new environments.

The individual with a high level of crystallized intelligence has different capacities. He will have learned many intelligent responses to problem situations. He will recognize an engineering problem as requiring solution by differential calculus, and he will diagnose a defective sentence by pointing to a dangling participle. He could not have acquired these skills, however, unless he had the fluid ability to see them.

To illustrate a case where crystallized ability is clearly higher than fluid ability, we must take either a person in

Primary Abilities of Specific Batteries	Research I: Boys (57) and Girls (5) of 6½ Years Old		Research II: Boys (151) and Girls (154) of 9, 10, & 11 Years Old		Research III: Boys and Girls (277) of 12 & 13 Years Old		Research IV: Men and Women (297) Adult Range	
	g_f	g_c	g_f	g_c	g_f	g_c	g_f	g_c
Verbal	−17	74	22	63	15	46	10	69
Spatial			73	03	32	14	30	−07
Reasoning	10	72			08	50	23	30
Number	43	19	47	35	05	59	24	29
Fluency					07	10	−03	25
Series: Culture Fair					35	23		
Classification; Culture Fair	58*	−11*	78*	09*	63	−02	48*	−08*
Matrices: Culture Fair					50	10		
Topology: Culture Fair					51	09		
Perceptual Speed							20	06
Flexibility							−03	03
Induction							55	12
Intellectual Speed							51	10
Mechanical Information							−15	48
Ego Strength	−07	−09					01	43
Self Sentiment							01	43
Super Ego								
Surgency								
Anxiety	10	−33	04	−04			−05	−26

Figure 1. Fluid and crystallized general ability factors at various ages.

whom there has been some recession of fluid ability, as through aging or brain damage, or a person who has been overeducated for his ability—say, someone like Sheridan's Mrs. Malaprop, taught a bigger vocabulary than natural judgment permits handling.

Crystallized and fluid intelligence abilities could not be isolated until technical progress in factor analytic experiments made their recognition possible. These two structures have been confirmed repeatedly by researchers over the whole age range, from five to fifty.

Fluid and crystallized ability factors are positively correlated. According to the theory of two broad intelligences, fluid intelligence is a general relation-perceiving capacity, independent of sensory area, and it is determined by the individual's endowment in cortical, neurological-connection count development. It is a broad factor because such integrating power can be brought to bear in almost any perceptual or reasoning area. Crystallized ability, on the other hand, appears as a related circle of abilities—verbal, numerical, reasoning—that normally are taught at school. The extent to which an individual takes or leaves what he is taught depends on

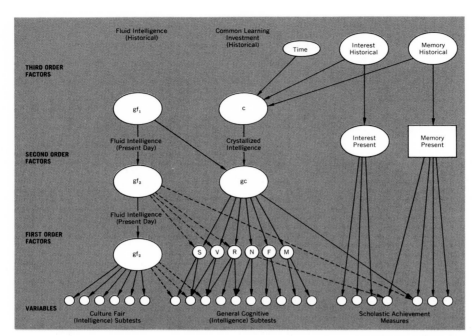

Figure 2. Causal relations between fluid and crystallized ability factors. Arrows indicate the direction of influence, and solid arrows show major lines of influence.

his fluid ability, on his years of formal education, and on his motivation to learn. Thus, crystallized general ability reflects both the neurological integrative potential of the individual and his fortune in cultural experience.

Crystallized ability is not identical with scholastic achievement. Many scholastic skills depend largely on rote memory, whereas what factor analysis shows is crystallized ability in that section of school learning involving complex judgment skills that have been acquired by the application of fluid ability (see Figure 2).

Further Differences

Once these two general abilities are located and independently measured, further distinguishing characteristics appear. The age curve of growth for the two abilities turns out to be quite different. Fluid ability follows a biological growth curve and approaches a plateau at about fourteen years, whereas crystallized ability shows an increase to sixteen, eighteen, and beyond. The evidence points to some steady decline in fluid intelligence after about twenty-two years of age, but crystallized intelligence keeps its level as far into later years as adequate samples have been taken (see Figure 3).

The standard deviation of the calculated IQ—mental age divided by actual age—is almost exactly 50 percent greater for fluid than for crystallized ability, 24 points instead of 16 points. Socioeducational research might determine whether arranging brighter and duller streams of classroom instruction would permit more divergence of crystallized IQ.

There are substantial indications that fluid and crystallized intelligence respond differently to brain damage.

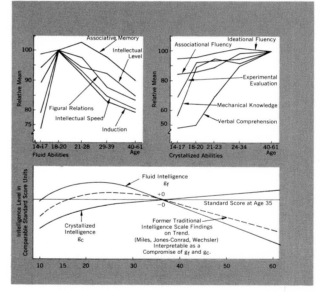

Figure 3. Age curves compared for fluid and crystallized general ability and traditional tests.

Localized injury may produce localized loss of skills, while leaving other abilities untouched. By the nature of fluid ability, an impairment in any cortical locality should produce some loss of general fluid-ability performance.

A pilot study on nature-nuture ratios suggests that heredity bears a greater relation to fluid than to crystallized intelligence. Tentative estimates of relative variance are 90 percent for g_f and 70 percent for g_c. An independent demonstration of the higher hereditary influences of fluid-ability levels has been given by John Loehlin, who compared the primary factor within pairs of both fraternal and identical twins. Verbal ability, fluency, and reasoning primaries naturally showed environmental influence, but a general genetic factor corresponding to fluid ability was apparent.

My own research and that of others indicates that day-to-day changes do occur in intelligence. Our subjective conviction that we are brighter on some days than we are on others is borne out by measures of g_f variability over time, as might be expected from the closer dependence of fluid intelligence upon total physiological efficiency.

Many of the puzzling phenomena in intelligence testing are explained if we consider that the traditional intelligence test actually is a mixture of fluid and crystallized factors. Discoveries of different ages for the end of intelligence growth, significant differences in the standard deviation of IQs, and different ratios of the weight of heredity and environment on the IQ all result from a confusion of the two factors in the usual intelligence test.

Culture Fair Test

When I first called attention to the flaws in the general intelligence theory, I at once proceeded to investigate the correlations with the general fluid ability factor of a variety of perceptual tests. From my research came the culture fair intelligence test associated with present uses in cross-cultural studies and Head Start programs. But whatever its present practical importance, the origin of these culture fair tests was in the first place the theoretical goal of defining the new form of intelligence.

In our first attempt at developing a fluid-ability test appropriate to all cultures, I took such common elements as parts of the human body, sun, moon, rain, and stars, as well as random blotches. But only the perceptual forms have been retained in later tests, for experiment has shown that these give accurate results (see Figure 4).

In choosing test elements, the effect on the score of cultural experience can be reduced by taking either what is overlearned in all cultures or what is absolutely strange to all. Anything in between these extremes is bound to show the influence of the culture in the test scores. To take overlearned items is more practicable, because valuable test time is wasted in getting responses on completely strange items.

To avoid pointless sociological arguments, we called fluid-ability measures culture *fair* rather than culture *free*. Objection from teachers to a culture-free concept arises from confusion between the cultural familiarity and test sophistication effects on test scores. *All* tests, culture fair tests included, are susceptible to test sophistication, and scores may continue to improve for some four to six retests. Scores increase due to familiarity with instructions, with layout, with timing, and with

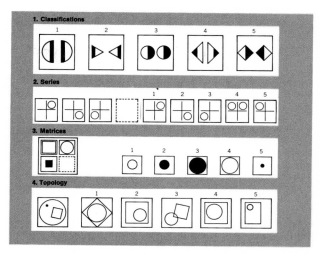

Figure 4. Sample items from the IPAT Culture Fair Test. (Reproduced by kind permission of the Institute for Personality and Ability Testing, Coronado Division, Champaign, Illinois.)
1. Which one of these is different from the remaining four? (No. 3)
2. Which of the 5 figures on the right would properly continue the 3 on the left (fill the blank)? (No. 5)
3. Which of the figures on the right should go into the square on the left to make it look right? (No. 2)
4. At the left, the dot is outside the square and inside the circle. In which of the figures on the right could you put a dot outside the square and inside the circle? (No. 3)

the tricks any good person being tested can learn. Studies by Sarason, Feingold, and myself have shown that practice in the culture fair type of spatial and analogies perception produced no real gain, unlike training in the verbal and numerical fields that dominate the traditional intelligence test. But with subjects unused to paper-and-pencil tests, and with subjects from other cultures, it would be ideal always to repeat testing several times and to throw away the results of the first three or four encounters.

The culture fair concept does not imply that no significant differences ever should be found between different populations living in different cultures or subcultures or social classes. The bright people in most societies tend to migrate to higher socioeconomic levels. The correlation of .20 to .25 between fluid ability measures and social status presumably is a measure of the relation of real ability to status, but the correlation of .38 found with traditional intelligence tests represents also the scholastic gain of those with the luck to be born into more educated families.

Cultural Differences

Where ulterior evidence suggests that peoples *are* equally gifted, a culture fair test must show absolutely no difference of score despite profound differences of culture. None have been demonstrated on the Cattell

Culture Fair Scales among American, British, German, French, and Italian samples. A more severe test was made by William Rodd, who compared Chinese (Taiwanese) and American school children and university students on identically printed culture fair tests. The raw scores are identical to three significant figures for Midwestern American and Taiwanese school children. American college students do not differ from the Taiwanese, but there is a significant difference between Taiwanese and mainland Chinese, which could be the result of differences in methods of student selection (see Figure 5).

It is such findings of complete equality of performance across wide differences of culture on tests of this kind that give the lie to the dogmatic statement of conservatives that "You cannot have a culture free intelligence test." It is obvious that no test can be 100 percent culture free, just as no water is truly "pure." But we all prefer what we call pure water to ditch water.

But testing also suggests that significant mean population differences *can* exist. Samples have shown higher

means in the south than in the north of Japan, in the north than in the south of Italy, and in New Zealand migrants as compared with unselected British Isles stock. Further research might develop a world map of intelligence resources.

For school-age children, when intelligence tests are most used, the correlation between g_f and g_c scores is positive and substantial. It will probably become even higher if regular school attendance becomes universal and methods used in more efficient school systems become uniform. From this high correlation, casual administrators may argue that one kind of test—the old kind, of course—is enough. Indeed, hard-headed realism may assert that the traditional IQ test is preferable, because the g_c test predicts this or next year's scholastic performance slightly but systematically better than does the g_f test (see Figure 6).

But if a maximum prediction of next year's academic achievement were all that one desired, one would not use an intelligence test at all. For a higher correlation can be obtained from this year's grades, or from a proper combination of intelligence, personality, and motivation measures, as our research has shown.

The purpose of an intelligence test is different. It should help us to understand the causes of a given person's good or poor grades or to predict what he will do in the future in radically changed circumstances. Over an interval of a year or so we can expect habits and situations and the momentum of interest to make scholastic performance *now* the best predictor of grades in the future. But when a person's life turns a corner, as when he goes from liberal education in the school to technical education in a career, the crystallized-ability measure may be quite misleading. A fluid-ability IQ from a culture fair test is likely to be a better predictor of performance.

The same principle holds if we compare children of fundamentally different backgrounds. The Binet in French, administered to a mixed group of 100 French, 100 American, and 100 Chinese children, would show a correlation of IQ with French language skills, but the Binet score would be no general predictor of language

1. Comparison of American and Chinese Children, 10 Years of Age, by IPAT Culture Fair Scale 2 (Rodd, 1960).

	American (1007)		Chinese (Hong Kong) (1007)	
	Mean	Stand. Dev.	Mean	Stand. Dev.
Culture Fair Form 2A	24.10	6.66	24.04	5.70

2. Comparison of American and Chinese College Students (Mean Age 18 yrs.) by IPAT Culture Fair Scale 3 (Rodd, 1960).

	American (1100)		Taiwanese (765)		Chinese Mainland Chinese (525)	
	Mean	Stand. Dev.	Mean	Stand. Dev.	Mean	Stand. Dev.
Culture Fair Form 3A	21.99	4.50	21.99	4.50	22.88	4.47
Culture Fair Form 3B	26.90	4.50	26.95	4.47	27.23	4.53

3. Correlation of Culture Fair and Traditional Tests with Social Status (McArthur and Elley, 1964).

1. Traditional Test (California Test of Mental Maturity)	+0.38
2. Traditional Test (Modified) (Lorge-Thorndike)	+0.27
3. Fluid Ability (IPAT Culture Fair) (On 271 12- and 13-Year-Olds)	+0.24

Figure 5. Cultural differences and culture fair scores. American and Chinese scores on the same test are shown. The correlation between g_f and social status measures the relation of real ability to the status.

	Validity General Factor	Marks by Teacher Amer. Chin.		Stand. Ach. Test	Correlation with School Total Achievement English Amer. Chin.		Read-ing	Math Amer. Chin.		Other Intelligence Tests Calif. Test of Mental Maturity Verb. Numer.		Wisc. I.Q.
Fluid Abil. (IPAT Cult. Fair Scale 2)	.79*	.34*		.35*			.52++					.72++
Fluid Abil. (IPAT Cult. Fair Scale 3)	.78c	.35**	.35**	.59 .49	40	30+		64	47+	42	56	
Crystal. Abil. (Cal. Test Ment. Mat.)	.58*	.66*	0?	.65*		0?			0?			
Crystal. Abil. (Lorge-Thorndike)	.52*	.43*	0?	.35*		0?			0?			
Army Beta						25		34		27	58	
Henmon Nelson				.81								
Pintuer						.85++.						.80++

* McArthur & Elley, 271, 12 and 13 year olds   + Rodd & Goodman (Atten. corrected on school test)   ° Bajard
** Domino, 94 college students   ++ 79 children in Bridge Project School

Figure 6. Correlations of fluid and crystallized intelligence tests with other measures. The validity in terms of general ability saturation is highest for the culture fair scales, but correlation with school grades is higher when the traditional intelligence test is used.

ability among the Americans and Chinese. In the same situation, a culture fair test would correlate with the native-language performance about equally in each of the three language groups.

During the school years, culture fair tests are both theoretically and practically useful, especially in localities with language or cultural differences. But the dual IQ becomes indispensable almost anywhere when testing adults. The two IQ values for a given person may be very different, and the kinds of prediction made from each will differ. Crystallized ability may remain steady or even climb, for it increases with age and experience, but fluid ability falls after age twenty-two. A middle-aged man handles most situations in our culture more intelligently than he would have when he was twenty, but if a younger and an older man were transferred to an absolutely new society, the probably higher fluid-intelligence level of the younger man would be likely to show itself. Where performance in radically different situations is involved, the man of fifty will perform very differently from what would be predicted for him on the basis of his g_c mental age. The g_f mental age would have predicted this difference.

Despite the tremendous accumulation of experience concerning intelligence testing between ten and twenty years of age, there has been comparatively little over the twenty- to seventy-year range, and we know little about what happens to age trends, distribution, or sex differences of intelligence in that period.

Decision Must Be Made

Our society, which values high intelligence, must make some kind of policy decision on *which* kind of intelligence should be given emphasis in this period. A decision on culture fair and traditional test usage becomes even more imperative for the psychologist whose testing helps determine jobs and clinical outcomes. As men leave school and go into their special occupational fields, the statistical general factor begins to disintegrate, or to

persist only as a historical relic. Vocabulary tests for the average man reveal a distinct falling off in ability after school. And if women in middle age are tested by intelligence tests (at least as mostly designed by men), they undergo an apparent drop in crystallized ability not shown by men.

To continue to regard the traditional intelligence tests as a general intelligence measure when applied after the age of twenty is pure illusion. If a g_c score predicts relation-perceiving capacity in new fields, it does so indirectly by harking back to the fact that scholastic ability at eighteen was a measure of g_f intelligence. If that happens not to be true for a person, or if such things as brain damage have occurred since, the g_c prediction can be badly in error.

The need for a dual IQ score is rooted not only in what happens to the man but in what happens to the culture. A comparison that I made of all eleven-year-olds in a city of 300,000 before World War II with eleven-year-olds in the same city after the war and thirteen years later showed no trace of any significant difference on a culture fair test. Yet Godfrey Thomson's comparisons on the British Binet at about the same period showed a very significant upward shift. Results in America by Frank Finch with various traditional crystallized-ability tests showed an even greater upward shift. The standardization of a traditional test becomes unanchored from the moment it is made, and it drifts in whatever direction the tide of educational investment happens to take. In this more prosperous age, the direction is upward. Since no such drift is demonstrable with culture fair, fluid-ability measures, error of prediction is less flagrant.

New answers to educational, political, and social questions may be reached through culture fair intelligence testing. Culture fair tests are not toys for anthropologists to take to remote cultures. They need to be used here and now to open equal educational opportunity to all our subcultures of class and race.

V
Reinforcement and Learning

the range of interactions available to a child. In many instances the interactions that are terminated may be needed for further development (speaking, for example), and the situations that are avoided may be critical to a normal child-rearing environment (such as those involving the father) and may affect other similar aspects of the environment (all male adults). Thus, stimuli and responses that were not directly involved in the aversive interaction may come to have aversive properties in themselves.

Third, aversive stimuli may evoke physiological responses (such as gastric reactions to a fear-producing event) that affect biological functioning of the child and thereby reduce his potential for serviceable interactions.

While the consequences of strong aversive stimulation are most frequently discussed in the literature of child psychopathology under the heading of severe emotional disturbances (referred to as psychoneurotic, psychotic, and autistic), they are discussed here because

aversive stimulation also retards development. Just as biological anomalies and social insufficiencies limit opportunities for development, so do strong avoidant reactions. All three foreclose many occasions for a child to make new adjustments.

I have singled out for discussion here the retarding effects of abnormal anatomical structure and functioning, inadequate reinforcement and discrimination histories, reinforcement of undesirable behavior, and severe aversive stimulation. There are, however, other processes. For example, there is the possibility that the termination (say, through death) of interactions with a mother-figure after a strong affection bond has been established can have strong retarding effects. It can weaken or even eliminate well-established behavior by removing the cues on which the behavior depended. It should be emphasized, however, that these other processes do *not* include assumed conditions such as "defective intelligence," "clinically inferred brain damage" and "familial factors."

Learning and Lollipops

Todd Risley

When we raise the question of the black child's lack of preschool preparation, we should be clear whether we are asking a question about arbitrary demands of a middle-class school administration or about skills and knowledge that are unequivocal prerequisites for all school learning. If Todd Risley's article convinces you that the verbal and imitative responses reinforced are basic prerequisites, then you may not object to his program of behavior control using candy rewards, smiles, and praise.

Particularly unique and appealing about the Juniper Gardens program he describes is the use of reinforcement to teach the children's mothers to teach their own and other children. Why were the mothers more approving with other children than with their own? Also, how do black children learn personal, social, and ethical autonomy in a learning system that rewards only those responses preselected by adults?

Play with a play car.

Play with a truck, play with a play car, get on a seesaw and play with a train.

My mama bought them last night when Dan's daddy took her to the Salvation Army.

The Salvation Army is uptown, uptown.

All the way up there in the projects, Dan lives in the projects.

Dan lives across the street from Edward's house.

Me and Dan. Me and Dan went to the store and bought some candy. Here's one that was on the floor.

We found it on the ground.

Some money.

We found it; we found it on the ground. One penny, two penny.

We found it.

A penny.

And we ride the play cars to the store.

Some sugar and a sucker for to eat.

We eat a candy sucker.

These lines are not blank verse, or at least they were not intended as such. They were spoken by a four-year-old boy receiving narration training at a preschool for culturally deprived children. His teacher has asked, "What do you do when you go home from school? . . . And what else . . . and what else . . . and what else?" This boy is an inarticulate child from an inarticulate family, the kind of child who grows up in our society to be Stanley Kowalski.

As a child grows up, he acquires "culture" chiefly from three sources: from his parents, from his peers, and from the public schools. In view of that fact, it is hardly surprising that those who are culturally deprived as infants usually become culturally deprived adults. Parents and peers cannot easily transmit what they themselves lack, and the public schools apparently offer too little too late—or, to put it another way, too much too soon.

When the culturally deprived child enters kindergarten, he lacks the social and language skills that the schools assume a child of five will possess. Since his parents do not stress the importance of school achievement, he also lacks motivation. In addition, the situation at home may be such that he is not particularly sensitive to the smiles and frowns with which his teacher will attempt to shape his behavior.

One way to attack this problem is to find a way to

modify the behavior of the deprived preschool child so that when he enters school, he will be in a better position to learn what is being taught there. This is the purpose of the Juniper Gardens Children's Project.

The residents of Juniper Gardens, an area located in northeastern Kansas City, Kansas, have the lowest median annual income in the city: 90 percent of them belong to the poverty class; 99.5 percent are Negro; and about 70 percent of those over twenty-five have not graduated from high school.

Under the auspices of the University of Kansas, my colleagues and I are conducting two preschool programs with the children and parents from Juniper Gardens. One is for members of the "hard-core" poverty class, the other for members of the "upwardly mobile" poverty class. The chief difference between the two programs is that the first is for children only, whereas the second is for children and their mothers, and especially for the mothers.

Turner House

In the program for the hard-core group, the Turner House program, we teach the children skills that we hope will be useful to them in public school—to follow directions, to describe objects and events, and so forth. In the program for the upwardly mobile group, the Parent-Teacher Cooperative Preschool, we teach mothers how, in general, to communicate more effectively with their children and how, specifically, to teach them skills they will need in school. That is, the Turner House program supplements, while the Parent-Teacher Preschool attempts to modify, the home environment of the child.

For Turner House, we recruited four-year-olds from families characterized by multiple problems: absence of a father, many children, extreme poverty, ramshackle housing, child neglect, and histories of unemployment, poor health, criminal and deviant behavior, alcoholism, and the like. In some cases, it proved necessary to offer the mother a weekly cash fee for her "trouble" in getting the child ready for preschool; thus some of the twelve children in the program were, in effect, rented.

Most children arrived at school without breakfast. We therefore fed them supplementary meals, and we also experimented, very successfully, with the use of food as a reinforcement for behavior we wanted maintained. This is quite a departure from the usual teaching techniques of both public and nursery schools, which are based chiefly on positive social reinforcement. But with these children, warm praise rarely proved powerful enough to rapidly effect extensive changes in behavior.

The teachers carried about, in baskets and in their plastic-lined jumper pockets, sugar-coated cereals, grapes and pieces of apple, tiny sandwiches, M&M candies, and cookies. When the children worked at tables, teachers carried pitchers and poured small quantities of milk, juice, or warm soup into mugs for each child.

These snacks invariably were accompanied by smiling, warm-voiced statements of approval, appreciation, or affection, and these statements very often were offered without food. We hoped in this way to increase the effectiveness of social reinforcement with the children, and thus prepare them for the public-school classroom.

Some of the behavior we tried to teach the children at first may seem trivial. For example, we spent considerable time teaching them to say "good morning" to their teachers. This may not seem the stuff from which successful scholars are made. However, the child who says "good morning" cheerfully and consistently when he arrives at school will dispose most teachers quite favorably toward him—our own teachers testified to this during the experiment—and the credit he gains may survive a good deal of academic bumbling later in the day. This credit is useful, because it may make the teacher more likely to praise approximations of learning in the child. A similar rationale lay behind several other "social" projects, such as teaching the child to be quiet in some work situations and to converse in others, and to raise his hand and wait to be recognized before speaking in group discussions.

Rightly or wrongly, formal schooling is chiefly an exercise in language, so we gave considerable attention to developing the language skills of the children. We tried to improve their skill at imitation, so that they might make linguistic gains from any language community in which they found themselves. We also picked one especially inarticulate child—the author of the "poem" that opens this chapter—and taught him to describe, in logically connected, meaningfully elaborated, and even factually correct narratives, his own experiences.

These projects will serve to illustrate the kind of thing we tried to do and the way we tried to do it, but there were others, of course. For example, we trained the children in the use of color and number adjectives and studied the effect the training had on their spontaneous conversation. And we experimented with various kinds of reinforcement and reinforcement conditions. One, in addition to food, that proved especially powerful was the materials and equipment of the schoolroom. It seemed that, when a child wanted to ride a tricycle, nothing in his environment was as important to him as that tricycle. Teachers therefore made it available to the child only after he had performed some task, such as naming or describing it.

"Good Morning"

As each child entered the preschool in the morning, removed his coat, and proceeded to his seat, each of the three teachers (Nancy Reynolds, Dianetta Coates, and Betty Hart) smiled at him and said, "Good morning." At the beginning of the school year, only about 20 percent of the children answered any teacher appropriately. These the teachers would reinforce with social approval. Over the next three months, the average number of children answering the teachers' greetings rose from 20 percent to between 70 and 80 percent.

By mid-December, it was clear that no further improvement was likely. So, as a test of the durability of this new skill, the teachers discontinued the stimulus to which the children had responded. They stood at the door as usual, but they did not speak to the children as they entered. Although the children who continued to say "good morning" were answered and praised as usual, the number who did so fell immediately to 20 percent and fluctuated from 15 to 45 percent for six days. Then it collapsed to zero.

It appeared that behavior with social consequences would not be maintained unless supported at both ends, by a preceding stimulus as well as by subsequent approval. When the teachers began greeting the children with a smiling "good morning" again, 80 percent of the children promptly began replying.

However, our aim was to teach the children to say "good morning" whether greeted first by the teacher or not. Therefore we brought a more powerful reinforcer into play. Each teacher gave an M&M to each child who answered her greeting appropriately. The number of children replying rose at once to 100 percent and remained there for the last five days of this condition. Then the teachers again discontinued their initial greetings. As before, some children stopped saying "good morning" as they entered, but far fewer stopped than before. As long as the M&Ms were used, about 95 percent continued to greet the teachers despite the teachers' silence.

To make sure it was the candy that made the difference, we stationed all three preschool teachers at the door but supplied only one of them with M&Ms. We thought that over the weeks, when first one teacher and then another had the M&Ms, the children would speak most often to the teacher who distributed the candy. This turned out to be true (see Figure 1). However, we also expected the children to behave with a modicum of consistency toward the third teacher, who throughout the whole ten weeks of the experiment offered social reinforcement only, no candy.

Instead, most children spoke to the third teacher whenever they spoke to the first teacher. During the first seven weeks of the experiment, when the first teacher had M&Ms and the third did not, most children said "good morning" to both of them; during the last three weeks, when the first teacher had no candy, greetings to the third teacher fell off as well. I am sorry to report that this seemed to indicate racial discrimination in our children: the first and third teachers were white, and the second was Negro.

The public school, of course, does not offer M&Ms for desirable behavior. However, our results indicate the need for something more powerful than friendly approval to establish durable behavior in the children, especially if the behavior is to remain despite minimal stimulus support. Had we not run out of time, we would have begun shifting the behavior maintained by candy to the control of social approval only, a process that requires consistent social reinforcement combined with a gradual cutback on the distribution of candy.

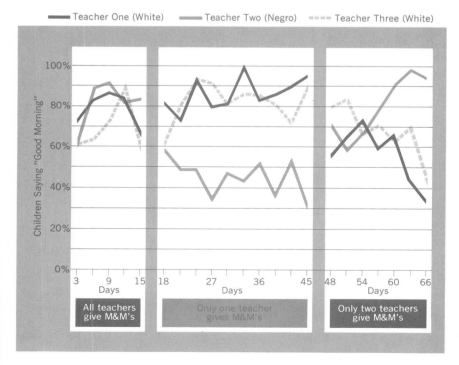

Figure 1. Effect of candy distribution on children's morning greeting to teacher.

Imitation

An ability to imitate the teacher, especially her use of language, is particularly valuable for the child from a culturally deprived background. Most culturally deprived children learn a different dialect at home from the one they will hear in school. Consequently they will have trouble understanding what they hear and being understood when they speak. It is unlikely that the child's dialect will be modified in school unless he undertakes the modification himself, a possible task—many a Midwesterner has done it at Harvard—but one that requires what is called a "good ear."

Therefore we set out to develop the children's ability to imitate. We did not begin by asking them to imitate verbal statements. We started with gross motor imitations, progressed to fine motor imitations, and then to facial responses, and only at the end added verbalizations. The program had two parts: training sessions that stressed each kind of imitation in turn, and nontraining sessions, or probes, that tested the effects of the training.

In the training sessions, three children worked with a model teacher. At first, the teacher did nothing more than sit down on a rug and take a bit of snack for herself from a bowl. The children were prompted by another teacher to do as the model teacher had done, including taking a bit of snack in their own cups.

Then the second teacher took charge of the snack bowl, and she provided food only when the child imitated the part of the model teacher's behavior that was the subject of training. In early sessions, the child was given a snack whenever he imitated the model teacher's gross motor behavior—raising the arms, leaning to one side, and the like. Later, training passed to more detailed motor imitations, and finally to speech.

Periodically, the model teacher tested each child's ability to imitate a complex performance. The tests consisted of four acts performed simultaneously: a gross motor act, a fine motor act, a facial expression, and a verbal statement. For example:

Probe I. Arms out to the side, palms of hands turned back, face frowning, statement: "This too shall pass away." During the test each child was reinforced if he imitated the teacher's gross motor act, whether he imitated the other components of her performance or not.

As it turned out, the children imitated all the teacher's actions with increasing accuracy. They imitated best the act that was the subject of training at the time, but they did not lose the skills they had learned earlier. So, when speech finally was added to the training, the children began to imitate it reliably, and they continued at the same time to imitate gross, fine motor, and facial acts. This apparently represented a growing ability to observe and imitate a complex performance, even when unreinforced, which was exactly the result we wanted.

It is always important in studies like this one to demonstrate that the outcome was indeed the result of the conditions applied. Otherwise one finds one's self clinging superstitiously to useless procedures. So, after the children were far into the program, we began giving bits of food to one child in each group of three when he did *not* imitate the model teacher. The procedure did greatly reduce the child's tendency to imitate. When snacks again were given for imitation, the child also began to imitate again, as well as or better than he had before (see Figure 2).

The ultimate intent of imitation training was to give the children the ability to listen to novel language performances and to repeat them. In one year, it was possible to develop training only to the point where the children consistently imitated fairly short sentences. To be useful, the program would have to increase the children's skill with longer and longer verbal performances. Whether that can be done remains to be seen; it is one subject of the current year's research. But the success of the program so far suggests that the extension of verbal imitative skills to complex statements is probably a practical goal.

Verbal Skill

Any child may have a much more elaborate verbal repertoire than he demonstrates in a spontaneous account of some happening. To find out whether we could bring that repertoire into use, and perhaps add to it as well, we chose a child who was probably the least articulate in the group.

We began by finding out just how inarticulate he was. The teacher asked, repeatedly over a period of thirteen days, five questions such as "Who do you like to play with?" In answer to these questions, the child usually answered with one word or two, yielding a grand average over repeated inquiries of one and one-half words per answer.

Then the teacher began training. She asked, "What did you see on the way to school?" When she prompted the boy's answers with "What else," he simply repeated one- and two-word answers, alternating between the two responses, "A doggie" and "TV," and repeating the pair over and over.

When it had become clear that this pattern was not likely to change by itself, the teacher provided a more logical prompt: "What kind of doggie?" The boy replied that it was a German shepherd, and the teacher praised him and gave him a bit of snack. Then she asked again what he saw on the way to school. He answered, "A doggie." At this point, the teacher raised her eyebrows, cocked her head, and waited. Presently the child amended his answer: "A German shepherd doggie," and was praised and fed.

When the original question was asked again, with the reply "A German shepherd doggie," the child was given a second prompt: the teacher asked what the doggie was doing. In this way the training proceeded, with the teacher prompting each logical step, waiting for all

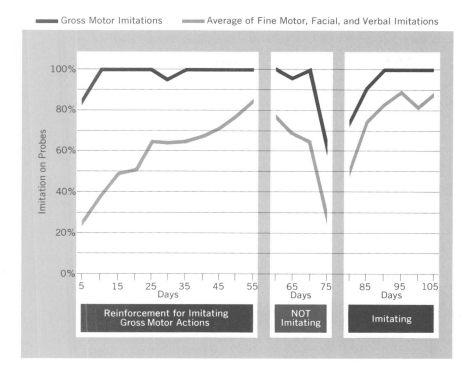

Gross Motor Imitations — Average of Fine Motor, Facial, and Verbal Imitations

Imitation on Probes

100%
80%
60%
40%
20%
0%

5 15 25 35 45 55 65 75 85 95 105
Days   Days   Days

Reinforcement for Imitating Gross Motor Actions

NOT Imitating

Imitating

Figure 2. Effect of reinforcement (snacks) on imitating.

previous steps to be chained together in reasonable sequence, and reinforcing only increasingly long and meaningfully connected sequences. The child's average answer to this first question eventually rose to about 200 words per ten-minute sessions, which amounted to about fifty words per session if duplications were eliminated.

Then the teacher asked a new question, "What do you do when you go home from school?" The child's answer showed that he had profited from the training on the first question; therefore the teacher reduced her logical prompts and asked simply, "what else" or "what then," while continuing to dispense praise and snacks only for more and more elaborate phrases.

The child was trained on five questions in all (see Figure 3). After each of them, the teacher asked five other questions on which he had not been trained. The child answered them at length, in a meaningfully connected and understandable way. The average length of his answers to these questions was over five times greater than that of his answers to the questions that preceded training.

Although the boy's narrative skill developed admirably as the program progressed, it was thought that the accuracy of his stories was perhaps questionable. So the last training question was one that the teacher could check: "What have you been doing at school today?" The boy was reinforced only for accurate elaborations, and his answers to the question were not only longer and longer but more and more accurate.

We do not know yet whether this technique will work with other children, or whether it can be used with groups. But it is encouraging to discover that narrative ability can grow without step-by-step and word-by-word training. In many cases, the child seems to know the words and how to use them, so that virtually all he needs is an invitation.

How Turner House Is Different

Visitors to Turner House are sometimes surprised to find that it looks very much like any other nursery school, except that the children are somewhat better behaved. They enjoy the usual activities—playing house, painting pictures, "dancing" to piano music—and get along well with each other and with their teachers. It is true that every now and then a child receives a bit of food, and that observers with clipboards and stopwatches are scattered about the room, but the general atmosphere is warm, cheerful, and distinctly unmechanical.

Despite appearances, Turner House is in fact quite different from the traditional nursery school and from its stepchild, the "enrichment" preschool for the culturally deprived. It is unfortunate that enrichment nursery schools tend to be modeled on middle-class nursery schools, because middle-class nursery schools are for middle-class children. For example, they attempt to develop the child's ability to get along with other children, but skill at social interaction rarely is lacking in a child with a large family and many siblings near his own age. They try to enhance motor skills and uninhibited activity, but those skills are usually well developed in a child whose playground is the street. They try to stimu-

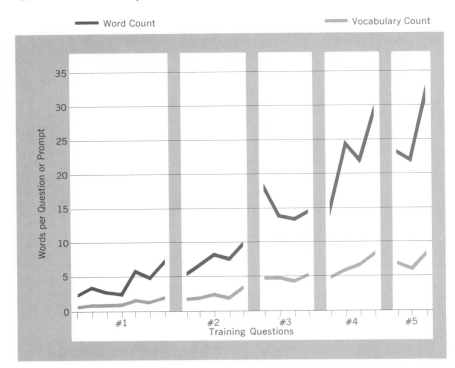

Figure 3. Effect of reinforcement (snacks) on one boy's vocabulary and sentence-making growth.

late intellectual development with puzzles, books, and manipulative toys, but the content of these items is as meaningless to the culturally deprived preschool child as to the culturally deprived kindergartner.

In addition, the methodology of the middle-class nursery school is inappropriate for the culturally deprived child. For example, fighting and "making trouble" are likely to be regarded as symptoms of insecurity, and therefore to be met by the teacher with understanding, acceptance, and love. In the culturally deprived child (and, indeed, in the middle-class child), aggressive and disruptive behavior may be nothing more sinister than a useful social tool—a tool that the child must replace if he is to get along well in public school. It is therefore more suitable to ignore the child when he behaves badly, and to reserve attention for behavior that one wants him to maintain.

Finally, though an atmosphere of warmth and approval is certainly helpful, its chances of success in effecting radical changes in the child's behavior are slim. For one thing, since responses to social reinforcement are usually weak and deficiencies in skills are unusually large in culturally deprived children, it may be necessary to begin with something to which they *do* respond, like food, in order to establish new skills rapidly. For another, if social reinforcement is to be effective at all, it must be specific. It must *immediately follow* the behavior to which it relates. Teachers who are not trained to praise a child's small achievements at once often fail to do so because without close attention and also considerable patience, it is easy to miss the brief and infrequent moments of desirable behavior that occur at first.

The Parent-Teacher Cooperative Preschool

It would be better, in the long run, to modify the home environment of the culturally deprived child than to try to make up for its deficiencies through a supplementary program. As a small step in this direction, the Juniper Gardens Parent-Teacher Cooperative Preschool provides daily lessons for mothers on how to teach their preschool children the skills that they will need for elementary-school work.

For this project we chose thirty four-year-olds and their mothers from upwardly mobile poverty families. The parents had a considerable amount of ambition for their children, and our aim was to channel that ambition into constructive behavior.

Compared to the children in the hard-core group, the upwardly mobile children had somewhat more motivation to achieve in school and somewhat stronger responses to social reinforcement. In addition, their mothers were willing to participate in the program. We did find, however, that it was useful to provide a bonus for attendance: we gave each mother a place setting of inexpensive china each week, at the rate of a dish a day, for coming to the preschool with her child.

The Parent-Teacher Preschool included many traditional preschool group activities, plus a carefully graded sequence of 150 daily lessons. The lesson series trained the mothers in teaching techniques and also showed them what their children should be learning—colors, numbers, rhymes, and so forth.

For the first six months of the program, each mother taught lessons to her own child. At a certain time during the day, she and the child would retire to one of several booths, each containing two chairs, a TV tray, and a shoebox of lesson materials such as crayons, toys, and pictures of various objects.

At first, the mothers were poor teachers. They used almost no praise or approval, and they showed very little grasp of the technique of attacking a complex problem by starting with its simplest form. Their usual pattern was to present a difficult problem and then to punish errors or silence with nagging or threats. They told the child to sit up, to pay attention; they informed him that they knew he knew the answer, so he had better say it.

Therefore we devised written instructions for the mothers to read before each lesson. Early instructions were very detailed. For example, Lesson One on naming objects began: "Hold up an object in front of the child. Say 'Can you tell me what this is?' Praise him by saying 'Good for you!' if he names it right." The same lesson ended with a general plea: "When he names something right, praise him."

Later in the lesson series, unless radically different materials or procedures were called for, the instructions were simple statements of what the child was to learn from the lesson.

Using these instructions, and with help from preschool teachers, the mothers' skill increased rapidly. But by the end of the year, though they praised their children's appropriate behavior much more often, they still did not praise it often enough. And the tendency to nag and threaten persisted.

So, at the start of the next school year, we made two changes in the program. First, we had each mother begin not with her own child, but with someone else's.

Second, we had the preschool teacher keep track of how often the mother dispensed praise, and flash a red light, mounted where the mother could see it, each time praise was recorded. We explained the purpose of the record and the light to the mothers, and we encouraged them to inspect the record after each lesson.

Under these revised conditions, all the mothers began to be much more liberal with praise (see Figure 4). At the same time, nagging and threats almost disappeared. Then we asked the mother to press a foot pedal whenever the child answered a question right. Her record of correct answers eventually corresponded to the preschool teacher's record of the mother's praise. At this point, except for covert reliability checks, we allowed each mother to record her own praise rate under the guise of recording the child's right answers.

After the mothers had learned to praise other people's children, we allowed them to begin teaching their own. In general, they continued to praise and to refrain from nagging. However, they did not teach their own children in quite the same way that they taught other children. When a mother taught her own child a lesson she already had taught to other children, she tended to praise him more than she had the others. When she taught him a lesson she had not taught before, she praised her child less than she later praised other children.

During the part of the day that was not taken up with lessons, the mothers supervised the children's group activities. As the rate at which they dispensed praise during the lessons rose, it also rose during play periods. However, it quickly became apparent that the

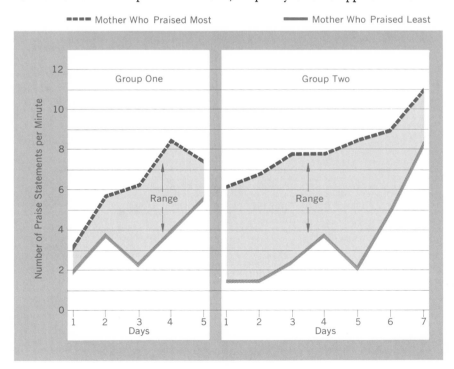

Figure 4. When mothers' praises in teaching their children were recorded, the number of praise statements dispensed grew considerably.

mothers had little skill in maintaining order. They responded to shouting and fighting by shouting back, shaking the children, and so forth. This was not only ineffective but directly contrary to the guiding principle of the program, which was to reinforce with attention only the behavior that they wanted the children to continue.

To remedy this situation, we developed a system for structuring the activities of the playroom. We defined the boundaries of each area—doll corner, block corner, and so forth—and then required the children to complete a "switching requirement" before moving from one area to another.

The switching requirement was a simple matching problem involving pegs on a pegboard. The child was told to go to the board, complete the problem, and raise his hand. At that point a mother would come over, approve of his work, and allow him to choose a ticket to a new play area.

We imposed the requirement more for immediate, practical reasons than for training in skills that mothers or children could use outside the preschool. It did, however, have some interesting results. Noting that a one-row problem increased the average time a child spent in one activity area from ten minutes to twenty-six, we decided to see what effect a four-row problem would have. In addition to reducing the switching rate still further, the four-row problem taught the children a good deal about matching. The first time one boy tried the problem, it took him half an hour; his eighth attempt took a mere nine minutes. In other words, moving from area to area served as an effective reinforcement for learning, just as did the use of equipment and materials at Turner House.

The Parent-Teacher Preschool was primarily a training program for mothers, but it did, of course, affect the children as well. Its benefits can be inferred from the marked change in their IQ scores. At the beginning of the program, the average child's score on the Peabody Picture Vocabulary Test was 69 and the range was from 48 to 81. At the end of the program, the average child's score on the same test was 87 and the range was 67 to 117.

As for the mothers, we found that they can learn to become fairly good teachers. However, they tend to teach other children better than they do their own, and they have trouble putting principles of positive reinforcement into practice in unstructured situations. These are problems that we are working on this year.

An important by-product of the project is that the mothers have participated in a community project, many of them for the first time. Indeed, we have tried to involve the community as closely as possible both at Turner House and at the Parent-Teacher Preschool. For example, one of the three full-time teachers at Turner House is a girl of nineteen from Juniper Gardens, who came to us from the neighborhood Youth Corps. The Parent-Teacher Preschool is supervised this year by one professional teacher instead of three; now the two assistant teachers are mothers who participated in the program last year.

In summary, it seems best simply to repeat the logic that led us to develop the Turner House program and the Parent-Teacher Preschool. One characteristic of culturally deprived children is that they have trouble in school, and in the United States we rely on the public schools to teach children the behavior that our society considers useful. The right kind of preschool might make it possible for culturally deprived children to learn what the public schools set out to teach.

Ideally, the schools will be teaching something meaningful, and teachers will see these particular children as valuable people for whom it is worth opening the doors to knowledge.

VI
Language and Technology

Language and the Mind

Noam Chomsky

Noam Chomsky's theory of language and language acquisition constitutes the most serious challenge to behavioral studies of language learning. Chomsky is interested in explaining how children who are only four have the competence to generate an infinite number of novel sentences. According to Chomsky, such competence is innate (it is not a product of learning) and consists of an intuitive, tacit, and unconscious grasp of the rules whereby sentences are properly generated.

The grammar of a language is a transformational grammar, which describes the operations we use to relate to its deep structure. Traditional grammar analyzes only surface structure.

Psycholinguistic research on the relationship between memory and deep structure has generally supported Chomsky's theory of deep structure. If language capacity is innate rather than learned, what is the role of language teaching in the school?

How does the mind work? To answer this question we must look at some of the work performed by the mind. One of its main functions is the acquisition of knowledge. The two major factors in acquisition of knowledge—perception and learning—have been the subject of study and speculation for centuries. It would not, I think, be misleading to characterize the major positions that have developed as outgrowths of classical rationalism and empiricism. The rationalist theories are marked by the importance they assign to *intrinsic* structures in mental operations—to central processes and organizing principles in perception, and to innate ideas and principles in learning. The empiricist approach, in contrast, has stressed the role of *experience* and control by environmental factors.

The classical empiricist view is that sensory images are transmitted to the brain as impressions. They remain as ideas that will be associated in various ways, depending on the fortuitous character of experience. In this view a language is merely a collection of words, phrases, and sentences, a habit system, acquired accidentally and extrinsically. In the formulation of Williard Quine, knowledge of a language (and, in fact, knowledge in general) can be represented as "a fabric of sentences variously associated to one another and to nonverbal stimuli by the mechanism of conditioned response." Acquisition of knowledge is only a matter of the gradual construction of this fabric. When sensory experience is interpreted, the already established network may be activated in some fashion. In its essentials, this view has been predominant in modern behavioral science, and it has been accepted with little question by many philosophers as well.

The classical rationalist view is quite different. In this view the mind contains a system of "common notions" that enable it to interpret the scattered and incoherent data of sense in terms of objects and their relations, cause and effect, whole and part, symmetry, gestalt properties, functions, and so on. Sensation, providing only fleeting and meaningless images, is degenerate and particular. Knowledge, much of it beyond immediate awareness, is rich in structure, involves universals, and is highly organized. The innate general principles that underlie and organize this knowledge, according to Leibniz, "enter into our thoughts, of which they form the soul and the connection . . . although we do not at all think of them."

This "active" rationalist view of the acquisition of knowledge persisted through the romantic period in its essentials. With respect to language, it achieves its most illuminating expression in the investigations of Wilhelm von Humboldt. His theory of speech perception supposes a generative system of rules that underlies speech production as well as its interpretation. The system is generative in that it makes infinite use of finite means. He regards a language as a structure of forms and concepts based on a system of rules that determine their interrelations, arrangement, and organization. But these finite materials can be combined to make a never-ending product.

Innovative Quality of Language

In the rationalist and romantic tradition of linguistic theory, the normal use of language is regarded as characteristically innovative. We construct sentences that are entirely new to us. There is no substantive notion of analogy or generalization that accounts for this creative aspect of language use. It is equally erroneous to describe language as a habit structure or as a network of associated responses. The innovative element in normal use of language quickly exceeds the bounds of such marginal principles as analogy or generalization (under any substantive interpretation of these notions). It is important to emphasize this fact because the insight has been lost under the impact of the behaviorist assumptions that have dominated speculation and research in the twentieth century.

In Humboldt's view, acquisition of language is largely a matter of maturation of an innate language capacity. The maturation is guided by internal factors, by an innate "form of language" that is sharpened, differentiated, and given its specific realization through experience. Language is thus a kind of latent structure in the human mind, developed and fixed by exposure to specific linguistic experience. Humboldt believes that all languages will be found to be very similar in their grammatical form, similar not on the surface but in their deeper inner structures. The innate organizing principles severely limit the class of possible languages, and these principles determine the properties of the language that is learned in the normal way.

The active and passive views of perception and learning have elaborated with varying degrees of clarity since the seventeenth century. These views can be confronted with empirical evidence in a variety of ways. Some recent work in psychology and neurophysiology is highly suggestive in this regard. There is evidence for the existence of central processes in perception, specifically for control over the functioning of sensory neurons by the brain-stem reticular system. Behavioral counterparts of this central control have been under investigation for several years. Furthermore, there is evidence for innate organization of the perceptual system of a highly specific sort at every level of biological organization. Studies of the visual system of the frog, the discovery of specialized cells responding to angle and motion in the lower cortical centers of cats and rabbits, and the somewhat comparable investigations of the auditory system of frogs—all are relevant to the classical questions of intrinsic structure mentioned earlier. These studies suggest that there are highly organized, innately determined perceptual systems that are adapted closely to the animal's "life space" and that provide the basis for what

we might call acquisition of knowledge. Also relevant are certain behavioral studies of human infants, for example those showing the preference for faces over other complex stimuli.

These and other studies make it reasonable to inquire into the possibility that complex intellectual structures are determined narrowly by innate mental organization. What is perceived may be determined by mental processes of considerable depth. As far as language learning is concerned, it seems to me that a rather convincing argument can be made for the view that certain principles intrinsic to the mind provide invariant structures that are a precondition for linguistic experience. In the course of this article I would like to sketch some of the ways such conclusions might be clarified and firmly established.

Input-Output Models

There are several ways linguistic evidence can be used to reveal properties of human perception and learning. In this section we consider one research strategy that might take us nearer to this goal.

Let us say that in interpreting a certain physical stimulus a person constructs a *percept*. This percept represents some of his conclusions (in general, unconscious) about the stimulus. To the extent that we can characterize such percepts, we can go on to investigate the mechanisms that relate stimulus and percept. Imagine a model of perception that takes stimuli as inputs and arrives at percepts as outputs. The model might contain a system of beliefs, strategies for interpreting stimuli, and other factors, such as the organization of memory. We would then have a perceptual model that might be represented graphically, as in Figure 1.

Consider next the system of beliefs that is a com-

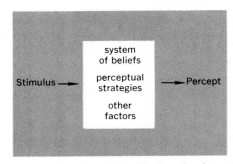

Figure 1. A perceptual model, with the stimulus representing the input and a percept representing the output.

ponent of the perceptual model. How was this acquired? To study this problem, we must investigate a second model, which takes certain data as input and gives as output (again, internally represented) the system of beliefs operating in the perceptual model. This second model, a model of learning, would have its own intrinsic structure, as did the first. This structure might consist of conditions on the nature of the system of beliefs that can be acquired, of innate inductive strategies, and again, of other factors such as the organization of memory (see Figure 2).

Under further conditions we could take these perceptual and learning models as theories of the acquisition of knowledge, rather than of belief. How then would the models apply to language? The input stimulus to the perceptual model is a speech signal, and the percept is a representation of the utterance that the hearer takes the signal to be and of the interpretation he assigns to it. We can think of the percept as the structural description of a linguistic expression that

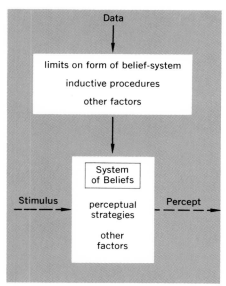

Figure 2. A learning model, with data representing the input and a system of beliefs representing the output.

contains certain phonetic, semantic, and syntactic information. Most interesting is the syntactic information, which best can be discussed by examining a few typical cases.

Surface Structure

The three sentences in Figure 3 seem to have the same syntactic structure. Each contains the subject *I*, and the predicate of each consists of a verb (*told, expected, persuaded*), a noun phrase (*John*), and an embedded predicate phrase (*to leave*). This similarity is only superficial, however—a similarity in what we may call the surface structure of these sentences, which differ in important ways when we consider them with somewhat greater care.

The differences can be seen when the sentences are paraphrased or subjected to certain grammatical operations, such as the conversion from active to passive forms. For example, in normal conversation the sentence *I told John to leave* can be roughly paraphrased as *What I told John was to leave*. But the other two sentences cannot be paraphrased as *What I persuaded*

John was to leave or *What I expected John was to leave*. Sentence 2 can be paraphrased as *It was expected by me that John would leave*. But the other two sentences cannot undergo a corresponding formal operation, yielding *It was persuaded by me that John would leave* or *It was told by me that John should leave*.

Sentences 2 and 3 differ more subtly. In Sentence 3 *John* is the direct object of *persuade*, but in Sentence 2 *John* is not the direct object of *expect*. We can show this by using these verbs in slightly more complex sentences: *I persuaded the doctor to examine John* and *I expected the doctor to examine John*. If we replace the embedded proposition *the doctor to examine John* with its passive form *John to be examined by the doctor*, the change to the passive does not, in itself, change the meaning. We can accept as paraphrases *I expected the doctor to examine John* and *I expected John to be examined by the doctor*. But we cannot accept as paraphrases *I persuaded the doctor to examine John* and *I persuaded John to be examined by the doctor*.

The parts of these sentences differ in their grammatical functions. In *I persuaded John to leave, John* is both the object of *persuade* and the subject of *leave*. These facts must be represented in the percept since they are known intuitively to the hearer of the speech signal. No special training or instruction is necessary to enable the native speaker to understand these examples, to know which are wrong and which right, although they may all be quite new to him. They are interpreted by the native speaker instantaneously and uniformly, in accordance with structural principles that are known tacitly, intuitively, and unconsciously.

These examples illustrate two significant points. First, the surface structure of a sentence, its organization into various phrases, may not reveal or immediately reflect its deep syntactic structure. The deep structure is not represented directly in the form of the speech signal; it is abstract. Second, the rules that determine deep and surface structure and their interrelation in particular cases must themselves be highly abstract. They are surely remote from consciousness, and in all likelihood they cannot be brought to consciousness.

Syntactic Structure

A study of such examples, examples characteristic of all human languages that have been carefully studied, constitutes the first stage of the linguistic investigation outlined above, namely the study of the percept. The percept contains phonetic and semantic information related through the medium of *syntactic structure*. There are two aspects to this syntactic structure. It consists of a surface directly related to the phonetic form, and a deep structure that underlies the semantic interpretation. The deep structure is represented in the mind and rarely is indicated directly in the physical signal.

A language, then, involves a set of semantic-phonetic percepts, of sound-meaning correlations, the correlations being determined by the kind of intervening syntactic structure just illustrated. The English language correlates sound and meaning in one way, Japanese in another, and so on. But the general properties of percepts, their forms and mechanisms, are remarkably similar for all languages that have been carefully studied.

Returning to our models of perception and learning, we can now take up the problem of formulating the system of beliefs that is a central component in perceptual processes. In the case of language, the system of beliefs would now be called the *generative grammar*, the system of rules that specifies the sound-meaning correlation and generates the class of structural descriptions (percepts) that constitute the language in question. The generative grammar, then, represents the speaker-hearer's knowledge of his language. We can use the term *grammar of a language* ambiguously, as referring not only to the speaker's internalized, subconscious knowledge but to the professional linguist's representation of this internalized and intuitive system of rules as well.

Theory of Language Acquisition

How is this generative grammar acquired? Or, using our learning model, what is the internal structure of the device that could develop a generative grammar?

We can think of every normal human's internalized grammar as, in effect, a theory of his language. This theory provides a sound-meaning correlation for an infinite number of sentences. It provides an infinite set of structural descriptions; each contains a surface structure that determines phonetic form and a deep structure that determines semantic content.

In formal terms, then, we can describe the child's acquisition of language as a kind of theory construction. The child discovers the theory of his language with only small amounts of data from that language. Not only does his theory of the language have an enormous predictive scope, but it also enables the child to reject a great deal of the very data on which the theory has been constructed. Normal speech consists, in large part, of fragments, false starts, blends, and other distortions of the underlying idealized forms. Nevertheless, as is evident from a study of the mature use of language, what the child learns is the underlying ideal theory. This is a remarkable fact. We must also bear in mind that the child constructs this ideal theory without explicit instruction, that he acquires this knowledge at a time when he is not capable of complex intellectual achievements in many other domains, and that this achievement is relatively independent of intelligence or the particular course of experience. These are facts that a theory of learning must face.

A scientist who approaches phenomena of this sort without prejudice or dogma would conclude that the acquired knowledge must be determined in a rather specific way by intrinsic properties of mental organization. He would then set himself the task of discovering the innate ideas and principles that make such acquisition of knowledge possible.

It is unimaginable that a highly specific, abstract, and tightly organized language comes by accident into the mind of every four-year-old child. If there were not an innate restriction on the form of grammar, then the child could employ innumerable theories to account for his linguistic experience, and no one system, or even small class of systems, would be found exclusively acceptable or even preferable. The child could not possibly acquire knowledge of a language. This restriction on the form of grammar is a precondition for linguistic experience, and it is surely the critical factor in determining the course and result of language learning. The child cannot know at birth which language he is going to learn. But he must "know" that its grammar must be of a predetermined form that excludes many imaginable languages.

The child's task is to select the appropriate hypothesis from this restricted class. Having selected it, he can confirm his choice with the evidence further available to him. But neither the evidence nor any process of induction (in any well-defined sense) could in itself have led to this choice. Once the hypothesis is sufficiently well confirmed, the child knows the language defined by this hypothesis; consequently, his knowledge extends vastly beyond his linguistic experience, and he can reject much of this experience as imperfect, as resulting from the interaction of many factors, only one of which is the ideal grammar that determines a sound-meaning connection for an infinite class of linguistic expressions. Along such lines as these one might outline a theory to explain the acquisition of language.

Sentence Interpretation

As has been pointed out, both the form and meaning of a sentence are determined by syntactic structures that are not represented directly in the signal and that are related to the signal only at a distance, through a long sequence of interpretive rules. This property of abstractness in grammatical structure is of primary importance, and it is on this property that our inferences about mental processes are based. Let us examine this abstractness a little more closely.

Not many years ago, the process of sentence interpretation might have been described approximately along the following lines. A speech signal is received and segmented into successive units (overlapping at the borders). These units are analyzed in terms of their invariant phonetic properties and assigned to *phonemes*. The sequence of phonemes, so constructed, is then segmented into minimal grammatically functioning units (morphemes and words). These are again categorized. Successive operations of segmentation and classification will lead to what I have called surface structure—an analysis of a sentence into phrases, which can be represented as a proper bracketing of the sentence, with the bracketed units assigned to various categories (see Figure 3). Each segment—phonetic, syntactic, or semantic—would be identified in terms of certain invariant properties. This would be an exhaustive analysis of the structure of the sentence.

With such a conception of language structure, it made good sense to look forward hopefully to certain engineering applications of linguistics—for example, to voice-operated typewriters capable of segmenting an expression into its successive phonetic units and identifying these, so that speech could be converted to some form of phonetic writing in a mechanical way; to mechanical analysis of sentence structure by fairly straightforward and well-understood computational techniques; and perhaps even beyond to such projects as machine translation. But these hopes have by now been largely abandoned with the realization that this conception of grammatical structure is inadequate at every level, semantic, phonetic, and syntactic. Most important, at the level of syntactic organization, the surface structure indicates semantically significant relations only in extremely simple cases. In general, the deeper aspects of syntactic organization are representable by labeled bracketing, but of a very different sort from that seen in surface structure.

There is evidence of various sorts, both from phonetics and from experimental psychology, that labeled bracketing is an adequate representation of surface structure. It would go beyond the bounds of this paper to survey the phonetic evidence. A good deal of it is presented in *Sound Pattern of English*, by myself and Morris Halle. Similarly, very interesting experimental work by Jerry Fodor and his colleagues, based on earlier observations by D. E. Broadbent and Peter Ladefoged, has shown that the disruption of a speech signal (for example, by a superimposed click) tends to be perceived at the boundaries of phrases rather than at the point where the disruption actually occurred, and that in many cases the bracketing of surface structure can be read directly from the data on perceptual displacement. I think the evidence is rather good that labeled bracketing serves to represent the surface structure that is related to the perceived form of physical signals.

Grammatical Transformations

Deep structures are related to surface structures by a sequence of certain formal operations, operations now generally called *grammatical transformations*. At the levels of sound, meaning, and syntax, the significant structural features of sentences are highly abstract. For this reason they cannot be recovered by elementary data-processing techniques. This fact lies behind the search for central processes in speech perception and the search for intrinsic, innate structure as the basis for language learning.

How can we represent deep structure? To answer this question we must consider the grammatical transformations that link surface structure to the underlying deep structure, which is not always apparent.

Consider, for example, the operations of passivization and interrogation. In the sentences (1) *John was examined by the doctor*, and (2) *Did the doctor examine John*, both have a deep structure similar to the paraphrase of Sentence 1, (3) *The doctor examined John*. The same network of grammatical relations determines the semantic interpretation in each case. Thus, two of the grammatical transformations of English must be the operations of passivization and interrogation that form such surface structures as Sentences 1 and 2 from a deeper structure, which in its essentials also underlies Sentence 3. Since the transformations ultimately produce surface structures, they must produce labeled

Figure 3. The superficial similarity of surface structures is revealed when sentences are paraphrased or converted to passive form.

(1) I told John to leave
(2) I expected John to leave
(3) I persuaded John to leave

First Paraphrase:

(1a) What I told John was to leave (ACCEPTABLE)
(2a) What I expected John was to leave (UNACCEPTABLE)
(3a) What I persuaded John was to leave (UNACCEPTABLE)

Second Paraphrase:

(1b) It was told by me that John would leave (UNACCEPTABLE)
(2b) It was expected by me that John would leave (ACCEPTABLE)
(3b) It was persuaded by me that John would leave (UNACCEPTABLE)

(4) I expected the doctor to examine John
(5) I persuaded the doctor to examine John

Passive replacement as paraphrase:

(4a) I expected John to be examined by the doctor (MEANING RETAINED)
(5a) I persuaded John to be examined by the doctor (MEANING CHANGED)

bracketings (see Figure 4). But notice that these operations can apply in sequence: we can form the passive question *Was John examined by the doctor?* by passivization followed by interrogation. Since the result of passivization is a labeled bracketing, it follows that the interrogative transformation operates on a labeled bracketing and forms a new labeled bracketing. Thus a transformation such as interrogation maps a labeled bracketing into a labeled bracketing.

By similar argument, we can show that all grammatical transformations are structure-dependent mappings of this sort and that the deep structures that underlie all sentences must themselves be labeled bracketings. Of course, the labeled bracketing that constitutes deep structure will in general be quite different from that representing the surface structure of a sentence. Our argument is somewhat oversimplified, but it is roughly correct. When made precise and fully accurate it strongly supports the view that deep structures, like surface structures, are formally to be taken as labeled bracketings, and that grammatical transformations are mappings of such structures onto other similar structures.

Mental Operations and Grammar

Recent studies have sought to explore the ways in which grammatical structure of the sort just described enters into mental operations. Much of this work has been based on a proposal formulated by George Miller as a first approximation, namely, that the amount of memory used to store a sentence should reflect the number of transformations used in deriving it. For example, H. B. Savin and E. Perchonock investigated this assumption in the following way: they presented to subjects a sentence followed by a sequence of unrelated words.

They then determined the number of these unrelated words recalled when the subject attempted to repeat the sentence and the sequence of words. The more words recalled, the less memory used to store the sentence. The fewer words recalled, the more memory used to store the sentence. The results showed a remarkable correlation of amount of memory and number of transformations in certain simple cases. In fact, in their experimental material, shorter sentences with more transformations took up more space in memory than longer sentences that involved fewer transformations.

Savin has extended this work and has shown that the effects of deep structure and surface structure can be differentiated by a similar technique. He considered paired sentences with approximately the same deep structure but with one of the pair being more complex in surface structure. He showed that, under the experimental conditions just described, the paired sentences were indistinguishable. But if the sequence of unrelated words precedes, rather than follows, the sentence being tested, then the more complex (in surface structure) of the pair is more difficult to repeat correctly than the simpler member. Savin's very plausible inference is that sentences are coded in memory in terms of deep structure. When the unrelated words precede the test sentence, these words use up a certain amount of short-term memory, and the sentence that is more complex in surface structure cannot be analyzed with the amount of memory remaining. But if the test sentence precedes the unrelated words, it is, once understood, stored in terms of deep structure, which is about the same in both cases. Therefore, the same amount of memory remains, in the paired cases, for recall of the following words. This is a beautiful example of the way creative experimental studies can interweave with theoretical

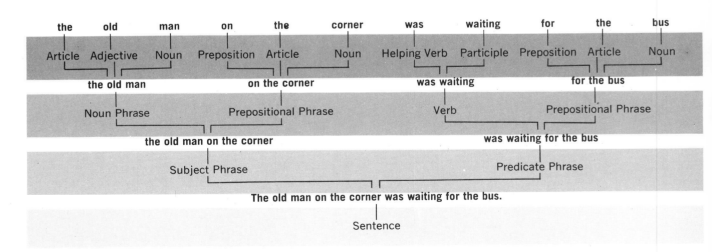

Figure 4. This type of sentence analysis (labeled bracketing) is now considered inadequate; it analyzes the sentence by successive division into larger units, with each unit assigned to its own category.

work in the study of language and of mental processes.

Perceptual Theory

In speaking of mental processes we have returned to our original problem. We can now see why it is reasonable to maintain that the linguistic evidence supports an active theory of acquisition of knowledge. The study of sentences and of speech perception, it seems to me, leads to a perceptual theory of a classical rationalist sort. Representative of this school, among others, were the seventeenth-century Cambridge Platonists, who developed the idea that our perception is guided by notions that originate from the mind and that provide the framework for the interpretation of sensory stimuli. It is not sufficient to suggest that this framework is a store of neural models or *schemata* that are in some manner applied to perception (as is postulated in some current theories of perception). We must go well beyond this assumption and return to the view of Wilhelm von Humboldt, who attributed to the mind a system of rules that generates such models and schemata under the stimulation of the senses. The system of rules itself determines the content of the percept that is formed.

We can offer more than this vague and metaphoric account. A generative grammar and an associated theory of speech perception provide a concrete example of the rules that operate and of the mental objects that they construct and manipulate. Physiology cannot yet explain the physical mechanisms that affect these abstract functions. But neither physiology nor psychology provides evidence that calls this account into question or that suggests an alternative. As mentioned earlier, the most exciting current work in the physiology of perception shows that even the peripheral systems analyze stimuli into the complex properties of objects, and that central processes may significantly affect the information transmitted by the receptor organs.

The study of language, it seems to me, offers strong empirical evidence that empiricist theories of learning are quite inadequate. Serious efforts have been made in recent years to develop principles of induction, generalization, and data analysis that would account for knowledge of a language. These efforts have been a total failure. The methods and principles fail not for any superficial reason such as lack of time or data. They fail because they are intrinsically incapable of giving rise to the system of rules that underlies the normal use of language. What evidence is now available supports the view that all human languages share deep-seated properties of organization and structure. These properties—these linguistic universals—can be plausibly assumed to be an innate mental endowment rather than the result of learning. If this is true, then the study of language sheds light on certain long-standing issues in the theory of knowledge. Once again, I see little reason to doubt that what is true of language is true of other forms of human knowledge as well.

There is one further question that might be raised at this point. How does the human mind come to have the innate properties that underlie acquisition of knowledge? Here linguistic evidence obviously provides no information at all. The process by which the human mind has achieved its present state of complexity and its particular form of innate organization are a complete mystery, as much of a mystery as the analogous questions that can be asked about the processes leading to the physical and mental organization of any other complex organism. It is perfectly safe to attribute this to evolution, so long as we bear in mind that there is no substance to this assertion—it amounts to nothing more than the belief that there is surely some naturalistic explanation for these phenomena.

There are, however, important aspects of the problem of language and mind that can be studied sensibly within the limitations of present understanding and technique. I think that, for the moment, the most productive investigations are those dealing with the nature of particular grammars and with the universal conditions met by all human languages. I have tried to suggest how one can move, in successive steps of increasing abstractness, from the study of percepts to the study of grammar and perceptual mechanisms, and from the study of grammar to the study of universal grammar and the mechanisms of learning.

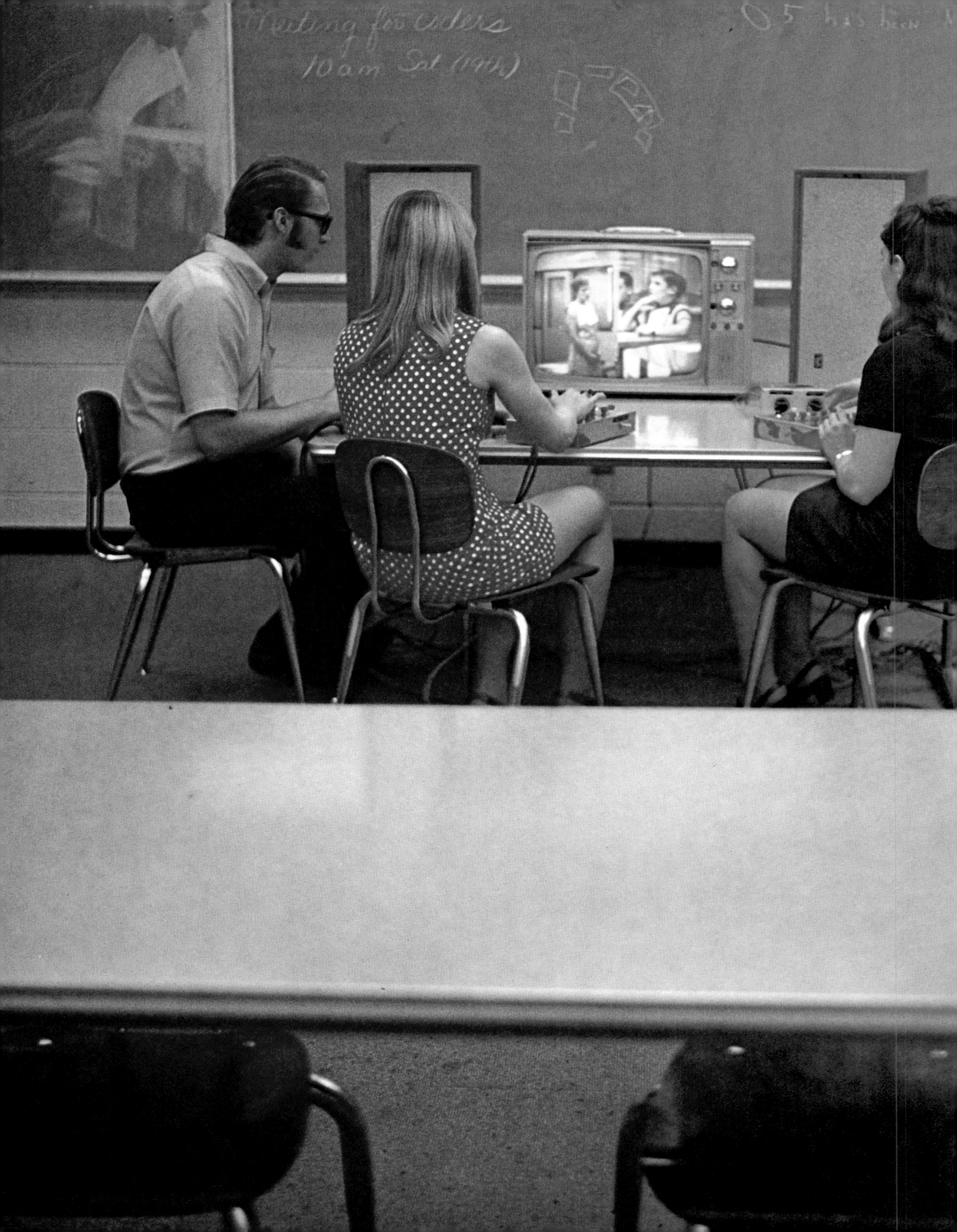

Teaching and Machines
William R. Uttal

William Uttal argues that teaching machines controlled by complex computers may someday provide the student with all the teaching flexibility and creativity of the best flesh-and-blood teacher. Such technological marvels Uttal calls "generative computer teaching machines." These machines will be able to analyze *what the student states and* construct *appropriate responses. Consequently, they must contain programs that can change internally while they are in use.*

Perhaps the most exciting implication of Uttal's research is the clarity that knowledge of computer teaching functions brings to highly complex human teaching functions. For two examples (you may find many others), we can now clearly see that the focus of classroom learning should be on the student's learning *not the teacher's* teaching, *and that bookkeeping models of teaching are no more workable for computer than for human instruction.*

It is more than somewhat humbling to be forced to admit that we still know all too little about the phenomenon of learning. Psychologists have yet to discover exactly what marvelous internal change makes it possible for the infant to say his first word, the twelve-year-old to divide 3,254 by 589, and the adult to distinguish Bach from Beethoven. We do know a considerable amount about the conditions that facilitate learning, enough to tell us that the educational techniques currently used in most of our classrooms are far from ideal.

For one thing, we know from experimental evidence that the most elaborate educational plant yet constructed is worth far less to a student than the undivided attention of a great teacher. We know that students tend to learn less in a lecture class than in a discussion group, and far less in a large discussion group than in a small one. Ideally, each student should have his own personal tutor—and a good one, at that. The trouble is that there are not enough teachers, good or otherwise, to go around. We need an army where we have only a regiment. And we need an army of generals, not sergeants.

Computer teaching machines offer great promise for the future, and far from being the depersonalizing threat many people envision, such machines can give better individual instruction than one might dream. Someday they may even carry on "conversations" with students. This goal is not quite as distant as it seems. Now that computer teaching machines are beginning to be able to process natural languages, they can simulate, at least to some extent, the normal conversation of teacher and student. A program devised by one teacher can be fed into as many machines as we have the raw materials and the inclination to produce. And, though computer technology still lags far behind theory, it appears that we someday may be able to produce a machine that will respond to the student with as much imagination and flexibility as a flesh-and-blood tutor.

'Round and 'Round It Goes

In a paper discussing the motivating properties of a two-person conversation, I drew an analogy between the loop systems used in control theory and certain educational processes. An *open loop system* is one in which input gives way to output with no modification from feedback; a *closed loop system*—which control engineers have come increasingly to regard as the superior type—is one in which feedback is taken into account. An example of an open loop system in human education is the lecture; an example of a closed loop system is the teacher-student dialogue. Through conversational interaction, each speaker actively participates in the learning process and receives from his partner responses adapted to his own stream of thought and manner of expression.

Given the obvious superiority of conversational interaction, why does the classroom lecture dominate our current educational technology? The most important reason is that it is *administratively simple* to assemble a class and present an open loop lecture. A lecture is superficially efficient, because information may be transmitted to a very large class by a single lecturer.

The computer teaching machine shares with the human lecturer—and with educational television and other audiovisual devices—the ability to amplify and diverge information from a single master, directing it to a very large number of students. However, the computer teaching machine is happily exempt from the most serious drawback of other information amplifiers, the loss of the flow of information from student to teacher. Because they do not utilize feedback, one-way information systems such as films and television are simply communication systems. They are not "new" teaching methods; they merely serve to enhance the demonstrated limitations of the conventional lecture.

Education is an information processing activity that requires the teacher not only to communicate information, but to adapt to his student, to interpret the student's response, and to generate new specific material. The ability of the computer teaching machine to perform these last three tasks—though as yet it cannot perform them all well—is what allies it with the human tutor and distinguishes it both from other types of teaching machines and from the nonautomated teaching techniques now in use.

In the usual school or college classroom, the presentation of information, practice and drill, recitation, and evaluation all are separate functions, occurring more or less sequentially and at widely spaced intervals. Recitation or practice, rather than coming at each step, usually occurs after a large block of material has been presented. Thus the teacher's evaluation of his students' performance cannot influence his presentation until it is too late. By the time the teacher discovers that his students did not understand him, the critical moment for modifying his presentation is gone.

The situation is quite different with the human teacher or with the computer teaching machine. These provide for a homogeneous, smooth, two-way flow of information between teacher and student. The presentation of information, practice, and testing occur much closer to each other in time, so that the teacher's efforts can be modified at once as it becomes apparent what the student has or has not understood.

A particularly important feature of this smoothly flowing process is that, since "tests" precede the presentation of each new step, failure on a given test precludes presentation of the next step. In other words, the student stays with each step of the curricular sequence until he has mastered it.

Note that this apparently simple idea represents a crucial difference between education as it is now practiced and education as it could be. In the conventional classroom, each student spends the same amount of time to learn an amount of material that varies from student to student. With a computer teaching machine (or a human tutor), each student spends a variable amount of time to learn a constant amount of material,

and there is no a priori reason that the amount of time taken should not be that required for complete mastery. Computer teaching machines offer the hope that the emphasis in education can be taken off *efficiency* of information transmission and put back where it belongs, on mastery of the subject.

Model Modern Major General

The vital characteristic of the modern computer—the characteristic that allows it to do what media merely transmitting information cannot do—is that the program stored in its memory can be modified internally while the machine is in use. The computer's ability to adapt to feedback means that it can, in theory at least, be programmed to simulate the human intellectual process of tutoring or, for that matter, of thinking. This truly revolutionary idea is distressingly undervalued by many computer theoreticians and technologists. Instead of devoting their financial and intellectual resources to the development of conceptual models for internal program modification, they concentrate on the perfection of details of communication and on the exploitation of basically inadequate systems. Where we need creativity, we get bookkeeping.

Many of the devices now in use are little more than bookkeeping machines, for they use only a fraction of the computer's capacities. For example, some machines ask the student to indicate his response by choosing among a small set of multiple-choice buttons instead of, say, by typing his response on a computer-controlled typewriter. This expedient reduces the demand on the computer's central processer, but it also disastrously diminishes the effectiveness of the tutorial process and can be a bore to the student. The repertoire of responses allowed the student is too small and stereotyped; the kinds of analysis that can be applied to this type of response are few. With such machines, the question "Why do you need a computer at all?" is justified and difficult to answer.

Another shortcoming of many teaching machines is that they use a storage medium such as microfilm for the material to be presented to the student. A frame of microfilm contains a great deal of information; presenting the material in large blocks instead of in a series of small steps makes it impossible to identify the exact point at which the student loses his way. Thus, analysis of the student's responses becomes general instead of specific, and the educational program again approximates the lecture-cum-quiz instead of the student-tutor conversation. In addition, microfilm cannot be erased as can magnetic storage devices, so it becomes more difficult to modify a program in response to new insights into the educational process or into the subject at hand.

In short, many computer teaching machines now in use are typified by extremely limited input media and by output display devices that are relatively static and unrefined in step size. In general, these teaching machines

must be considered automated conventional teaching machines rather than actual computer teaching machines. I classify them as degenerate teaching machines.

A more serious attempt to utilize the computer's power to provide solid tutorial aid is represented by machines whose programs include *branching*. Conventional teaching machines, by and large, proceed in a linear fashion. Degenerate computer teaching machines do branch in simple ways but not with the elaborations found in the excitingly effective applications of computer teaching. The computer teaching machine can adapt to the student's progress. It can be programmed for a large amount of decision making at critical points.

The basic idea of branching is that the student's response determines which of several alternatives the machine presents next. There are a great many types of branching trees, or decision logics, that a computer can use. One major type is the *main trunk* tree, in which, after a short remedial digression, the student always returns to some central sequence. To the *fully branched* tree-type, the student never returns once he has left a given sequence.

What You Forgot to Remember

Since branching is implemented through a process of storage, comparison, and, finally, selection, computer teaching machines that use such a process can be called *selective* computer teaching machines. All possible questions, statements, and remedial hints or queries—indeed, any action of the computer—are prestated by the author of the program. They then are stored in the computer's large and, it is hoped, randomly accessible memory. The computer compares the student's answers, perhaps after slight editing, with a list of possible correct answers and anticipated incorrect answers. If there is a match between any answer in the list and the student's answer, that match determines which of the prestored statements from the computer memory is next displayed to the student. The analysis, then, is very simple: The input is compared with alternative answers, and a match determines the next statement.

Most computer teaching machines that deal with general verbal material are members of this category. They take advantage of the computer's ability to store and to compare small chunks of material. They also allow the author freedom to change easily and quickly the contents of a single statement or question. Thus, as quickly as improvements become apparent to the human author, they can be added to the existing program—and, superficially, this type of computer teaching machine can imitate the tutorial dialogue.

What Tomorrow Brings

The teacher does not compare his student's response with other possible responses and then select an appropriate reply; he does not store in his memory specific branches, outcomes, and statements. Instead, he uses his understanding of the subject, his awareness of the difficulties it is likely to present, and his knowledge of the student to *analyze* the student's response and to *construct* his own next statement. What we need, then, is a computer that can analyze and construct as well as compare and select—a computer that thinks vertically as well as horizontally, so to speak.

Such computers, since they generate responses not specifically written into their memories, could be called *generative* computer teaching machines. This kind of teaching machine would be an exceedingly economical way to achieve powerful teaching programs, and tedious and exhaustive programming of teaching steps would be unnecessary.

One of the first examples of a generative teaching machine was J. C. R. Licklider's imaginative use of a computer and a cathode ray oscilloscope to permit powerful tutorial interaction in the study of analytical geometry. Like the human teacher, this technique used no fixed, prestored dialogue, but rather had a small number of algorithms that could perform generally useful functions. It could *plot* a graph on the face of an oscilloscope, or *substitute* parameters presented by the student into the algebraic expression of a geometrical curve. With this small library of standard equations for various two-dimensional curves, the student could explore the effects of changing intercepts, slopes, and other parameters that defined one or another curve. He also could track a photoelectric pointer, alter the ge-

ometry of the curve itself, and observe how the analytical expression corresponding to a particular curve affected the various parameters. So Licklider's visual display of a cathode ray tube allowed additional rhetorical tools to be brought into play—a critical point could be circled.

Another example of a generative computer teaching machine, in which the special analog properties of the subject matter allow algorithmic generation of an almost unlimited number of computer responses, is illustrated by the work of Roger Buiten and Harlan Lane at the University of Michigan. Their machine was designed to teach students how to pronounce foreign language words. The student was presented with an audio recording of a given word. Then he repeated that sound into a microphone. The microphone was connected to an analog-to-digital converter, which fed a digitized representation of the speech sound into the computer. The computer analyzed the speech for pitch, amplitude, and rhythm, and then responded to the student by means of meters that indicated how far the student had deviated from the sample sound. The important feature of this computer teaching machine is that, unlike the usual "language laboratory," the student does not have to rely upon his untrained ear to decide whether his performance is acceptable. The analysis and evaluation are made on an individual word basis by an impartial, discriminating computer.

Some laboratories are using random number generation as a means of varying the terms of mathematical problems in computer teaching machines. In this way many new problems can be generated for a variety of students, or for one student in a continuing way as he deals with a special class of problem. Some researchers claim success for editing routines that recognize nearly equivalent spellings or phonetic equivalents. This sort of input to the computer will, of course, be a very important part of the generative computer teaching machine of the future.

Perhaps the most intriguing representation of a true generative teaching program is that described by Leonard Uhr of the University of Wisconsin. Uhr attacks the problem of the generation of teaching programs to achieve the old-fashioned classroom question-and-answer atmosphere. His current programs handle well-defined problems in elementary arithmetic and word-for-word language translation. He uses prototype problem formats, such as "How much is A plus B?", which previously have been stored in the computer. Questions are generated either by a random number calculator or by a reaction to the student's performance on previous problems. Uhr goes on to suggest that there really is no limit to the prototypes of many different problems that can be presented, and that almost any problem that can be stated formally can be presented. However, analysis of the answer is quite another thing—and a knotty problem for the scientist to solve for his machine. For example, presentation of a theorem proof to a student would require that the computer be able to deal with the many possible equivalent paths. This is a problem that goes far beyond the simple statement that 3 + 4 is, indeed, equal to 7.

Ultimately, of course, this problem will be solved, and inevitably the real breakthrough in programmed learning will be conversational interaction between the student and the generative computer teaching machine.

Already J. Weizenbaum of the Massachusetts Institute of Technology has developed a program system called ELIZA, in which dialogues with the machines are directed strongly by the human conversant. The machine detects key words and context and responds to the human's message with the most appropriate of many prestored sentences.

This is only the beginning, the very beginning, for generative computer teaching machines. The future is fantastic to contemplate. It is hard for most people to believe that any machine could teach with as much insight, flexibility, and imagination as a human tutor; it is equally difficult to conceive of the enormous numbers of people who could be educated to high levels of mastery through conversations with such machines. But who, fifty years ago, would have believed we would ever land men on the moon?

The intersection of an initial unit row and a final unit column determines the entry in any given cell.

The problem format for the construction of each cell is divided into four parts: Parts A and D are standard instructional sections, and Parts B and C are remedial sections. Parts B and C are branches from Part A, and may be presented independently or in combination.

On the cathode ray screen the student first sees an empty cell with its associated initial and final units and an array of response choices. He hears a message to touch and say the word that belongs in the empty cell. If the student makes the correct response, in this case touches *ran* with his light-pen, he proceeds to Part D, where he sees the word written in the cell and is told "Good, you have put *ran* in the cell. Touch and say *ran*."

The array of multiple-choice responses in Part A is designed to identify three types of errors: final unit incorrect; initial unit incorrect; both initial and final units incorrect.

If in Part A the student responds with *fan* instead of *ran*, he is branched to remedial instruction (Part B), where attention is focused on the initial unit of the cell. If a correct response is made in the remedial section, the student is returned to the beginning for a second attempt. If an incorrect response is made in the remedial section, an arrow is displayed on the screen to indicate the correct response, which the student then is asked to touch.

If in Part A the student responds with *rat* instead of *ran*, he is branched to remedial instruction (Part C) on the final unit of the cell. The procedure is similar. However, it should be noted that in the remedial instruction the initial letter is never pronounced by the audio system, whereas the final unit always is pronounced. If the student responds in Part A with *bat* instead of *ran*, then he has made an error on both the initial and the final units, and he is branched through both sets of remedial instruction.

When the student returns to the beginning after completing a remedial section, a correct response will advance him to Part D. If a wrong response is made on the second attempt, an arrow is placed beside the correct response area and held there until a correct response is made. If the next response is still an error, a message is sent to the proctor terminal, and the sequence is repeated from the beginning.

When a student has responded correctly in Parts A and D, he is advanced to the next cell of the matrix, which is a problem identical to that just described. As a student makes correct responses, he constructs a matrix of word cells. When the matrix is complete, the rows and columns are reordered and the full matrix is displayed. The student is asked in a criterion test to identify the words in the cells. He completes the entire test without interruption, even if he makes mistakes. Errors are categorized as initial, final, and other. If the percentage of total errors on the criterion test exceeds a predetermined value, then appropriate remedial exercises are provided. After working through one or both of the remedial sections, the student is branched back for a second pass through the criterion matrix. The second pass is a teaching run, and the student receives additional correction and optimization routines.

| COMPUTER PROGRAM | Let us consider briefly the problem of translating the curriculum materials into a language that can be understood by the computer. The particular computer language we use is called Coursewriter II, a language developed by IBM in close collaboration with Stanford University. A coded lesson is a series of Coursewriter II commands that cause the computer to display and manipulate text on the cathode ray screen, to display images on the film screen, to position and play audio messages, to accept and evaluate keyboard and light-pen responses, to update the performance record of each student, and, with a set of switches and counters, to implement the branching logic of the lesson.

A typical lesson in the reading program, which takes the average student about thirty minutes to complete, requires more than 9,000 Coursewriter commands for its execution.

An example from a task designed to teach both letter discrimination and the meaning of words will illustrate some of the complexities of the coding problem. A picture illustrating the word being taught is presented on the film screen. Three words, including the word illustrated, are presented on the cathode ray screen. A message is played on the audio system asking the child to touch the word on the cathode ray screen that matches the picture on the film screen.

Using the light-pen, the student then can make his response. If he makes no response within thirty seconds, he is told the correct answer, an arrow points to it, and he is asked to touch it. If he makes a response within the time limit, the point that he touches is compared by the computer with the correct-answer area. If he places the light-pen within the correct area, he is told that he was correct, and goes on to the next problem. If the response was not in the correct area, it is compared with the area defined as a wrong answer. If his response is within this area, he is told that it is wrong, given the correct answer, and asked to touch it. If his initial response was neither in the anticipated wrong-answer area nor in the correct-answer area, then the student has made an undefined answer. He is given the same message that he would have heard had he touched a defined wrong answer; however, the response is recorded on his data record as undefined. The student tries again until he makes the correct response, at which time he goes on to the next problem.

To prepare an instructional sequence of this sort, the programmer must write a detailed list of commands for the computer. He also must make a tape recording of all

TABLE 2   Macro Commands for Instructional Sequence in Table 1

Command	Audio Information			Film Strip	
	Address	Message		Address	Picture
Problem 1 CM PW]FO1]bat]bag]rat]AO1] ABCD1]AO4]AO2]AO3]7]1,7,3,18]C1]	AO1	Touch and say the word that goes with the picture.		FO1	Picture of a bag.
	AO2	Good. Bag. Do the next one.			
	AO3	No.			
	AO4	The word that goes with the picture is bag. Touch and say bag.			
Problem 2 CM PW]FO2]card]cart]hard]] ABCD2]AO7]AO5]AO6]5]1,5,4,18]C2]	AO5	Good. Card. Do the next one.		FO2	Picture of a card.
	AO6	No.			
	AO7	The word that goes with the picture is card. Touch and say card.			

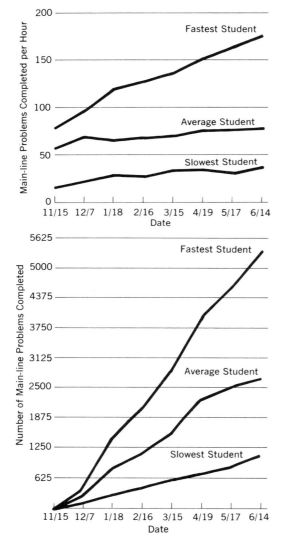

Figure 3. Rate of learning throughout the course. Note the wide range of speeds and total problems completed, showing the great potential for the individual child to learn to capacity.

We also wanted to see whether sex differences affected accuracy. On four standard types of problems—letter identification, word-list learning, matrix construction, and sentence comprehension—the only difference between boys and girls that was statistically significant was for word-list learning. These results, while not conclusive, do lend support to the notion that when students are removed from the normal classroom environment and given computer instruction, boys perform as well as girls in overall rate of progress. The results also suggest that with computer-assisted instruction the sex difference is minimized as the emphasis moves toward analysis and away from rote memorization. The one kind of problem on which the girls achieved significantly higher scores than the boys, word-list learning, is essentially a memorization task.

How did the computer-instructed first-graders compare with the control group? Both groups were tested extensively before the project began and again near the end of the school year. The two groups were not significantly different at the start of the year, but at the end of the year the group that received computer-assisted reading instruction performed significantly better on almost all of the reading achievement tests, including the California Reading Test, the Gates-MacGinitie Test, and the Hartley.

The average Stanford-Binet IQ score for the students (both experimental and control) was 89. There was considerable variation, but by and large these were not exceptional or gifted children. Students, teachers, and parents reacted quite favorably to the introduction of computer-assisted instruction into the classroom.

Initially, students were given only a few minutes per day on the teaching machines. The time was increased to twenty minutes after the first six weeks; in the last month we allowed students thirty to thirty-five minutes. We wanted to determine how well first-grade students would adapt to machine instruction for relatively long periods of time. We found that they adapt quite well, and this year we have been using thirty-minute periods for all students. This may seem like a long session for a first-grader, but our observations suggest that their span of attention is well over a half-hour if the programming is dynamic and responsive to their inputs.

Various optimization routines were evaluated during the year. These evaluations, in turn, have suggested a number of experiments and analyses that might be profitable. Such analyses, combined with the potential for additional research under the highly controlled conditions offered by computerized instruction, could lay the groundwork for a theory of instruction truly useful to the educator. The theory will have to be based on a highly structured model of the learning process, and it must generate optimization strategies that are compatible with the goals of education. The development of a viable theory of instruction is a major scientific undertaking, and substantial progress in this direction could well be one of psychology's most important contributions to society.

Biographies

ATKINSON   BIJOU   BOBBITT   BRUNER   CATTELL   CHOMSKY   M. COLE   S. COLE

RICHARD C. ATKINSON ("The Computer as a Tutor") joined the faculty of Stanford University in 1956, after receiving his Ph.B. from the University of Chicago and his doctorate from Indiana University. He is a professor of psychology and holds courtesy appointments in the Schools of Education and Engineering. Dr. Atkinson is coauthor of the fourth edition of Ernest Hilgard's textbook, *Introduction to Psychology* (1967), and a frequent contributor to scholarly and professional journals. His chief research interest is learning theory, particularly the formation and testing of mathematical models for human learning and memory.

SIDNEY W. BIJOU ("The Mentally Retarded Child") is a professor of psychology and director of the Child Behavior Laboratory at the University of Illinois. Before joining the Illinois faculty, he taught psychology and served as director of the Developmental Psychology Laboratory at the University of Washington for almost 20 years.

Bijou received his B.S. from the University of Florida, his M.A. from Columbia, and his Ph.D. from the University of Iowa. He has been editor of the *Journal of Experimental Child Psychology*, associate editor of the *International Review of Research in Mental Retardation*, and a frequent contributor to professional journals. He is a member of the Research Advisory Board for the National Association for Retarded Children, the American Psychological Association, and the Society for Research in Child Development.

RUTH A. BOBBITT (coauthor, "Monkeying with the Mother Myth") received her B.A. from the University of Denver, her M.A. from Mills College, and her Ph.D. from the University of Iowa in 1947. She is a clinical associate professor of psychology at the University of Washington, and a member of the core staff of the Regional Primate Research Center. The observational methods and computer programs that she helped devise are now being used in research with human subjects. Dr. Bobbitt says that she has always been more interested in methods of behavioral measurement than in particular psychological problems. Her clinical studies convinced her that a better means of determining patterns of social interaction was needed to advance psychological analysis in this area.

JEROME BRUNER ("Up from Helplessness"), who helped found Harvard's Center for Cognitive Studies in 1960, is a graduate of Duke University. Bruner received his Ph.D. from Harvard in 1941, joined the Harvard faculty in 1945, and has been a professor of psychology there since 1952. He has published many books and articles on the nature of cognitive processes, including *On Knowing: Essays for the Left Hand* and *Toward a Theory of Instruction*.

Dr. Bruner has served on committees advising the White House, the State Department, the United Nations, the Department of Defense, the National Science Foundation, and the National Institutes of Health; he is a founding member of the National Academy of Education and a past president of the American Psychological Association. In 1962, the APA awarded him its Distinguished Scientific Award.

RAYMOND BERNARD CATTELL ("Are IQ Tests Intelligent?") is Distinguished Research Professor in the Department of Psychology, University of Illinois, where he directs the Laboratory of Personality and Group Analysis. His study of intelligence began forty years ago, when his Ph.D. research was done under the direction of Charles Spearman and Sir Cyril Burt at the University of London. He later received his D.Sc. from the same institution.

Dr. Cattell came to the United States at the invitation of E. L. Thorndike and has taught at Clark and Harvard Universities. He has published 265 articles, contributed 31 chapters to books, and written 28 books of his own.

NOAM CHOMSKY ("Language and the Mind") holds the Ferrari P. Ward Professorship of Modern Languages and Linguistics at the Massachusetts Institute of Technology. He received his Ph.D. in linguistics at the University of Pennsylvania, where his dissertation was on transformational analysis. He is the author of books and articles not only on linguistics but on philosophy, intellectual history, and contemporary issues.

MICHAEL COLE (coauthor, "Russian Nursery Schools") is taking part in a new interdisciplinary program for the study of language and development at the Irvine campus of the University of California. In this program anthropologists, linguists, psychologists, and other social scientists bring their skills to bear on the problem of cultural change and development.

Dr. Cole began his research on human learning during his doctoral program at Indiana University. Then, as a postdoctoral fellow in the Soviet-American Exchange Program, he studied at Moscow University under Alexander Luria. There he was introduced to cross-cultural research on the development of cognitive processes.

While at Stanford University, he became interested in a mathematics-learning project in Africa and now commutes regularly between California and Liberia.

SHEILA COLE (coauthor, "Russian Nursery Schools") with her husband, Michael, spent the summer of 1966 in the Soviet Union, helping with preparations

DECECCO   FARSON   FLACKS   THE HARLOWS   JENSEN   KAGAN   KELLOGG

for the 18th International Congress of Psychologists and gathering material on Soviet nursery schools.

Mrs. Cole received her B.A. from Indiana University and her M.S. from the Columbia Graduate School of Journalism. She has worked on several newspapers, usually as an education writer, and is now a free-lance journalist.

JOHN P. DeCECCO (contributing editor) majored in biology at Allegheny College, where he earned his B.S. degree; he received his M.A. and Ph.D. degrees in history from the University of Pennsylvania. It was not until he started teaching at the University of Detroit that his interest in educational psychology became strong, so that for several years he pursued postgraduate studies in the field at Wayne State and Michigan State universities. He currently holds a joint appointment at San Francisco State College as professor of education and psychology.

He has been active in a number of research projects in the field and in 1968–1969 was visiting professor at Teachers College, Columbia University, to coordinate a research project aimed at developing a behavioral taxonomy of educational objectives for civic participation; this research was sponsored by the U.S. Office of Education and the Center for Research and Education in American Liberties under the auspices of Columbia Teachers College. Dr. DeCecco is the author of numerous articles and *The Psychology of Learning and Instruction: Educational Psychology*, a new and most successful textbook in the field. He is in the process of writing a history of psychology, wherein he can combine his training in the two fields to synthesize a historical view of how man has speculated about and studied animal and human behavior.

RICHARD E. FARSON ("Emotional Bar-

riers to Education") was one of the founders of Western Behavioral Sciences Institute, the "only nonprofit, interdisciplinary institute in the country looking at the broad field of human relations." A former student of Carl Rogers, Dr. Farson was a psychologist in private practice before WBSI. He is currently vice president for ecological affairs, California Institute of the Arts.

His research has been in the area of small-group processes, leadership and social power, and organizational behavior. The application and communication of behavioral-sciences knowledge and new ways of dealing with human problems of the future are among his special interests.

RICHARD FLACKS ("Student Activists: Result, Not Revolt"), a former national officer of Students for a Democratic Society, is now assistant professor of sociology at the University of Chicago. His Ph.D. work, done with Theodore Newcomb, was a study of Bennington College, its alumnae and students, published as *Persistence and Change* (Wiley, 1967).

HARRY and MARGARET HARLOW ("The Young Monkeys") are famous for their work with surrogate mothers, both wire and cloth. During the last ten years the Harlows have discovered a variety of affection ties in monkeys. They have experimentally produced social and asocial monkeys, good and bad mothers, as well as sexually adjusted and maladjusted monkeys.

Dr. Harlow, a past president of the American Psychological Association, received his Ph.D. from Stanford and went to the University of Wisconsin in 1930 to "enrich the literature on rodents." When he arrived, he found that the university had demolished its animal laboratory to make room for a building finally erected thirty years later. In desperation,

he turned to the Madison Zoo—and to the monkeys. "For better or worse," he says, "I became forever a monkey man."

Mrs. Harlow came to the university as a specialist in human development but soon broadened her interests to include other primates.

GORDON D. JENSEN (coauthor, "Monkeying with the Mother Myth") began his career as a specialist in child care and development. After 10 years as a practicing and teaching pediatrician, he went into the field of psychiatry. He is now associate professor of psychiatry and a member of the core staff of the Regional Primate Research Center at the University of Washington in Seattle. The research described in the article was supported by a grant from the National Institutes of Health.

Since his student days at Yale, where he received his M.D. in 1949, Dr. Jensen has been concerned with the behavioral and social problems that face man. He has written two books and has published more than 40 articles on child development, mental health, and animal behavior.

JEROME KAGAN ("The Many Faces of Response" and "Sex-Role Identity") is a professor of developmental psychology at Harvard. Doctoral studies at Yale and a position at Ohio State University preceded his Army service, during which Kagan did a research study on attrition at West Point. He found that the poor risks were youths who were aware of a bad or hostile relationship with their fathers.

Later research at the Fels Research Institute, Antioch College, resulted in *Birth to Maturity*, 1963 winner of the Hofheimer Prize for research by the American Psychiatric Association.

RHODA KELLOGG ("Understanding Children's Art") is the executive director of San Francisco's 80-year-old Golden Gate

KOHLBERG   LENT   NEILL   PRESSMAN   RISLEY   SCHEIN   SIZER

Kindergarten Association and administrator of the Phoebe A. Hearst Preschool Learning Center, a model kindergarten operated by the Association. With more than 40 years' experience in working with and observing children, Miss Kellogg has received widespread recognition for her work in preschool education. She is perhaps better known, however, as an international authority on preschool art. She hopes to show that certain children's reading difficulties can be prevented by analyzing the way they draw as preschoolers.

LAWRENCE KOHLBERG ("The Child as a Moral Philosopher") received his Ph.D. in psychology at the University of Chicago. A postdoctoral residence at Children's Hospital, Boston, "confirmed my opinion that psychoanalysis had little to offer the systematic study of the development of moral ideals and feelings." Dr. Kohlberg then spent two years at Yale, studying psychosexual development and identification in early and mid-childhood. A year at the Center for Advanced Study in the Behavioral Sciences was followed by five years at the University of Chicago. Dr. Kohlberg then spent a year at the Harvard Human Development Laboratory and has now settled at Harvard as professor of education and social psychology.

JAMES R. LENT ("Mimosa Cottage: Experiment in Hope") specializes in applying the principles of operant conditioning to the problems of handicapped children. He is particularly interested in programs that allow the placement of mentally retarded children in the community.

After receiving his doctorate in special education from Syracuse University, Lent worked with handicapped children in several states. He joined the staff of the Parsons Research Center in 1964. The Mimosa Cottage Project, financed by a National Institute of Mental Health grant, is conducted by the Research Center under the joint auspices of Parsons State Hospital and Training Center and the Bureau of Child Research at the University of Kansas.

ALEXANDER SUTHERLAND NEILL ("Can I Come to Summerhill?"), headmaster of Summerhill School, was born 86 years ago in Scotland. His ideas remain as controversial today as when they caused his resignation from the staff of King Alfred School in 1920. The forerunner of Summerhill was founded in 1921, when Neill set up an international school in Dresden, Germany. He moved this school first to the Austrian Tyrol and then, after seven months of harassment by the local peasants and the Austrian government, to England.

Neill, who holds the M.A. degree, is a graduate of Edinburgh University, where his major subject was English. He has written a number of books on education and child psychology.

HARVEY PRESSMAN ("Schools to Beat the System") was until recently associate director of the Regional Educational Laboratory program and director of the Office of Planning Services at the Education Development Center, Newton, Massachusetts. Before joining EDC, he was director of the 1964 Brandeis Enrichment Program for Disadvantaged Youth, a program designed to develop the intellectual talents of junior-high-school students from inner-city areas of Boston. He is now director of the Boston Area Project for Volunteers for International Technical Assistance (VITA).

He completed his undergraduate work at Brandeis University and moved on to Harvard for his Ph.D.

TODD RISLEY ("Learning and Lollipops") began his professional career by studying the uses of operant conditioning with autistic and severely retarded children. Now, at preschools for culturally deprived four-year-olds, he is trying to apply behavioral analysis to the problems of more normal children.

Dr. Risley was born in Alaska, graduated from San Diego State College, and received his M.S. and Ph.D. degrees in psychology from the University of Washington. Before joining the University of Kansas faculty, he taught psychology at Florida State University. In addition to his preschool research, Risley conducts laboratory research on basic questions of animal behavior.

EDGAR H. SCHEIN ("The First-Job Dilemma") is a professor of organizational psychology and management at the Alfred P. Sloan School of Management, Massachusetts Institute of Technology.

He obtained his first degrees at the University of Chicago and at Stanford and received his Ph.D. in social psychology from Harvard in 1952. He spent the next four years as a research psychologist with the Walter Reed Army Institute of Research. He became known for his studies of the Communists' brainwashing of American prisoners during the Korean war. Since joining MIT in 1956, Dr. Schein has found himself increasingly preoccupied with how young graduates are adapting to organizations in the early part of their careers. He also has begun to study how schools and universities indoctrinate or "socialize" students toward certain attitudes and values.

THEODORE SIZER (coauthor, "A Proposal for a Poor Children's Bill of Rights") is dean of the Faculty of Education at Harvard.

Dean Sizer received his B.A. from Yale, his M.A. and Ph.D. from Harvard. At Harvard he has been assistant professor of education, director of the Master of Arts Teaching Program, and a Member of the John F. Kennedy School of Government. He has served as a

TRABASSO   UTTAL   WHITTEN   WOHLWILL

member of the National Advisory Council on Education Professions Development, as director of the Education Development Center, and as secretary of the Navy's Advisory Board on Education. His publications include *Secondary Schools at the Turn of the Century* (Yale University Press, 1964), *The Age of the Academies* (Teachers College, Columbia University, 1964), and (editor) *Religion and Public Education* (Houghton Mifflin, 1967).

Tom Trabasso ("Pay Attention") is a professor of psychology at Princeton University. At the time his article was written, he was at the University of California, Los Angeles. He teaches courses in general and quantitative psychology, learning, and cognitive processes. Prior to going to UCLA he did postdoctoral work at Stanford University. Dr. Trabasso did his undergraduate work at Union College, where he majored in psychology, and went on to receive his M.A. and Ph.D. degrees from Michigan State University. His research interests have centered on human conceptual behavior and the application of mathematical models to these problems. His recent book with Gordon Bower, *Attention in Learning* (Wiley, 1968), represents a synthesis of these methods and interests.

William R. Uttal ("Teaching and Machines") is a professor of psychology and research psychologist at the Mental Health Research Institute, University of Michigan. Dr. Uttal has maintained a dual interest in sensory psychology and computer applications to psychology since being converted from physics during a stay in the U.S. Air Force. Before joining the University of Michigan faculty he had been the leader of the IBM research center group that developed the teaching machine versions of the IBM 650 and 1410 computers.

In 1965–1966, Uttal was a visiting professor at Japan's Kyoto Prefectural University of Medicine, a residence that gave him a chance to pursue his interest in Japanese history and culture. Two years ago, he published *Real Time Computers: Technique and Application in the Psychological Sciences* (Harper & Row).

Phillip Whitten (coauthor, "A Proposal for a Poor Children's Bill of Rights") is a doctoral candidate at the Graduate School of Education, Harvard University. He received his B.A. in foreign languages and M.A. in sociology from San Jose State College and his M.A. in education from Harvard, where he is currently a member of the Faculty Committee on Academic Policy. A former all-American swimmer, Whitten was a student leader at San Jose and helped bring about various reforms there such as the Community Involvement Program and the Experimental College.

Joachim F. Wohlwill ("The Mystery of the Prelogical Child") is a professor of psychology and director of the Graduate Training Program in Developmental Psychology at Clark University. Dr. Wohlwill worked with Jean Piaget at the Institut Rousseau in Geneva. He was graduated from Harvard in 1947 and received his Ph.D. in 1957 from the University of California, Berkeley. His main present interests are the development of perception and thinking in the child and formal instruction as opposed to spontaneous activity. This has led him to a related interest—people's responses to their physical environments, both natural and man made.

Bibliographies

I. School and Society

Can I Come to Summerhill?

FREEDOM, NOT LICENSE! A. S. Neill. Hart, 1966.

SUMMERHILL: A RADICAL APPROACH TO CHILD REARING. A. S. Neill. Hart, 1960.

Schools to Beat the System

CLASH OF CULTURES IN THE CLASSROOM. K. Clark in *Learning Together: A Book on Integrated Education.* M. Weinberg, ed. Integrated Education Associates, 1964.

DEATH AT AN EARLY AGE. THE DESTRUCTION OF THE HEARTS AND MINDS OF NEGRO CHILDREN IN THE BOSTON PUBLIC SCHOOLS. J. Kozol. Houghton Mifflin, 1967.

OUR CHILDREN ARE DYING. N. Hentoff. Viking, 1966.

THE SCHOOL-CHILDREN. GROWING UP IN THE SLUMS. M. F. Greene, O. Ryan. New American Library, 1967.

A TALK TO TEACHERS. J. Baldwin in *The Saturday Review,* December 21, 1963.

36 CHILDREN. H. Kohl. New American Library, 1967.

THE WAY IT SPOZED TO BE. J. Herndon. Simon and Schuster, 1968.

YOUTH IN THE GHETTO: THE CONSEQUENCES OF POWERLESSNESS. Harlem Youth Opportunities. HARYOU, 1964.

A Proposal for a Poor Children's Bill of Rights

CAPITALISM AND FREEDOM. M. Friedman. University of Chicago Press, 1962.

COMPULSORY MISEDUCATION. P. Goodman. Vintage Books, 1964.

EQUALITY OF EDUCATIONAL OPPORTUNITY. J. Coleman *et al.* U.S. Department of Health, Education and Welfare, U.S. Government Printing Office, 1966.

THE FAILURE OF THE PUBLIC SCHOOLS AND THE FREE MARKET REMEDY. H. M. Levin, February, 1968 (to be published in *The Urban Review*).

IS THE PUBLIC SCHOOL OBSOLETE? C. Jencks in *The Public Interest,* Winter 1966.

THE NEW INDUSTRIAL STATE. J. K. Galbraith. Houghton Mifflin, 1967.

THE OTHER AMERICA. M. Harrington. Penguin Books, 1963.

THE RIGHTS OF MAN. T. Paine. J. M. Dent, 1961.

THE ROLE OF GOVERNMENT IN EDUCATION. M. Friedman in *Economics and the Public Interest.* R. A. Solo, ed. Rutgers University Press, 1955.

SPECIAL ISSUE ON EQUALITY OF EDUCATIONAL OPPORTUNITY. *Harvard Educational Review,* 1968.

TOM PAINE'S VOUCHER SCHEME FOR EDUCATION. E. G. West in *Southern Economic Journal,* January 1967.

THE WEALTH OF NATIONS. A. Smith. Random House, 1937.

Russian Nursery Schools

A HANDBOOK OF CONTEMPORARY SOVIET PSYCHOLOGY. M. Cole, I. Maltzman, eds. Basic Books, 1968.

PROGRAMMA VOSPITANIIA V DETSKOM SADU [The Program of Education in Nursery School]. M. V. Zaluzhskaia, ed. *Gosidarstvennoe Uchebno-Pedagogicheskoe Izdatel'stvo Ministerstua Prosveshcheniia* [Ministry of Education, RSFSR]. Moscow, 1962.

TEORIIA I PRAKTIKA SENSORNOV VOCPITANIIA V DETSKOM SADU [The Theory and Practice of Sensory Training in Nursery School]. A. P. Usovoi, N. P. Sakulinoi, eds. Proveshcheniia, Moscow, 1965.

II. The Student in Transition

Emotional Barriers to Education

DAEDALUS, Fall, 1967.

DESIGNING EDUCATION FOR THE FUTURE: AN EIGHT-STATE PROJECT. E. L. Morphet, Project Director. Denver, 1967.

EDUCATION AND ECSTASY. G. Leonard. Delacorte Press, 1969.

THE NEXT THIRTY-THREE YEARS. H. Kahn, A. Wiener. Macmillan, 1967.

The Child as a Moral Philosopher

THE DEVELOPMENT OF CHILDREN'S ORIENTATIONS TOWARD A MORAL ORDER: 1. SEQUENCE IN THE DEVELOPMENT OF MORAL THOUGHT. L. Kohlberg in *Vita Humana,* Vol. 6, pp. 11–33(b), 1963.

DEVELOPMENT OF MORAL CHARACTER AND IDEOLOGY. L. Kohlberg in *Review of Child Development Research.* M. L. Hoffman, ed. Russell Sage, 1964.

EQUALITY. J. Wilson. Hutchison, 1966.

THE LANGUAGE OF MORALS. R. M. Hare. Oxford University Press, 1952.

MORAL EDUCATION IN THE SCHOOLS: A DEVELOPMENTAL VIEW. L. Kohlberg in *School Review,* Vol. 74, pp. 1–30, 1966.

MORALS IN EVOLUTION: A STUDY OF COMPARATIVE ETHICS. L. T. Hobhouse. London, 1951.

THE PSYCHOLOGY OF CHARACTER DEVELOPMENT. R. F. Peck, R. J. Havighurst. Wiley, 1960.

STAGES IN THE DEVELOPMENT OF MORAL THOUGHT AND ACTION. L. Kohlberg. Holt, Rinehart & Winston (in preparation).

Student Activists: Result, Not Revolt

ACTIVISM AND APATHY IN CONTEMPORARY ADOLESCENTS. J. H. Block, N. Haan, M. Smith in *Contributions to the Understanding of Adolescents.* J. F. Adams, ed. Allyn & Bacon, 1967.

FROM GENERATION TO GENERATION. S. N. Eisenstadt. Free Press, 1956.

THE LIBERATED GENERATION. R. Flacks in *Journal of Social Issues,* Vol. 23, pp. 52–75, July, 1967.

THE PORT HURON STATEMENT. Students for a Democratic Society, 1962.

A PROPHETIC MINORITY. J. Newfield. New American Library, 1967.

STUDENT POLITICS. S. M. Lipset, ed. 1967.

THE UNCOMMITTED. K. Keniston. Harcourt, Brace and World, 1965.

The First-Job Dilemma

ATTITUDE CHANGE DURING MANAGEMENT EDUCATION. E. H. Schein in *Administrative Science Quarterly,* Vol. 11, No. 4, 1967.

HOW TO BREAK IN THE COLLEGE GRADUATE. E. H. Schein in *Harvard Business Review,* Nov.–Dec., 1964.

ORGANIZATIONAL PSYCHOLOGY. E. H. Schein. Prentice-Hall, 1965.

ORGANIZATIONAL SOCIALIZATION IN THE EARLY CAREER OF INDUSTRIAL MANAGERS. E. H. Schein. M.I.T. School of Management Working Paper No. 39–63, 1963.

PROBLEMS OF THE FIRST YEAR AT WORK: REPORT OF THE FIRST CAREER PANEL REUNION. E. H. Schein. M.I.T. School of Management Working Paper No. 03–62, 1962.

III. The Roots of Development

The Young Monkeys

AFFECTION IN PRIMATES. M. K. Harlow, H. F. Harlow in *Discovery,* Vol. 27, pp. 11–17, 1966.

BEHAVIORAL ASPECTS OF REPRODUCTION IN PRIMATES. H. F. Harlow, W. Danforth Joslyn, M. G. Senko, A. Dopp in *Journal of Animal Science,* Vol. 25, pp. 49–67, 1966.

LEARNING TO LOVE. H. F. Harlow, M. K. Harlow in *American Scientist,* Vol. 54, pp. 244–272, 1966.

LOVE IN INFANT MONKEYS. H. F. Harlow in *Scientific American,* June, 1959.

MATERNAL BEHAVIOR OF RHESUS MONKEYS DEPRIVED OF MOTHERING AND PEER ASSOCIATION IN INFANCY. H. F. Harlow, M. K. Harlow, R. O. Dodsworth, G. L. Arling, in *Proceedings of the American Philosophical Society,* Vol. 110, pp. 329–335, 1967.

Tell us what you think

All over the country today students are taking an active role in the quality of their education. They're telling administrators what they like and what they don't like about their campus communities. They're telling teachers what they like and what they don't like about their courses.

This response card offers you a unique opportunity as a student to tell a publisher what you like and what you don't like about his book.

FIRST CLASS
PERMIT NO. 59
DEL MAR, CALIF.

BUSINESS REPLY MAIL
No Postage Stamp Necessary if Mailed in the United States.

Postage will be paid by

CRM BOOKS

Del Mar, California | 92014

INFANT DEVELOPMENT UNDER ENVIRON-MENTAL HANDICAP. W. Dennis, P. Najarian in *Psychological Monographs General and Applied*, Vol. 71, No. 7, Whole No. 436, 1957.

POSITIVE REINFORCEMENT AND BEHAVIOR DEFICITS OF AUTISTIC CHILDREN. C. B. Ferster in *Child Development*, Vol. 32, pp. 437–456, 1961.

REINFORCEMENT AND PUNISHMENT IN THE CONTROL OF HUMAN BEHAVIOR BY SOCIAL AGENCIES. C. B. Ferster in *Psychiatric Research Reports*, Vol. 10, pp. 101–118, 1958.

Learning and Lollipops

CHILD DEVELOPMENT. S. W. Bijou, D. M. Baer. Appleton-Century-Crofts, 1961, 1965. Vols. 1 and 2.

CONTROL OF HUMAN BEHAVIOR. R. Ulrich, T. Stachnik, J. Mabry. Scott, Foresman, 1966.

EFFECTS OF ADULT SOCIAL REINFORCE-MENT ON CHILD BEHAVIOR. F. Harris, M. M. Wolf, D. Baer in *Young Child*, Vol. 20, pp. 8–17, 1964.

ESTABLISHING FUNCTIONAL SPEECH IN ECHOLALIC CHILDREN. T. R. Risley, M. M. Wolf in *Behaviour Research and Therapy*, Vol. 5, pp. 73–88, 1967.

SCIENCE AND HUMAN BEHAVIOR. B. F. Skinner. Macmillan, 1953.

Mimosa Cottage: Experiment in Hope

THE EFFECT OF AN INSTITUTION EN-VIRONMENT UPON THE VERBAL DE-VELOPMENT OF IMBECILE CHILDREN. J. G. Lyle in *Journal of Mental Deficiency Research*, Vol. 3, pp. 122–128, 1959.

ENVIRONMENTAL INFLUENCE ON VERBAL OUTPUT OF MENTALLY RETARDED CHILDREN. B. B. Schlanger in *Journal of Speech and Hearing Disorders*, Vol. 19, pp. 339–345, 1954.

PROGRAMMED INSTRUCTION AS AN AP-PROACH TO TEACHING OF READING, WRITING, AND ARITHMETIC TO RE-TARDED CHILDREN. S. W. Bijou *et al.* in *Psychological Record*, Vol. 16, pp. 505–552, 1966.

RESIDENTIAL CARE OF MENTALLY HANDI-CAPPED CHILDREN. J. Tizzard in *British Medical Journal*, Vol. 1, pp. 1041–1046, 1960.

SHIFTING STIMULUS CONTROL OF ARTICU-LATION RESPONSES BY OPERANT TECH-NIQUES. J. McLean. Unpublished doctoral dissertation, University of Kansas, 1965.

A STUDY OF THE EFFECTS OF COMMUNITY AND INSTITUTIONAL SCHOOL CLASSES FOR TRAINABLE MENTALLY RETARDED CHILDREN. L. F. Cain, S. Levine. San Francisco State College, 1961.

VI. Language and Technology

Language and the Mind

ASPECTS OF THE THEORY OF SYNTAX. N. Chomsky. M.I.T. Press, 1965.

CARTESIAN LINGUISTICS. N. Chomsky. Harper & Row, 1966.

GRAMMATICAL STRUCTURE AND THE IM-MEDIATE RECALL OF ENGLISH SEN-TENCES. H. Savin, E. Perchonock in *Journal of Verbal Learning and Verbal Behavior*, Vol. 4, pp. 348–353, 1965.

THE PHILOSOPHY OF LANGUAGE. J. Katz. Harper & Row, 1966.

THE PSYCHOLOGICAL REALITY OF LIN-GUISTIC SEGMENTS. J. Fodor, T. Bever in *Journal of Verbal Learning and Verbal Behavior*, Vol. 4, pp. 414–420, 1965.

SOUND PATTERN OF ENGLISH. N. Chomsky, M. Halle. Harper & Row, 1968.

STRUCTURE OF LANGUAGE: READINGS IN THE PHILOSOPHY OF LANGUAGE. J. Fodor, J. Katz, eds. Prentice-Hall, 1964.

Teaching and Machines

THE AUTOMATIC GENERATION OF TEACH-ING MACHINE PROGRAMS. L. Uhr, August, 1965. Copies available from the author: Computer Sciences De-partment, University of Wisconsin.

CERTAIN MAJOR PSYCHOEDUCATIONAL IS-SUES APPEARING IN THE CONFERENCE ON TEACHING MACHINES. S. L. Pressey in *Automatic Teaching: The State of the Art*, pp. 187–198. Wiley, 1959.

THE COMPILATION OF NATURAL LAN-GUAGE TEXT INTO TEACHING MACHINE PROGRAMS. L. Uhr in *AFPIS Confer-ence Proceedings*, pp. 26 and 35–44, 1964.

COMPUTER-AIDED INSTRUCTION. J. A. Swets, W. Feurzeig in *Science*, Vol. 150, pp. 572–576, 1965.

"ELIZA"—A COMPUTER PROGRAM FOR THE STUDY OF NATURAL LANGUAGE COMMUNICATION BETWEEN MAN AND MACHINE. J. Weizenbaum in *Com-munications of the ACM*, Vol. 9, pp. 36–45, 1966.

EXPERIMENTAL SYSTEM GIVES LANGUAGE STUDENT INSTANT ERROR FEEDBACK. R. Buiten, H. S. Lane in *Digital Equipment Corporation Computer Application Note*, 1965.

ON CONVERSATIONAL INTERACTION. W. R. Uttal in *Programmed Learning and Computer-Based Instruction*, pp. 171–190. Wiley, 1962.

PRELIMINARY DISCUSSION OF THE LOG-ICAL DESIGN OF AN ELECTRONIC COM-PUTING INSTRUMENT. A. W. Burks, H. H. Goldstine, J. von Neumann. Institute for Advanced Study, 1947. Part I, Vol. I.

PRELIMINARY EXPERIMENTS IN COM-PUTER-AIDED TEACHING. J. C. R. Lick-lider in *Programmed Learning and Computer-Based Instruction*. Wiley, 1962.

The Computer as a Tutor

COMPUTER-ASSISTED INSTRUCTIONS IN INI-TIAL READING. R. C. Atkinson, D. N. Hansen in *Reading Research Quar-terly*. Vol. 2, pp. 5–25, 1966.

COMPUTER-BASED INSTRUCTION IN INI-TIAL READING: A PROGRESS REPORT ON THE STANFORD PROJECT. H. A. Wil-son, R. C. Atkinson in Technical Report 119, Institute for Mathemati-cal Studies in the Social Sciences, Stanford University, 1967. (To be published in *Basic Studies in Read-ing*, H. Levin, J. Williams, eds. Harper & Row.)

HUMAN MEMORY: A PROPOSED SYSTEM AND ITS CONTRACT PROCESSES. R. C. Atkinson, R. M. Shiffrin in *The Psychology of Learning and Motiva-tion: Advances in Research and The-ory*, Vol. 2. K. W. Spence, J. T. Spence, eds. Academic Press, 1968.

Index

CRM BOOKS
David A. Dushkin, *President and Publisher*, CRM BOOKS

Richard L. Roe, *Vice-President*, CRM BOOKS, *and Director, College Department*
Sales Manager, College Department: Richard M. Connelly
Fulfillment Manager, College Department: Nancy Le Clere
College Department Staff: Elaine Kleiss, Carol A. Walnum, La Delle Willett

Jean Smith, *Vice-President and Managing Editor*, CRM BOOKS
Senior Editor: Arlyne Lazerson
Editors: Gloria Joyce, Cecie Starr, Betsy H. Wyckoff
Editorial Assistants: Jacquelyn Estrada, Cynthia Macdonald, Johanna Price, Ann Scales

Jo Ann Gilberg, *Vice-President*, CRM BOOKS, *and Director, Manufacturing and Production*
Production Manager: Eugene G. Schwartz
Production Supervisors: Barbara Blum, E. Cecile Mayer, P. Douglas Armstrong
Production Assistants: Georgene Martina, Patricia Perkins, Toini Jaffee
Production Staff: Mona F. Drury, Margaret M. Mesec

Tom Suzuki, *Vice-President*, CRM BOOKS, *and Director of Design*

Art Director: Leon Bolognese
Promotion Art Director: John Isely
Designer: George Price
Associate Designers: Catherine Flanders, Reynold Hernandez
Assistant Designers: Robert Fountain, Pamela Morehouse
Assistant Promotion Designer: John Madison Hix
Art Staff: Jacqueline McLoughlin, Kurt Kolbe

Paul Lapolla, *Vice-President*, CRM BOOKS, *and Director, Psychology Today Book Club*
Assistant: Karen De Laria

Controller: Robert Geiserman

Assistant: Maryann Errichetti

Office Manager: Lynn D. Crosby
Assistant: Janie Fredericks

Officers of Communications/Research/Machines, Inc.
John J. Veronis, *President*; Nicolas H. Charney, *Chairman of the Board*;
David A. Dushkin, *Vice-President*; James B. Horton, *Vice-President*

This book was composed by American Book–Stratford Press, Inc., New York, New York.
It was printed and bound by Kingsport Press, Inc., Kingsport, Tennessee.